MODERN LIBRARY CHRONICLES

Currently Available

KAREN ARMSTRONG on Islam
DAVID BERLINSKI on mathematics
RICHARD BESSEL on Nazi Germany
IAN BURUMA on modern Japan
PATRICK COLLINSON on the Reformation
FELIPE FERNÁNDEZ-ARMESTO on the Americas
LAWRENCE M. FRIEDMAN on law in America
PAUL FUSSELL on World War II in Europe
F. GONZÁLEZ-CRUSSI on the history of medicine
PETER GREEN on the Hellenistic Age
ALISTAIR HORNE on the age of Napoleon
PAUL JOHNSON on the Renaissance
FRANK KERMODE on the age of Shakespeare
JOEL KOTKIN on the city
HANS KÜNG on the Catholic Church
MARK KURLANSKY on nonviolence
EDWARD J. LARSON on the theory of evolution

MARGARET MACMILLAN on the uses and abuses of history
MARTIN MARTY on the history of Christianity
MARK MAZOWER on the Balkans
JOHN MICKLETHWAIT and ADRIAN WOOLDRIDGE on the company
ANTHONY PAGDEN on peoples and empires
RICHARD PIPES on Communism
COLIN RENFREW on prehistory
KEVIN STARR on California
MICHAEL STÜRMER on the German Empire
GEORGE VECSEY on baseball
MILTON VIORST on the Middle East
A. N. WILSON on London
ROBERT S. WISTRICH on the Holocaust
GORDON S. WOOD on the American Revolution

Forthcoming

TIM BLANNING on romanticism
ALAN BRINKLEY on the Great Depression
BRUCE CUMINGS on the Korean War
SEAMUS DEANE on the Irish
JEFFREY E. GARTEN on globalization
JASON GOODWIN on the Ottoman Empire
BERNARD LEWIS on the Holy Land

FREDRIK LOGEVALL on the Vietnam War
PANKAJ MISHRA on the rise of modern India
ORVILLE SCHELL on modern China
CHRISTINE STANSELL on feminism
ALEXANDER STILLE on fascist Italy
CATHARINE R. STIMPSON on the university

UNCIVIL SOCIETY

STEPHEN KOTKIN
WITH A CONTRIBUTION BY JAN T. GROSS

UNCIVIL SOCIETY

1989 AND THE IMPLOSION
OF THE COMMUNIST ESTABLISHMENT

A MODERN LIBRARY CHRONICLES BOOK
THE MODERN LIBRARY
NEW YORK

Published in the United States by Modern Library, an imprint of
The Random House Publishing Group, a division
of Random House, Inc., New York.

MODERN LIBRARY and the TORCHBEARER Design are registered
trademarks of Random House, Inc.

ISBN 978-0-679-64276-3

Kotkin, Stephen.
Uncivil society: 1989 and the implosion of the communist establishment/
Stephen Kotkin; with a contribution by Jan T. Gross.
p. cm.
Includes bibliographical references and index.
ISBN 978-0-679-64276-3
1. Soviet Union—Politics and government—1985–1991. 2. Europe, Eastern—
Politics and government—1989– 3. Former communist countries—History.
4. Social change—Soviet Union—History. 5. Social change—Europe,
Eastern—History—20th century. 6. Civil society—Soviet Union—History.
7. Civil society—Europe, Eastern—History—20th century. 8. Soviet Union—
Social conditions—1970–1991. 9. Europe, Eastern—Social conditions—
20th century. I. Gross, Jan Tomasz. II. Title.

DK288.K68 2009
947.0009'048—dc22 2009012903

Printed in the United States of America on acid-free paper

www.modernlibrary.com

2 4 6 8 9 7 5 3 1

First Edition

To Paul Lendvai (b. 1929),
Journalist and leading light of
twentieth-century Eastern Europe

The party was shattered not by its opponents but—paradoxically—by the leadership.

—KÁROLY GRÓSZ,
the last Hungarian Communist-party chief, 1991

CONTENTS

PREFACE

The defeat in the Cold War of the Communist alternative to the market and a liberal order was momentous, and the repercussions for Europe, Russia, and the rest of the globe are still playing out. Already, though, the books on communism's demise in Eastern Europe in 1989 could probably be piled longer and higher than the old Berlin Wall. Some of this literature is first-rate. For instance, in a collection of essays written primarily in 1990–1991 and gathered by Vladimir Tismăneanu for the collapse's tenth anniversary in 1999, Daniel Chirot stressed the twin crises of economic malperformance and political illegitimacy, which magnified each other. Leszek Kołakowski highlighted the special roles of Mikhail Gorbachev and Poland, which crushed the system from both ends. And Katherine Verdery singled out Hungary's opening of its border with Austria, which helped turn the East German yearning for passage to West Germany into a Wall-bursting flood. Combined, these essays go a long way toward explaining what happened.[1] Elsewhere, Mark Kramer has shown that Gorbachev's Kremlin, far from having kept its hands off Eastern Europe, quietly intervened to prevent crackdowns by hard-liners in the satellites.[2] The resulting shock implosion of communism in Eastern Europe made thinkable a similar exit for the Soviet republics, especially the tiny Baltic republics and to a lesser extent Ukraine. Still, it was the Russian Republic's improbable quest for emancipation from Moscow that shattered the Soviet state by 1991. *"Pater sancte,"* as a monk attendant reminds the Holy Father during grandiose papal coronations, *"sic transit gloria mundi."*

What more could there be to say on this twentieth anniversary of 1989? Plenty. Most analysts continue to focus disproportionately, even exclusively, on the "opposition," which they fantasize as a "civil society." This fixation recalls the long and fruitless search for "the bourgeoisie" who supposedly caused the French Revolution of 1789. But just as "the bourgeoisie" were mostly an outcome of 1789, so "civil society" was more a consequence than a primary cause of 1989. Thanks to the repudiation of the single-party monopoly and its corollary, the state-owned and state-run economy, the 1989 revolutions would make civil society possible. That said, highlighting the opposition is understandable for Poland since, as we shall see, Poland *had* an opposition, which *imagined itself* as civil society. Such a focus almost works for Hungary, too, because, like Poland, Hungary had a negotiated exit from communism, though Hungary's proreform Communists in 1989 had to bolster the anti-Communist opposition in order to have a negotiating partner. Be that as it may, for all other Eastern European countries the focus on the opposition falls into the realm of fiction. And even for the Polish case, analysts too often leave out the side across the table from the opposition—namely, the Communist establishment. The often overlooked establishment, which we call "uncivil society," is a primary focus of our book, because that is where collapse happened.

The incompetent, blinkered, and ultimately bankrupt Communist establishments—party bosses and propagandists, secret policemen and military brass—deserve their due, but we do not examine every Eastern European country in depth. East Germany, Romania, and Poland are the case studies (in that unusual order) that we single out for extended treatment because, in our view, they best reveal how and why each establishment's implosion occurred. Seeking to use the opposition to help push through tough economic measures to save the system, uncivil society in Poland (as well as in Hungary) discovered that it had instead capitulated; in East Germany and Romania (and elsewhere) the establishment just collapsed. The causes behind both these outcomes had a lot to do with internal elite dynamics and

with geopolitics, as we shall show. But in cases where the uncivil society was determined to hold on, it had to be, and was, given a shove
by mass social mobilization. Paradoxically, therefore, in 1989 the
enormous street demonstrations took place not in the country with
the formidable organized opposition (Poland) but in the lands of the
formidable Securitate and Stasi—the dreaded security police of Romania and East Germany, respectively. No less paradoxically, the
mass protests broke out without equivalent mass social organizations.
Hence, a second goal of our book, beyond a close look at uncivil society, entails an explanation of the social mobilization absent corresponding societal organization.[3]

Eastern Europe ended up shaping the destiny of the Soviet Union,
but the Soviets had long held the fate of Eastern Europe in their hands.
The "Brezhnev Doctrine"—employing military force, as a last resort,
to uphold socialism in the bloc—was in many ways the Andropov
Doctrine. Yuri Andropov, the long-serving KGB chief (1967–82) and
briefly the successor to Leonid Brezhnev as general secretary (1982–
84), had long undergirded the Soviet resolve. Andropov played a hard-
line man-on-the-spot role as Soviet ambassador to Hungary during
the crackdown in 1956; he manipulated the more cautious Brezhnev
over using force in Czechoslovakia in 1968; and he took a tough stance
on Poland in 1980–81 during Solidarity's existence. The KGB underling who served as station chief in Poland from April 1973 through
October 1984 recalled that Andropov had refused to countenance
Poland taking the "capitalist" path, a scenario viewed as zero sum
geopolitically. Other evidence, though, indicates that behind closed
doors in 1981 Andropov lamented that the overtaxed Soviet Union
had reached the limits of its ability to intervene militarily in Eastern
Europe and goaded the Polish regime to conduct its own crackdown
(it did).[4] Be that as it may, in 1989 Mikhail Gorbachev's Kremlin not
only *formally* repealed the Brezhnev Doctrine but also worked to prevent Eastern Europe's uncivil societies from themselves using violence to prop up their regimes. Almost immediately thereupon, the
Communist systems in Eastern Europe were overturned. The ashes of
Andropov—who more than anyone had helped put Gorbachev into
power—must have been turning over in his Kremlin Wall urn.

Initially, almost no one had believed Gorbachev—not the bloc's uncivil societies, not the dissidents, not the West. He surprised everyone, including himself. Controlling the Warsaw Pact chain of command, his Kremlin held sway over all the major national military commanders of Eastern Europe (Romania excepted) and employed its formidable bully pulpit. In September 1988, one of Gorbachev's aides was authorized to tell *Le Monde* that "we [in Moscow] would not be frightened if Solidarity reemerged," undercutting Polish hard-liners and helping to cajole into being the roundtable process that would lead to Solidarity's relegalization. After China's crackdown against the more than one million demonstrators gathered in Beijing's Tiananmen Square in June 1989—during which hundreds died—Gorbachev stepped up the pressure on the Eastern Europeans to refrain from mass repression. When Solidarity was poised to take power in Poland after the June 1989 elections, Romania's Nicolae Ceauşescu urged other socialist countries to intervene—reversing Bucharest's famous anti-interventionist stance dating from the 1968 Prague Spring—but the Soviets publicly rebuked him. More than that, the Kremlin congratulated Prime Minister Tadeusz Mazowiecki of Solidarity and sent Vladimir Kryuchkov, the head of the KGB, in person to offer praise in public and to win over the new Polish premier in private. But Moscow's unintended "loss" of Eastern Europe in 1989—reinforced (also unintentionally) by the completion that same year of the Soviet withdrawal from Afghanistan in public view—placed the integrity of the USSR itself in question. The Soviet dissolution warrants a book unto itself, examining, among other factors, the shifting international context and superpower rivalry as well as Gorbachev's idealistic program of socialist renewal.[5] Here, in an epilogue, we highlight the significance of the momentous turnabout in Eastern Europe for the 1991 Soviet downfall.

In the popular imagination, communism's demise in Eastern Europe has given rise to two opposing grand narratives. The first tells of a breakthrough to freedom; the second, of a revolution stolen by the old establishment. Both are partly true. Freedom, meaning the messiness of democracy as well as the rewards and risks of the market in an age of globalization, came in varying degrees to the countries of Eastern

Europe, albeit with great assistance from the 1990s process of European Union accession. At the same time, much of the old Communist establishment in the East bloc survived and prospered, even in Poland (though not East Germany). Still, outcomes do not mean causation. The 1989 revolutions did not happen *because* of a broad freedom drive or an establishment self-enrichment grab. The cave-in was unintended, precipitated by Gorbachev's unilateral removal of the Soviet backstop, a move that had been intended to goad socialist-bloc countries to reform themselves. In other words, Gorbachev was looking to galvanize the reform-minded Gorbachevs of Eastern Europe. There was only one flaw in this approach: there were no East European Gorbachevs. True, inside the establishments there was some ferment even before 1985 (Romania excepted), but party types inspired by Gorbachev's Prague-Spring-style socialist revival were not numerous around the bloc. Romania's Communist party had no reform wing whatsoever. In Poland, which was run by a military man, the party reform wing was concentrated in a periodical (*Krytyka*). In East Germany, proponents of a socialist renewal were found mostly among dreamy intellectuals, not officialdom. Instead of galvanizing socialist reformers in Eastern Europe, Gorbachev's stunning repeal of the Brezhnev doctrine caught out the bloc's uncivil societies, exposing how they had long engaged in breathtaking mismanagement. Above all, they had clung to anticapitalism in the face of an ever-flourishing capitalist Western Europe—from which the uncivil societies had borrowed to avoid making hard choices, running up self-destructive debts in hard currency, as we shall see. Then they borrowed some more. What Gorbachev did was to lay bare how socialism in the bloc had been crushed by competition with capitalism and by loans that could be repaid only by ever-new loans, Ponzi-scheme style.

We offer, then, a third narrative of global political economy and a bankrupt political class in a system that was largely bereft of corrective mechanisms. It may seem a depressing tale, yet perhaps it is not as disheartening as that of ruinous elites in a market democracy. In the 1990s and 2000s, American elites colluded in the United States' descent into a sinkhole of debt to foreign lenders, enabling besotted consumers to indulge in profligate consumption of imported goods.

America's unwitting policy emulation of irresponsible uncivil societies was facilitated by communism's implosion in Eastern Europe, which opened the bloc economies to global integration, and by the rise of savings-rich Asia. It was in such an environment that the spectacular incomprehension, lucrative recklessness, and not infrequent fraud of elites—bankers, fund managers, enabling politicians—booby-trapped the entire world's financial system. After the meltdown that commenced in fall 2008, we can only hope that the market and democracy prove their resiliency and good governance and accountability return. In the meantime, if Eastern Europe's experience is any guide, those responsible will largely escape any reckoning.

For criticisms and suggestions on various parts of our manuscript, the authors would like to thank Scott Moyers of the Andrew Wylie Agency, Amir Weiner, Leonard Benardo, Eric Weitz, and Tim Borstelmann. The authors are also grateful to John Flicker, editor of the Modern Library at Random House. Our book originated in a seminar for Ph.D. students at Princeton University cotaught by the authors in fall 2007. Along with a group of top-notch students, Adam Michnik—a major participant in the events in Poland before, during, and after 1989—took part in the weekly class meetings and follow-up discussions. To absorb his tenacious spirit of resistance even so many years after the fact was to appreciate what the Communist establishment in Poland had faced. His presence and observations also furnished a challenge to figure out how the East bloc edifice could have been brought down when so few people there, as anywhere, were heroes.

CHRONOLOGY

1961   Erection of Berlin Wall

1961-62   Romania rejects assigned role of agricultural supplier to the rest of the East bloc in the Council for Mutual Economic Assistance (COMECON)

1964   Soviet KGB advisers withdrawn from Romania's Securitate

1965   Nicolae Ceaușescu succeeds Gheorghe Gheorghiu-Dej as ruler of Romania

1968   Prague Spring "socialism with a human face" reform movement, crushed by Soviet-led Warsaw pact forces (August); announcement of "Brezhnev Doctrine" (use of force, if necessary, to uphold Eastern European Communist regimes)

1970   Poland (under Edward Gierek) and East Germany (under Walter Ulbricht) begin the policy of borrowing from the West in hard currency

1970 (Dec.)   Mass strikes in Poland over price hikes

1971   Erich Honecker displaces Ulbricht as ruler of East Germany

1971   Leszek Kołakowski publishes essay "Hope and Hopelessness," arguing the impossibility of reforming socialism

1973   In first oil shock, world price of crude rises 400 percent in a few months

1976 (June)   Mass strikes in Poland over price hikes; formation of KOR (Workers' Defense Committee)

1976   Adam Michnik publishes "A New Evolutionism," urging the self-liberation of society

1978 (Oct.)   Election of Karol Wojtyła as Pope John Paul II, the first-ever Polish pope

1978 (Dec.)   Deng Xiaoping launches China's market reforms

1980 (Aug.)   Strikes in Poland lead to formation of independent trade union Solidarity

1981 (Oct.)   General Wojciech Jaruzelski becomes ruler of Poland

1981 (Dec.) Martial law in Poland, five thousand arrests in one night, Solidarity driven underground

1982 Ceaușescu begins imposing severe austerity measures in Romania to pay back the state's hard-currency debt

1982 Leipzig peace marches begin after church services at the St. Nicholas Church

1985 (March) Mikhail Gorbachev elevated to the Kremlin; soon launches perestroika and glasnost, and begins to state publicly that Eastern Europe is on its own

1987 (Nov.) Strikes and protests in Brașov, Romania, bloodily repressed

1988 (Nov.) Lech Wałęsa–Alfred Miodowicz debate on Polish TV before 25 million viewers

1989 East bloc hard-currency debt reaches a combined $90 billion, with no end in sight to further borrowing: Hungary needs $1 billion annually just to pay the interest; Poland needs $2 billion; Gorbachev repudiates the Brezhnev Doctrine, while also working to prevent Eastern European regimes from cracking down themselves

1989

Feb.–Apr. Roundtable negotiations in Poland between regime and opposition

May–June Gorbachev introduces real elections for USSR legislature

June 4 Elections in Poland, in which Solidarity wins almost every seat it is allowed to contest; Communist China cracks down on demonstrators in Tiananmen Square

June 27 Hungary demonstratively cuts barbed wire on its border with Austria, making a virtue of necessity; mass exodus of East Germans westward accelerates

Aug. 18 Solidarity prime minister takes over in Poland

Sept. 11 Leipzig Monday night peace marches grow to several thousand, with new chants of "We're staying" and "We are the people"

Oct. 9 Leipzig peace marchers reach seventy thousand; feared crackdown fails to materialize

Nov. 9 East German Politburo member Günter Schabowski bungles press conference about pending new travel policy; Berlin Wall breached

Nov.–Dec. German unification chants ("Helmut, Helmut") take over at the Leipzig peace marches and throughout East Germany

Dec. 15 László Tőkés, pastor of a Reformed (Calvinist) church in Timişoara, Romania, asks parishioners at Sunday services to stop the regime from evicting him; around forty mostly elderly people defy the Securitate to protect the ethnic Hungarian pastor

Dec. 17 Romanian troops massacre demonstrators in Timişoara

Dec. 18 Timişoara factory workers strike

Dec. 19–20 Romanian general in Timişoara withdraws troops, ceding city to demonstrators

Dec. 22 Romanian army chief General Vasile Milea commits suicide; Ceauşescu flees Bucharest by helicopter from the roof of the surrounded Central Committee building

Dec. 25 Ceauşescu tried and executed

1990

Feb.–March Free elections for the Supreme Soviets in the Soviet Union's fifteen republics

March Democratically elected Lithuanian Supreme Soviet votes 291 to 8 (3 abstentions) for independence from the Soviet Union

May Latvian Supreme Soviet votes for the republic's independence

June Boris Yeltsin elected president of the Russian Republic, campaigning for Russia's sovereignty and, eventually, independence

1991

July Dissolution of the Warsaw Pact

Aug. Failed coup by Soviet hard-liners hoping to save the USSR

Dec. Soviet Union formally dissolved; Soviet president Mikhail Gorbachev yields Kremlin to Russian president Boris Yeltsin

Communism in the six Soviet satellites ended peacefully in 1989; in Albania, it ended in 1991; in Yugoslavia, wars of dissolution began in the late 1980s and continued into the 1990s.

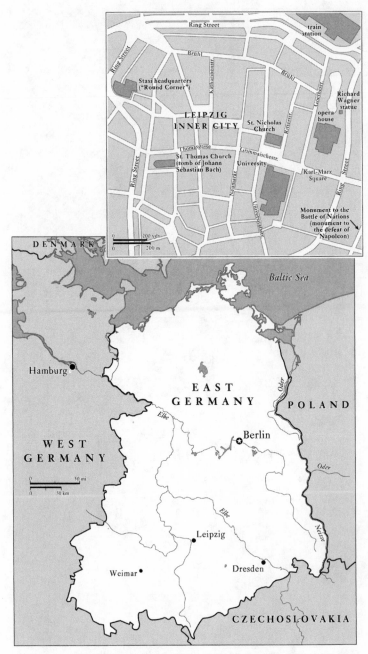

Leipzig, East Germany's second-largest city, had an illustrious history.

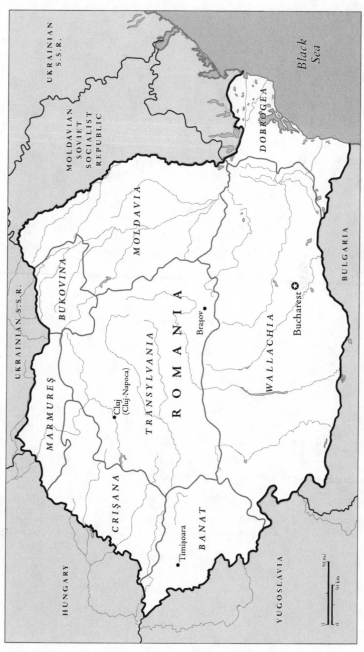

The large Romanian state (including a substantial Hungarian minority) was a product of World War I.

Under communism some 95 percent of Poland's population was Roman Catholic (baptized in a church), and more than half attended Mass regularly.

I

BANK RUN

"How did you go bankrupt?"
"Two ways. Gradually and then suddenly."
— ERNEST HEMINGWAY, *The Sun Also Rises*

The wry Romanian film *A fost sau n-a fost?* (2006), known in English as *12:08 East of Bucharest*, poses a seemingly passé question: Was there or was there not—"A fost sau n-a fost?"—a revolution in 1989? Most of the film takes place at a desk, as an on-air discussion inside a television studio. (It is often said that Romania's 1989 events took place mostly on TV.) The pompous host (who is given to quoting Herodotus) is called Virgil Jderescu, a provincial TV station owner whose talk show is called *Issue of the Day*. This particular day is December 22, 2005, and the issue is what happened on the same date sixteen years earlier. After some potential panelists bow out, Jderescu goes live with a debt-ridden, alcoholic history teacher named Tiberiu Mănescu and a grumpy, lonely pensioner named Emanoil Piscoci who dresses up as Santa Claus for children. The telecast backdrop shows the live image of a drab, unnamed Stalinist-style wide town square (thought to be Vaslui, the eastern Romanian hometown of the film's director, Corneliu Porumboiu). The film's nonaction is riveting: three men sitting in chairs. Jderescu keeps asking "Was there, or was there not, a revolution in our town?" Mănescu recounts how on December 22, 1989, he had gone to their town square with three other teachers—conveniently, two are now dead and one departed for Canada—before 12:08 P.M., as part of a protesting vanguard. The timing is crucial because Nicolae Ceaușescu, the Romanian dictator, fled Bucharest by helicopter precisely at that time. The Santa Claus impersonator claims that he, too, went to the square, albeit after 12:08. Jderescu takes a call to the show: it's the sentry on duty in the town square sixteen years ago, who denounces as a lie Mănescu's claim to have been on the square before 12:08. Another caller places Mănescu at the corner bar drinking the whole day and night. As callers along with the host impugn Mănescu's story, the latter interjects, "Why split hairs over such stupidity?" The broadcast winds down by depicting—live on the studio backdrop—forlorn gray buildings, a darkening sky, streetlights turning on, and beautiful snow falling. The last phone-in caller says, "I'm just calling to let you know it's snowing outside. It's snowing big white flakes. Enjoy it now, tomorrow it will be mud ... Merry Christmas, everybody!" The woman reveals that she lost her son on December 23, 1989, the day after the revolution.

The film seems to examine whether a revolution can take place if no one risks anything, at least in this town, and it seems to reinforce a general impression that Romania in 1989 was the grand exception. Romania, it is often said, was the only Eastern European country whose experience in 1989 was supposedly a coup, not a revolution. Or it is said that Romania did have a revolution, but it was stolen.[1] Adding to this sense of exceptionalism, Romania turned out to be the only country besides Yugoslavia where socialism's end was bloody. That carnage notwithstanding—officially Romania suffered 1,104 dead, mostly after December 22—it will be our argument that Romania in 1989 was not an exception but part of a continuum that includes East Germany as well as most other cases. Communist Romania had a minuscule opposition. It was a country of Tiberiu Mănescus and Emanoil Piscocis, as well as Virgil Jderescus, but, as we shall see, Romania offers a fine example of what could be called nonorganized mobilization, which in 1989 was actually the norm across Eastern Europe. It was Communist-era Poland, usually taken as paradigmatic, that proved to be the grand exception. In Poland, the opposition was not a small coterie of dissidents or groups of people arrayed around private kitchen tables, taking advantage of the mass construction of self-contained (noncommunal) apartments to commiserate in trusted company. The opposition in Poland was societal, with organizations and physical spaces, Sunday sermons and flying universities, and a fully articulated alternative to the regime.[2] Yet Romania, not Poland, experienced large street protests in 1989. That year, East Germany, too, had massive street demonstrations, even though, as in Romania, there was relatively little organized opposition.

Back in the 1970s, most commentators thought that the capitalist West, not communism, was nearing collapse, and even in the second half of the 1980s, Communist systems seemed not doomed but uncertain. Unexpectedly, however, 1989 turned out to be an *annus mirabilis,* producing revolutions in Eastern Europe that sparked repercussions around the globe, from apartheid South Africa to one-party Mexico. The Romanian case, like the East German one, indicates that much of the interpretive challenge consists in analyzing how East European Communist regimes fell in the absence of organized oppositions. This requires a different understanding of social process from the usual invocation of something called "civil society." The latter slogan has proved to be catnip to scholars, pundits, and foreign aid donors.[3] After "modernization theory" (the hugely influential 1950s–1970s developmental ideology) had morphed by the 1980s into "democracy promotion," the notion of "civil society" became the conceptual equivalent of the "bourgeoisie" or "middle class"—that is, a vague, seemingly all-purpose collective social actor.[4] It was claptrap. Several hundred (sometimes just several dozen) members of an opposition—with a handful of harassed illegal associations and underground self-publications (*samizdat*)—were somehow a "civil society"? Meanwhile, *hundreds of thousands* of party and state officials, political police operatives, army officers—who often went to school, worked, and even lived together, controlled all (state) property, public spaces, communications networks, and institutions, and had their own clubs, resorts, and shops—were somehow not a society?

Such widespread misapprehension transpires when normative thinking—imagining how things ought to be—gets the better of analysis. Needless to say, in 1989 "civil society" could not have shattered Soviet-style socialism for the simple reason that civil society in Eastern Europe did not then actually exist. The mostly small groups of dissidents, however important morally, could not have constituted any kind of society. On the contrary, it was the establishment—the "uncivil society"—that brought down its own system. Each establishment did so by misruling and then, when Mikhail Gorbachev's Kremlin radically shifted the geopolitical rules, by capitulating—or by refusing to capitulate and thus making themselves susceptible to political bank runs.[5] Suddenly, decades of bravery by disparate dissidents—the moral thunderbolts, the "antipolitics," the "living in dignity"—were swamped by a cascade of activism on the part of formerly inert masses and by elite opportunism. Would-be totalitarian states, which aspired to total control and total mobilization, by the same token proved to be totally vulnerable.

CIVIL SOCIETY UTOPIAS

Whence the reverie of "civil society"? Before the eighteenth century, the terms "civil society" and "the state" were nearly synonymous and meant essentially political society. But Adam Ferguson (1723–1816), along with other thinkers of the Scottish Enlightenment, helped divide the two terms into an opposition (a process continued by G. W. F. Hegel and Alexis de Tocqueville). Ferguson's *Essay on the History of Civil Society* (Edinburgh, 1767) contrasted a civilized rule-of-law society to a barbarous one. His text came out in eight editions up to 1819, but the next English edition had to wait until 1966. Not long thereafter, the term "civil society" would again burst into vogue, especially among analysts awestruck by the breakthrough of Solidarity in Communist-ruled Poland.[6] Suddenly, individuals and groups around Eastern Europe that opposed Communist systems were said to constitute an emergent civil society—that is, "autonomous" forces outside the state and, in these instances, against the state. Such recourse to the concept of "civil society" in fact exaggerated the role of intellectuals (at the expense of workers, churches, and the world economy).[7] More consequentially, the supposed mutual exclusiveness of civil society and state produced a skewed characterization of society in terms of how a society was (self-)organized. True, social organization is not to be taken for granted; it must be achieved, and sustained. But a society is also profoundly shaped by how the state is organized.[8] "Civil society" was in many ways the conceptual counterpart to the concept of totalitarianism, but if it was precisely the all-encompassing totalitarian despotism that made the term "civil society"—as something outside the state—so appealing, this very system also did not permit anything like a civil society to exist.

"Civil society," if it means anything, signifies people taking responsibility for themselves. That, however, requires the ability not just to self-organize but also to have recourse to state institutions to defend associationism, civil liberties, and private property. Obviously, dissidents living under Soviet-style systems could not attain that, no matter how brave they were, because of the nature of the Communist state. Founded on the suppression of private property and "bourgeois" rule of law, the Communist state lacked independent judiciaries, civil services, and independent media to help defend *against* state power. To be sure, determined individuals could appeal to international norms and laws, especially the 1975 Helsinki "basket three" human rights obligations signed by Communist regimes. And many of them cited the Communist regimes' own constitutions. On December 5, 1965, Soviet "Constitution Day," the mathematician Aleksander Esenin-Volpin organized a rally on Moscow's Pushkin Square of around two hundred people and held up a sign reading "Respect the Constitution." (He was promptly arrested.) Less quixotically, in Poland from the 1970s such a strategy—designed as a decisive break from any attempt to reform socialism—did become a powerful form of social organization, in a kind of self-fulfilling prophecy. " 'We're supposed to be citizens!' we thought," recalled the late historian and Solidarity activist Bronisław Geremek in an interview in 2007. "Even the socialist constitution of the Polish People's Republic refers to citizens' place in society, and we wanted society to belong to the citizens. And that was our organizing utopia. If there was any sort of utopia in 'Solidarity,' it was the utopia of civil society."[9] Elsewhere in the bloc, however, this practice of living *as if* one constituted a civil society had limited organizing effects, even as utopia.

"Civil society," explained the Hungarian novelist and essayist György Konrád (1933–) in 1984, "is still only an idea."[10] That characterization held right through 1989. East Germany's "New Forum," a very loose umbrella for various groups, was first announced only on September 21, 1989. Fair or not, it was no Solidarity (an independent labor union of 10 million members). True, some 3,000 people signed New Forum's founding appeal straight away, and more than 200,000 people eventually signed, but New Forum played little role in the events of 1989; it vanished soon thereafter.[11] Czechoslovakia's Civic Forum took shape in November 1989, partly in response to East German events, such as the occupation of the West German embassy in Prague by East Germans clamoring to go west, but also in response to the beatings of peaceful Czechoslovak student demonstrators. (Civic Forum's Slovak counterpart was Public Against Violence.) Civic Forum seemed liked an update of the rights movement Charter 77 (which had not aspired to become a mass movement), but Civic Forum did not even have a program. As late as the beginning of 1989, the Czechoslovak security service estimated the country's active dissidents at no more than 500 people, with a core of about 60 (a count similar to East Germany's).[12] Meanwhile, on Prague's Wenceslas Square some 10,000 people massed on October 28, 1989, and 200,000 people on November 19; eight days later, a general strike of some one million people shut down the country. But none of this was inspired or led by dissidents or Civic Forum, which was abolished not long after 1989. In other words, the social-movement analogies to Poland's mesmerizing Solidarity have been profoundly misleading, falsely generalizing a successful strategy in one special case to others.[13]

Romania in 1989 lacked even a New Forum or a Civic Forum from which to try to make false analogies to Poland, but consider Hungary, which is often placed alongside Poland because in 1989 Hungary, too, had a regime-opposition "roundtable." As András Sájo has written, however, Hungary in 1989 saw few street protests and little popular mobilization, and "the Hungarian opposition was rather isolated and few in number." The Hungarian roundtable—300 sessions, 500 participants, three months—began as a kind of regime self-negotiation (which had been going on internally for years).[14] From 1985, Hungary's state trade unions and party youth group had begun to shrink and one third of Hungarians' working time was being spent in the private sector for services, but the key factor leading up to 1989 in Hungary was that many Communists lost interest in preserving their own system. Not all, but a number, of party officials preferred to become an asset-owning bourgeoisie.[15] An even more substantial number had come to favor a multiparty political system. Whatever the motivations, the Communist faction seeking an exit from the Communist monopoly system pressured hard-liners, while also assisting reform circles in society. In short, elements in the party worked to fortify the loose anti-Communist opposition. Someone had to be on the other side of the table when the Hungarian roundtable opened six days after the June 4, 1989, elections in Poland. Moreover, even in Poland, as we shall see, the roundtable had to be launched by the regime.

UNCIVIL SOCIETY PARADOXES

Unlike the people in whose name they ruled, the regimes enjoyed a full panoply of institutions, associations, patronage, and other networks. They carried special identity cards that opened doors and, when flashed, advertised their status. Within a hierarchy, they shared life experiences, beginning in youth groups, places of training and work, and an ideology, which "appealed to the simpletons and to the sophisticates alike," explained Zbigniew Brzezinski. "It made its subscribers feel self-righteous, correct, and confident all at once. It left nothing uncertain."[16] They forged lifelong contacts at Romania's Ştefan Gheorghiu Party School, East Germany's party schools, or Poland's Higher School for the Social Sciences, as well as at Moscow's Higher Party School. Many attended special military or spy academies, such as the Securitate School in Băneasa or the Stasi College in Potsdam. With their former classmates they ran entire industries and provinces, had acquaintances and relatives in charge of parallel agencies and locales, and gossiped about the differing comfort levels of the various "closed" hospitals and spas. They sat for their portraits, wore party lapel pins and unbreakable "military" watches as a further sign of their fraternity, and signed their letters "with socialist greetings." They were allocated apartments ahead of the queue and above the state norm for space, had maids and chauffeurs (so they could be watched and eavesdropped upon), and patronized sports clubs such as Dynamo and Gwardia according to their rank and sphere of activity. They cultivated patrons at the feasts known as party congresses.

And when problems arose—such as how to erase a child's arrest record—they could approach the "party affairs" section.[17]

The swath of people in the elite formed a society, just not a "civil society," meaning not one constituted, protected, and held in check by rule of law. To put the matter another way, totalitarian or would-be totalitarian states did not eliminate society—they created their own societies. Our term "uncivil society" refers to these formidable bonds and forms of social organization that accompanied an illiberal state, particularly an illiberal state without private property. How extensive were they? In the East bloc, Communist-party membership averaged around 8 to 10 percent of each country's population, although identification with the regimes' power and values was wider. Still, only a minority of party members were actually apparatchiks, that is, those who held no jobs other than party work. But beyond the party apparatus proper, we also ought to include the state functionaries and the military caste, as well as the most privileged sectors of the intelligentsia. Thus, a rule of thumb is that uncivil society, including family members, made up somewhere around 5 to 7 percent of the populace. Clearly, the establishments were not everything, and we touch on the big workplaces around which the large proletarian communities were organized, as well as the Evangelical (Lutheran) Church in East Germany, the Reformed (Calvinist) Church in Romania, and the Catholic Church in Poland.[18] Some of these various inchoate nonestablishment realms have been deemed by one analyst a "second society," thereby building on the idea of the "second economy" (illegal market activities under central planning).[19] Combined, the disaggregated "second society" and the "uncivil society" might be dubbed socialism's "actually existing society."[20] Be that as it may, the truly organized part, with manifold instruments, was the establishment.

For analyzing the Communist establishment, the main approach has been *The New Class* (1957), a celebrated work by the jailed Yugoslav Communist official Milovan Djilas, who argued that Communist systems produced a bureaucracy that, out of class consciousness, perpetuated its privileges and would cause economic decline by placing its corrupt self-interest and survival above all else.[21] Before Djilas, this "revolution betrayed" thesis was usually associated with Leon Trotsky or George Orwell, though shorn of class rhetoric it also overlapped Friedrich von Hayek's *The Road to Serfdom* (1944), while back in 1873 the anarchist Mikhail Bakunin had predicted that if the Marxists came to power, a "new class, a new hierarchy" would form.[22] After Djilas, Jacek Kuroń (1934–2004) and Karol Modzelewski (1937–), then two young lecturers at Warsaw University, developed this line of analysis, indicting Poland's Communist ruling class for precipitating a system crisis by exploiting workers and calling for a new proletarian revolution in an "Open Letter to the Party" (1964). Kuroń and Modzelewski were sentenced to three years' imprisonment for "preparing and distributing works harmful to the interests of the Polish state"—meaning, the interests of the very state officials they were targeting.[23] Similarly, among nonintellectuals under communism a visceral version of this viewpoint took shape: for example, in 1977, 35,000 miners in Romania's Jiu Valley in Transylvania went on strike and jeered the authorities with shouts of "Down with the Red bourgeoisie!" The notion of a "Red bourgeoisie" or "new class" predated the concept of "civil society," but "new class" went out of fashion long ago. Its power consisted in wielding Marxism against Marxist regimes, but, as Djilas himself later conceded, that was also its limitation.[24]

Far from acting coherently, let alone out of class consciousness, the Communist establishments were often incoherent, riven by turf wars and hypersecrecy. Decision making remained a black box even within the upper echelons, while wiretapping and informing were so widespread that elites often hesitated to socialize. Indeed, the paradox of uncivil society was that its members had unlimited authority and command over almost all national resources, yet they were paralyzed. Establishments that could collectivize a peasantry and nationalize an entire country subsequently found themselves unable to take the slightest corrective actions when something failed to go according to plan. Their ubiquitous surveillance notwithstanding, they proved unable to gather or process elementary information about their countries, the first step in policy making. To be sure, despotic governments are not supposed to be troubled by the aspirations of those they rule, but they still need information about public preferences and available resources if only to engage in manipulation. Instead, uncivil society provided all manner of incentives for even loyalists to lie and report fairy tales. And officials rarely debated with opponents, as Lenin had been forced to do, to sharpen their skills and views.

Incompetence in Communist systems was therefore structural. To remove any possible threats of being unseated, and to increase the bonds of dependency, officials often preferred appointing the less able to be their direct subordinates, something that was repeated all the way down the hierarchy. Even insiders lamented that those who rose up in the system were narrow-minded and submissive. People with initiative, independent judgment, and integrity who had joined the party to lead politically active lives or to better their countries were generally weeded out or beaten down. True, most state bureaucracies to an extent promote personnel who are fitter to obey than to lead. But in the cruelly named "people's democracies" of Eastern Europe, the apparatus substituted itself for the independent political, economic, legal, and academic realms that in pluralist systems furnish a steady flow of talent into the political elite. The resulting stultification afforded satirists boundless material about functionaries' boorishness and ineptitude—about hamsters in search of a wheel. There were exceptions—officials of distinction, even vision and courage—who occasionally reached and remained in major positions. But they invariably had to waste vast amounts of time and energy to overcome the idiotic obstacles that the apparatus and planned economy kept throwing into their paths. Anyway, career-wise, it was always safest to stick to routine. Risk taking was usually confined to the pursuit of additional material comforts.

Larceny became a way of life in a system where property was theoretically public though actually under the private disposition of managers and officials. Uncivil society also turned out to be full of saboteurs, albeit not deliberate ones. Its members were better educated than most of their compatriots, but that education often equipped them with a cliché-ridden vocabulary and crimped worldview. Minimal experience of travel or foreign languages was combined with maximal experience of administering structures and circumstances, always created by someone else's power. And though their intriguing and prevaricating required certain gifts, the party-state fostered a kind of "negative selection"—rewarding loyalty and punishing all else. This affected the most highly technical professions and the professional political police, too. Worse, what Vilfredo Pareto had at the turn of the twentieth century bitingly noted about elites generally—that *classes dirigeantes* (ruling classes) turn into *classes digerantes* (digesting classes), fixated on consumption and self-preservation—in Communist systems proved inimical to correction. This structural lack of resilience was compounded by a deficiency in conflict management tools. On the night of December 13, 1981, some five thousand Solidarity activists in Poland were shocked that they could be put under detention by administrative fiat, that the army and the police could roll tanks and combat vehicles into the streets in a massive display of force, disconnect telephones all over the country, impose a curfew on the entire society, and prevent people from moving between cities—all this despite the 10-million-strong membership in the Solidarity labor union. Still, repression provides no lasting solution to social problems.

The regime's stubborn denials of the existence of *any* social conflict made elementary conflict into an existential threat. It was not just that Soviet-style socialism stoked working-class consciousness through proproletarian rhetoric and ritual, then blatantly functioned as a system of elite perquisites, producing ubiquitous grumbling. It was the near-complete absence of outlets or safety valves for basic popular grievance, beyond petitioning and letter writing to officials or to the media (increasingly to state television). Having imposed one-party rule and a centrally managed economy, having abolished independent labor unions and voluntary associations, having forced outward conformity through informer networks, uncivil society found itself unable to handle spontaneous social life.[25] Even a mere indication of a desire for privacy, a mere inaction, could constitute—in view of its total claim on people's lives—a challenge to such a regime. In Communist systems there turned out to be little difference between a group of people signing a protest against a government-proposed amendment to the Constitution, a workers' strike in a factory, a student meeting opposing suspension of a play in the national theater, or an angry crowd shouting against increases in meat prices. A tremendous overload resulted. Each protest action, each conflict, contained within it the equivalent of a near system crisis. If people could not strike without risking being killed or tortured, if a play's production could not be suspended without hundreds of students risking expulsion from university and incarceration, and if price increases could not be implemented without putting the jobs of high officials in jeopardy, the system was at latent risk of upheaval even in the absence of society-wide *organized* opposition.

DISSOLUTION ON THE RADIO (HUNGARY, 1956)

Communist regimes worked doggedly to force regime-centered mobilization of the people, at official holidays or other times, and to discourage any impulses toward nonregime gatherings. All the same, spontaneous acts of self-mobilization were always lurking. Consider what transpired in Hungary in 1956. Communist-party reformers there, in an internal struggle, launched a drive for a more democratic one-party socialism, which escalated into a rollback of the Soviet-style order (but not of *any* form of socialism).[26] Mátyás Rosenfeld, better known as Rákosi (1892–1971), who had been born in the Austro-Hungarian Empire, the fourth son of a Jewish grocer, liked to imitate a peasant accent and ruled Communist Hungary through terror.[27] But in the topsy-turvy months following Nikita Khrushchev's February 1956 secret speech denouncing Joseph Stalin, the Stalinist Rákosi was forced to retire, and his rival Imre Nagy (1896–1958)— only recently condemned as a "right deviationist"—was rehabilitated. Past events were suddenly being subject to reconsideration in light of de-Stalinization, and anniversaries of such events provided motivation for demonstrations. Seemingly out of nowhere, street gatherings spiraled to a quarter-million people. The Soviet ambassador to Hungary, Yuri Andropov, warned Moscow that "our friends hold power so weakly that the least little forceful shove and they will lose it, and the fate of socialism in Hungary will be decided in the street."[28] Student-led marches through Budapest on October 23—with marchers chanting "We vow, we vow, we will no longer remain slaves"—induced a Soviet intervention of 6,000 troops the next day, which in turn provoked the formation of Hungarian militias of around 15,000 men. It was war.

Nagy, a committed Communist, former secret Soviet NKVD accomplice, and, by October 27, Hungary's prime minister, defected to the rebellion. On October 30 he declared, in a radio address, that "the Cabinet abolishes the one-party system."[29] Monopoly gone! The next day various Hungarian political parties reestablished or established themselves (also, dispossessed landlords began to reappear, eliciting panicked calls from many of the anti-Soviet protesters to prevent a return to the "world of counts and bankers"). What was so extraordinary was not just how fragile the Communist system proved to be—abolished over the radio—but how quickly it could be restored. On November 4, three days after Nagy had further declared Hungary's "neutrality," meaning withdrawal from the Warsaw Pact (formed only the year before), a far larger 60,000-strong Soviet military force arrived and began bloodily crushing the rebellion. More than 2,500 Hungarians and 700 Soviet troops died. By November 7, under Hungarian party chief János Kádár, the party's monopoly was firmly reinstated. Stiffened by the Soviet crackdown, the Hungarian Communists now applied plenty of force. From 1956 to 1961, 100,000 people were arrested, 35,000 tried, 26,000 sentenced, and several hundred executed, Nagy included. Another 182,000 emigrated. The lessons drawn were far-reaching. Ambassador Andropov's car had been shot at in Budapest, and when he was forced to return to the embassy on foot he caught sight of Communists hanging from trees and lampposts—which made an indelible impression on the future Soviet KGB chief.[30] The Kremlin had begun to learn that even Communist-party–led reform could morph into "counterrevolution."

Amid the postcrackdown repressions, the Yugoslav apostate Djilas thundered that "the wound which the Hungarian Revolution inflicted on Communism can never be completely healed," adding that "Hungary means the beginning of the end of Communism."[31] But he turned out to be right only in the fullness of time. In the immediate aftermath, Kádár—born Giovanni Czermanik (1912–1989) in Austro-Hungarian Fiume—stabilized the situation. The then forty-four-year-old new-generation leader carried out the aforementioned arrests and severe repressions. He also terminated celebration of Bolshevik Revolution Day (November 7) as a Hungarian holiday, made Russian in schools optional, and raised wages. To be sure, between 1959 and 1961, Kádár completed the enforced collectivization of the peasantry (this was socialism, after all), but he also promulgated a gentler slogan, "He who is not against us is for us." He abolished the workers' councils at factories, but he allowed passports to be issued to many members of the intelligentsia, so that if they left the country they could return (unlike in Poland), rendering many less implacable and helping to produce, despite Hungary's small size, perhaps the bloc's most impressive constellation of intellectuals. None of this relative flexibility altered the fundamental makeup of the party-state and its state-owned economy, which were the hallmarks of Stalinism. In 1956, when a Hungarian crowd (with the help of heavy machines) had pulled down Budapest's thirty-foot statue of Stalin and decapitated it, Stalin's boots remained implanted on the pedestal. As one Hungarian journalist had presciently said back when this bronze had first gone up in 1951, "Stalin was with us earlier, now he will be with us even more."[32] Still, the system had shown itself to be both stable and precarious, monolithic and brittle. In Hungary, it had been abolished—and reestablished—during the course of just two weeks.

For the Kremlin, the overriding dilemma was that ideology (socialism) and geopolitics (Soviet security) had been made inseparable.[33] Nikita Khrushchev, the Soviet leader during the Hungarian crisis, told his Soviet Politburo colleagues on October 31, 1956, "If we depart from Hungary, it will give a great boost to the Americans, English, and French—the imperialists. They will perceive it as weakness on our part and go on the offensive. We would then be exposing the weakness of our positions." Further, according to the Yugoslav ambassador to Moscow, Khrushchev told the Yugoslav president, Josip Broz Tito, that "there are people in the Soviet Union who would say that as long as Stalin was in command, everyone obeyed and there were no great shocks, but now [that these new bastards] have come to power, Russia has suffered the defeat and loss of Hungary."[34] Yet even though Moscow interpreted America's irresponsible incitement of the Hungarian rebels in 1956 as proof of imperialist designs, the Hungarians had themselves seen that American promises of liberation were empty.[35] Life would have to be lived within the Cold War framework. That circumstance galvanized support over time for Kádár and his policy of carving out room for maneuver. Outliving his 1956 epithet as the "butcher of Budapest," Kádár lasted in power until 1988 (he died the next year). Under him, party membership, which had dropped to only around 100,000 in December 1956 from a precrisis total of nearly 800,000, by 1988 grew back to some 700,000 (out of 10 million people). Kádár's replacement as general secretary that year was Károly Grósz (1930–96), his younger prime minister (since 1987) and an experienced official propagandist. Grósz had become a Communist in 1945, before turning fifteen, and had lived his whole adult life in uncivil society. The system seemed well entrusted to such next-generation guardians. But in fact, that was the great unknown.[36]

SOCIALISM WITH A SMASHED HUMAN FACE
(CZECHOSLOVAKIA, 1968)

Václav Havel's parable of the greengrocer who places the slogan "Workers of the world, unite!" in his shop window alongside his fruits and vegetables is justifiably celebrated. Called "The Power of the Powerless" and first circulated in samizdat beginning in 1978, the essay illuminates how ordinary people's desire to be left in peace sustained Communist systems.[37] But when the time finally came for the powerless to exercise their power, in the late 1980s, Havel, who feared that mass protests would offer a pretext for deadly repression, continued to advocate for a moral nonpolitical politics. By contrast, the opposition in Poland, as Adam Michnik explained in his underground *Letters from Prison,* had long aimed to cultivate an entire parallel society with non-Communist civic values and history and had addressed itself not to the rulers but to society, striving for a nonrevolutionary self-liberation.[38] Michnik recounted that after he obtained a diplomatic passport as a newly elected deputy to the Polish parliament in June 1989, he headed for Prague, where he told Havel that the whole thing was falling apart. "Havel," according to Michnik, "insisted that Czechoslovakia was different—'a Svejk regime,' 'Kafka.' " A few months later, Havel was president.[39] But apparently, Michnik's own education had also been swift. On the eve of the June 1989 elections, one eyewitness wrote, "the members of Solidarity should have known they were going to win! Yet they didn't know at all. On that Sunday [of the elections], I had a snack with Adam Michnik, who was exhausted and dejected—and he had no idea."[40]

Whatever the dissidents' slowness in grasping the system's stunning disintegration in 1989, the real conundrum is what each Communist establishment had been thinking and doing *all along*. We need, in other words, to consider not just the Václav Havels but the Vasil Bilaks. No one has bothered to translate Bilak's two-volume memoir, *Memories of Vasil Bilak* (1991), into English.[41] Born in 1917 in the Austro-Hungarian Empire's Subcarpathian region, Bilak is a Rusyn (sometimes called a "Ruthenian" or even a "Ukrainian") who assimilated into Slovak culture. He participated in the August 1944 uprising of the Czechoslovak Forces of the Interior against the Nazi wartime puppet state in Slovakia. Many who did so were put to death after German forces occupied Slovakia and overwhelmed the revolt. Only the arrival in Bratislava of the Soviet army in April 1945 chased the Germans out. Zdeněk Mlynář (1930–97), a future ideologue of the Prague Spring, wrote of World War II that it produced "a black-and-white vision of the world, with the enemy on one side and its adversary on the other. It was either one side or the other—there was no middle ground." And so the teenage Mlynář chose "the side of those who were most consistently and radically against the past, ... who made no compromises with the past but rather strove to sweep it aside, to overcome it in a revolutionary way"—that is, he chose Stalin.[42] Bilak was no teenager in May 1945—he was twenty-eight— and he joined the antifascist Communist party as well. In Eastern

Europe Communist systems were imposed, but by indigenous Communists, too.

In 1946, in democratic elections, the Communists won 30 percent of the vote in Slovak territories and 40 percent in Czech lands—the highest ever in free circumstances in any country. Leftist parties together (as one slogan had it, "Vote Communist or at least Social Democrat") secured a clear Czech majority and a strong Slovak minority.[43] Following the February 1948 Czechoslovak coup that established a Communist monopoly—which took place in the absence of Soviet troops—Mlynář was invited to study at the Stalinist Moscow State University and returned to become a legal analyst at the Czechoslovak Academy of Sciences Institute of State and Law as well as a consultant to the Central Committee. Bilak learned the tailor's trade and in Bratislava rose to the presidency of the tailors' and dressmakers' union. His formal education was limited to some training at the party "college" in 1952. By then, some 300,000 Czechoslovaks had been forced out of public life for having the wrong class origins, but up to 400,000 new people had been advanced, their weight greatly magnified by the elimination of Czechoslovakia's middle classes (the number of privately owned shops and artisan studios declined from nearly 250,000 in 1948 to under 7,000 by 1958).[44] "For many people in Czechoslovakia after the war," wrote Heda Margolius Kovály, the wife of an early top official purged in Stalinist show trials, "the Communist revolution was just another attempt to find a way home, to fight their way back." But for others, she added, socialism "was a victory over one's own smallness," a way to imagine "an unselfish subordination of an individual's interests to the good of all society." Kovály observed that "to give up this ideal would be to disclaim the meaning of one's whole life."[45] In other words, the rise of the Communist system and the rise of myriad Communists closely coincided.

Uncivil society would become cut off from the rest of the populace, but its members were Eastern Europe's first-ever elite with popular roots. In a then predominantly peasant region, Czechoslovakia stood out for being industrialized, and many of its newly promoted came from working-class backgrounds, like Bilak, as well as another Slovak, Alexander Dubček (1921–92). In 1962, the year before the down-to-earth Dubček became the head of the Slovak party, one journalist noted that "this man Dubček is remarkable for his innocent honesty. He may reach the top of the party, but he is much more likely to find himself in prison. His ingenuousness is ridiculous, but astonishing and refreshing."[46] Bilak was a Dubček protégé in the Slovak machine. In January 1968, when Dubček became general secretary of Czechoslovakia, Bilak succeeded him as Slovak first secretary.[47] This entire generation of promotees rose quickly. Many of them occupied decision-making positions well above their educational levels, particularly in industrial management.[48] Fully one half of the regime's security personnel had only primary schooling, while 68 percent of security commanders were judged to lack the requisite (modest) qualifications in the 1960s. (By then, according to a classified opinion poll, the Czechoslovak political police—originally created to hunt down former Nazi collaborators—stood second to last in terms of professions, just above sewer cleaners.)[49] To be sure, below the huge initial bulge of those who advanced, the younger echelons were usually better educated. Having come of age under socialism and its promises, many of these engineers and degreed professionals struggled to attain positions commensurate with their training, a frustration exacerbated by growing suspicions in their minds about Western European capitalist prosperity. "We learned from reports of the district party committees," Dubček recalled of early 1967, "that the mood in both Slovak and the Czech lands was increasingly impatient and in favor of change."[50]

The Prague Spring of 1968—launched by the Communist establishment—married ambition to idealism, aiming to renew socialism. The party's so-called Action Program of April 1968, coauthored by Mlynář, proposed replacing many of the Stalin-era officials while also easing the party's iron hierarchy (but keeping its leading role); relaxing central controls over enterprises (while retaining socialist ownership); lifting censorship; and softening the Czechs' grip over Slovakia.[51] The only genuine Slovak institution in Czechoslovakia was the Slovak Communist party, and the ferment had actually begun back in 1962–63 over Slovak issues. (Slovak autonomy was all that would survive the Prague Spring.) Still, uppermost in the minds of the Czech Prague Spring protagonists in the party and among intellectuals close to the Central Committee was what they called "socialism with a human face." They also spoke about their "sovereignty." The rest of the bloc, though, could not help but be affected by Czechoslovakia's strivings for a new incarnation of socialism. President Ludvík Svoboda (1895–1979)—an officer in the Czech Legion during World War I, a commander against the Nazis in World War II, briefly imprisoned during Stalinist purges but elevated to the presidency in March 1968—defended Czechoslovakia's reform. "Not through any fault of our own," the president-general said, "has our internal struggle against dogmatic and sectarian interpreters of socialism and its uniform Stalinist model overstepped the frontiers of Czechoslovakia."[52] In fact, some Prague Spring advocates did envision attracting a Western audience for their brand of socialism, thereby pretending to the role of the vanguard of world socialism.[53]

The Prague Spring was opposed in the name of socialism by most leaders of the rest of the bloc, such as Walter Ulbricht in East Germany, Władysław Gomułka in Poland, and eventually Kádár in Hungary. Their countries' sovereignty was infringed not just by the Soviet overlord but by the intertwined fate of all bloc countries. The Prague Spring was also opposed on socialist grounds internally, by people such as Bilak. Mlynář, a former Stalinist turned reform Communist, later dismissed Bilak as "no more than a failed tailor, full of ambition, a lust for power, and malice," but Bilak was a conservative by conviction and no less a partisan of socialism than Mlynář.[54] In February 1968, during the twentieth anniversary of the 1948 coup, Bilak gave Leonid Brezhnev an earful about the Czechoslovak "open counterrevolution" and its threat to the Soviet alliance, which he deemed integral to the success of socialism in Czechoslovakia. In July, Bilak promised Petro Shelest, the party boss in the Soviet republic of Ukraine, a collective Czechoslovak letter inviting Soviet intervention. Following several weeks of unexplained delay, in early August, at a clandestine rendezvous during a bloc gathering in Bratislava, Bilak delivered. "The very existence of socialism in our country is under threat," said the signed intervention request, written in Russian. "We are appealing to you, Soviet Communists, the leading representatives of the Communist Party of the Soviet Union.... Only with your assistance can the Czechoslovak Socialist Republic be extricated from the imminent danger of counterrevolution."[55] To avoid detection at the gathering, Bilak passed the invitation through a KGB intermediary in a toilet.

Operation Danube, the Soviet-led Warsaw Pact crackdown on August 21, 1968, against the Prague Spring, was the largest armed action in Europe after World War II—two hundred thousand troops and two thousand tanks. Seventy-two Czechs and Slovaks were killed, and seventy thousand fled (more than a quarter million eventually emigrated). The Czechoslovak leadership was kidnapped to Moscow and browbeaten to legitimize the invasion post facto. Moscow was infuriated that Dubček had failed to carry out his repeated promises to reintroduce censorship and remove the most radical reformers, in a political compromise. During a Kremlin harangue, Mlynář noted that Brezhnev was insistent that the Soviet Union had sacrificed too much in World War II to allow the results to be jeopardized.[56] *Pravda* soon explained that "The peoples of socialist countries and the Communist parties have and must have freedom to determine their country's path of development. Any decisions they make, however, must not be harmful either to socialism in their own country or to the fundamental interests of other socialist countries." In the West this became known as the Brezhnev Doctrine.[57] In Prague, after some disarray, a new party leader took power—not the assimilated Slovak Bilak, whom Moscow viewed as "Ukrainian," but his rival, the natural-born Slovak Gustáv Husák (1913–91). Bilak remained in high posts.[58] In October 1980, during Polish Solidarity, he issued warnings and a wish "that none of the endeavors by the bourgeoisie, by the anticommunist centers, and by the antisocialist forces... will deceive the Polish working man to the point where he would allow himself to be led astray from the socialist path."[59] But the orthodox types such as Bilak and Husák, who outnumbered the reform Communists, were the cause of their own anguish.

Borrowing the Rope to Hang Themselves

In the late 1940s, the Communist establishments across Eastern Europe formed small minorities, yet their members seemed deeply assured. They had resisted and defeated fascism; they were part of the movement of history; therefore, their theories and actions were right, even if majorities of their compatriots did not appreciate it, and in the name of the cause they could (and did) lie at will. By the 1980s, the Communist establishments had become enormous and possessed massive force, well-developed censorship mechanisms, and tight border controls. But the much bigger Communist establishments of the 1980s displayed the opposite sense of what the minuscule Communist establishments had in 1948: namely, that history was moving in the wrong direction, that defections could not be ignored, that the pervasive lying was sapping the system's own functionaries. "All it will take to bring the entire house down," remarked one anxious Soviet general in the world's biggest armed force, "is just one spark."[60] In other words, sometime between the late 1940s and the 1980s, uncivil society suffered a psychological blow, a loss of arrogance. That shift occurred not primarily because of the Hungarian events of 1956 or even the Czechoslovak events of 1968 but because of economic shortcomings, against the backdrop of Western capitalist successes. Eastern European elites who had come to power with Communist systems viewed the latter as instruments to force a modernization leap (of a particular nonmarket kind) on their "backward" countries. That was indeed what had happened, with great violence, but it had failed to close the gap with the West.

Eastern Europe had lagged behind Western Europe well before the imposition of communism.[61] Between 1913 and 1950, per capita GDP growth in Eastern Europe was an anemic 1 percent annually, slower than world averages. But from 1950 to 1973, it jumped to 3.9 percent annually, above world averages. For those twenty-three years, Eastern Europe's growth per head was even slightly above Asia's (3.7 percent). Post–World War II—having been entirely within the Axis wartime orbit, which had culminated in vast destruction—

Eastern Europe underwent an impressive recovery led by heavy industry. But then the Communist tree ceased leafing. For example, Hungary's annual average growth rate of around 6 percent dropped to 1.6 percent in 1979 and to 0 percent in 1980. The immediate cause was the 1973 oil shock, which raised the world price of crude some 400 percent in a few months. Among rich capitalist countries, the oil shock sparked the formation in 1974 of the International Energy Agency (IEA) and, the next year, of the Group of Six, or G6, a coordinating forum consisting of the United States, Japan, West Germany, Great Britain, Italy, and France (Canada would be added the next year). The Soviet Union, a major oil exporter, was buoyed by rising revenues but feared the political fallout of sticking the satellites with the entire bill, so Moscow tried to adjust prices moderately, absorbing some of the costs yet enduring the fallout anyway. Despite this initial Soviet energy cushioning, the oil shock worsened the socialist countries' terms of trade with the USSR. In 1974, the Soviets accepted 800 units of Hungary's Ikarus bus in exchange for 1 million tons of oil, but by 1981 that same quantity of oil required 2,300 buses, and by the mid-1980s, 4,000 buses.[62]

Paying more for oil hurt, but the deeper cause of the doldrums was that socialist economies had locked in low productivity, even as they kept promising ever-higher living standards. Rather than by gains in productivity, Soviet-style economies grew mostly by ever-greater inputs of capital and labor (so-called extensive growth). They also had trouble innovating, unable to assimilate even the innovations their spy agencies managed to steal from abroad. Most fundamentally, they invested in but misused and abused their human capital. Shortages and queues became endemic to a planned economy's routine operation, but the mania for heavy industry, the collectivization of agriculture (Poland excepted), and the suppression of the service sector as capitalistic combined to ensure that even during high growth spurts, rises in consumption lagged. True, following Stalin's death, the regimes had made concessions to the consumer. But that only compounded the challenge; subsidies for housing, food, clothing, and other consumer items became ever more costly to maintain, while the smallest price hikes (when tried) sparked revolts that sometimes shook the regimes to their foundations. The problem was simple: on top of the outsized expenses for military-security and elite perquisites, the daily-life subsidies were ever more costly but indispensable because, unlike the Soviet Union in the 1930s (the time of the capitalist Great Depression), the Eastern European satellites faced a capitalist world—in many cases, right across the border—that underwent its greatest-ever consumer boom in the 1950s and '60s. This circumstance, despite the censorship and propaganda, was known. Eastern Europeans learned from the media (foreign but also official) and, thanks to détente, increasingly from direct contacts with visiting foreign tourists or even from their own travels westward.

Communism had an insurmountable problem: it was locked in competition with the better-performing West. Unlike the Soviet Union, the East bloc uncivil societies could not draw on a World War II victory to compensate for their comparative failings. So, predictably, they fell back on asserting the supposed social and moral superiority of socialism and on cultivating nationalism. With some irony, Communist regimes promoted national feeling partly on the basis of anti-Russian sentiment. In Romania, as we shall see, such nationalism forged a strong bond between the regime and intellectuals, enabling the party to incorporate Romanian national aspirations with some success. Poland was even more virulently anti-Russian than Romania, but the Polish party could never manage to be synonymous with the nation in the face of competition with the Catholic Church or the organized opposition. East Germany is often said to have lacked nationalist feeling, but there, too, the regime linked itself to national traditions, whether great leaders (Frederick the Great) or great movements (nineteenth-century wars of liberation for a unified Germany; organized labor). Still, for the German Democratic Republic (GDR), the Western competition was another German state, the Federal Republic (which was often governed by Social Democrats, political rivals of the Communists on the left). Nonetheless, whatever the straining of credulity on national grounds, each bloc country's "national communism" was linked to promises of economic and technical modernization, perhaps the core of the regimes' claims to legitimacy. And that was the killer: after all the exertions, violence, and sacrifice, far from outdueling the West, the bloc had fallen into dependency on the West.

This was a time, in the 1970s, when the second great globalization took off. (The first, which had commenced in the latter half of the nineteenth century, had ended badly.) Global trade flows were liberalized and taxes on trade reduced. Also, steps toward a separate global financial liberalization began, while multinational corporations undertook not just international portfolio investment but foreign direct investment. Still, it was the selfsame oil shock that had upended the East bloc that put surplus money into the hands of Western banks. Western bankers profitably recycled the gushing Middle East petrodollars as loans to the Communist bloc (as well as to Latin America). Although it was Tito's Yugoslavia that had first opened to Western funding, receiving around $2.7 billion between 1951 and 1960 from the United States alone, nominally in exchange for good behavior vis-à-vis Greece and Italy, East bloc borrowing became known as the "Polish disease." It could also have been called the East German disease. Ostensibly, the goal was to use the loans to buy advanced equipment in order to manufacture export-quality goods... to pay off the loans. But that depended on steady market demand for East bloc goods abroad. The Eastern Europeans used the Soviet Union as a dumping ground for their inferior goods (low-quality and outdated clothes, footwear, fabrics, leather ware, furniture), which they did not even try to sell in hard-currency export markets. But even Eastern Europe's supposedly Western-export-grade goods left a lot to be desired. Then came a market surprise. Edward Gierek, the Polish party chief during the fateful 1970s, who launched the "borrow West" strategy, exhorted, "Build a second Poland!" He meant doubling GDP in a decade. Such a great leap forward proved an utter fantasy—except in the capitalist world. No Communist propaganda could wish away the phenomenal post–World War II economic performance of the United States, Western Europe (especially West Germany), and Japan, whose export-led boom inspired and funded the "tigers" of South Korea, Taiwan, Hong Kong, and Singapore. In the 1980s, East Asian manufacturers blindsided the Eastern European uncivil societies. Lower-cost exports turned out to be a game others in the global economy could play, with far cheaper labor and higher quality.

The Eastern European borrowing strategy also depended on affordable interest rates and on foreign bankers' willingness to roll over their loans—something that the bankers belatedly began to question around 1979, at the time of the second oil shock and a sharp uptick in interest rates. By then, Poland's convertible-currency debt had reached around $20 billion; servicing that debt ate up 80 percent of its export earnings. (The neglect of agriculture, meanwhile, meant that food accounted for nearly a quarter of Polish imports in 1978, costing valuable hard currency.) Hungary's convertible-currency debt ballooned from around $1 billion in 1972 to $9 billion by 1979, a burden that could be serviced only by taking on more debt. By 1989, Hungary's debt hit $18 billion, meaning the country needed a surplus in hard currency from exports of more than $1 billion annually *just to pay the interest* (the corresponding figure for Poland was $2 billion). Across the bloc, total hard-currency debt shot up from $6 billion in 1970 to $21 billion by 1975, $56 billion by 1980, and $90 billion by 1989, with no end of the escalation in sight.[63] Beginning with Mexico in 1982, Latin American countries defaulted individually on their foreign debts. Perhaps the Eastern European countries could have united to default simultaneously, seeking to deal a blow to the global financial system that held them in a vise, or at least to gain leverage in a write-down. But they were Communists and not global casino players. "Most of Eastern Europe's economies had plunged head-first into the swimming pool" of Western capitalist finance, two scholars have written, "and instead of emerging refreshed and revitalized had surfaced gasping for air and saddled with unsustainable debt."[64]

Nicolae Ceaușescu's Romania would demonstrate the brutal cost of paying off the debt—blackouts, ice-cold interiors, severe rationing of food. This was a price the East German and Polish establishments could not pay. The bloc's uncivil societies lacked the political capital to slash the costly price subsidies, let alone to inflict the tough medicine of unemployment, in a painful restructuring of reality. On the contrary, they continued to employ everyone and to dole out the subsidies and still labored to burnish their legitimacy. Moreover, possessing, as did Romania's dictatorship, the muscle to impose significant additional consumer deprivation (without mass layoffs) was not the same as having the wisdom and wherewithal to address the fundamental problem; namely, the inbuilt low productivity and waste of the planned economy. Staring at Romania's debt-reduction despair on one side and, on the other, at West Germany's relentless cornucopia, uncivil societies took out ever more foreign-currency loans to pay back their old foreign-currency loans. The bloc had become a Ponzi scheme.

GEOPOLITICS AND IDEOLOGY

After World War II, and particularly from the 1970s, profound structural changes radically altered the global geopolitical context for Eastern Europe, demanding a response from its uncivil societies. Having built socialism, they responded essentially with two opposed versions of trying to make it better. One involved the reformers' dream—socialism with a human face—which, however, had repeatedly shown itself to be not a renewal of socialism but its unwitting liquidation. Party conservatives were properly wary of Gorbachev's 1980s revival of socialism with a human face. But their alternative, conservative modernization—meaning a further tightening of "discipline" as well as profligate investment in technological panaceas—also failed to reenergize the systems. This left just muddling through, which held out great appeal. After all, the system had raised up the members of uncivil society, and they hoped the system would somehow save them, especially if capitalism finally descended into the second great depression that Communists had long predicted for it. But someone forgot to tell the post–World War II capitalist world to go into a death spiral. Instead, the competition in living standards all but bankrupted the Communist systems economically, because they were politically and morally bankrupt. Consciously or not, borrowing from the West amounted to a substitute for conceding the uncivil society's monopoly on power, but the bill came due. "There is no socialism with a human face," Adam Michnik liked to say, "only totalitarianism with its teeth knocked out."

Predictably, the bloc's uncivil societies upped their pleas to Moscow, but the Soviets could not bear the extra burden. From the 1970s, after having long paid below-world-market prices for imports from Eastern Europe while extracting higher prices for Soviet exports, Moscow found itself providing its satellites with raw materials at below-world prices, while importing shoddy goods in return.[65] Worse, after the world price of oil tumbled precipitously in 1985–86, the Soviet Union—which could not beg *itself* for more money—eventually became contaminated with the "Polish disease," too, borrowing from the capitalists to satisfy consumer desires in a socialist country. Meanwhile, Moscow fumed that the inhabitants of the satellites were living better than the Soviets, yet these beneficiaries were not even satisfied. But rank-and-file Eastern European dissatisfaction could not be directed at abstractions such as "the market" or "globalization"; the regimes were held responsible. Many members of uncivil society expressed outrage at the "petit-bourgeois" hankering for dachas and cars, washing machines and refrigerators (as did many dissidents, including Havel). Of course, the elites, along with their wives and children, enjoyed the best access to Western goods and services, not to mention domestic dachas (Bilak was preoccupied with restoring an old castle for himself). Be that as it may, those who decried "refrigerator socialism" were spitting in the wind. And yet, even the dim-witted comprehended the depth of the trap: If socialism was merely aiming to placate consumers just like capitalism, only not as well, was socialism's existence even justified? To put the matter in its starkest terms, how long could muddling through continue if Western bankers refused to roll over the loans?

What to do?[66] Communist rulers in China—who endure as of this writing—discovered a solution: a police-state market economy. On June 4, 1989, when multicandidate elections took place in Poland that would culminate in the formation of a Solidarity-led government, the tanks rolled into China's Tiananmen Square. It was a coincidence, but an extraordinary one: one Communist uncivil society capitulated, the other stood firm. But after bloodying its people who were demonstrating for political openness, the leadership in China also ended up deepening the country's turn toward economic openness. Who would have guessed it would be the Chinese Communists, rather than the Eastern Europeans, who would embrace the market and global integration? Unlike Mao Zedong and his homicidal Cultural Revolution (1966–76)—which, unintentionally, destroyed China's economic planning capacities—the Eastern European establishments had ceased to be militant. Albania excepted, the Eastern Europeans had not railed against the USSR for being in bed with imperialism (détente) and abandoning world revolution.[67] Rather, they turned out to be conservative, which derived from their long terms in power but also seemed vindicated by events in Prague in 1968. Indeed, 1968 helped formalize conservatives' identities across the bloc as the resolute "healthy forces." They branded their nemeses—the reformers—as counterrevolutionaries. But the reformers, too, fought *to defend socialism.* Neither side could imagine abandoning socialism. In sum, the uncivil societies of Eastern Europe, whether conservative or reformist, remained largely bound by the ideology, unlike the Leninist-type copycat single party in non-Communist Taiwan or the recovering post-Mao Communist party on mainland China.[68]

The mundane fact about the Communist establishments in Eastern Europe was that they were full of...Communists. This is abundantly clear from the single most important fact about the formerly secret archives: behind closed doors the Communists evidenced the same vocabulary and worldview that they did in public. For the Eastern European systems, the reformers such as Mlynář were the more immediately dangerous, since reform amounted to autoliquidation, but the conservatives such as Bilak and Husák bear the greater responsibility for the happy circumstance of the implosion. By July 1989, Bilak—by then recently ousted from the panicked Communist-party Presidium—was observed to be "genuinely frightened to see that the situation in Poland and Hungary has already reached the borderline of dramatic events."[69] Husák—elbowed aside as party chief in December 1987 by a younger cohort—remained president right until the collapse in December 1989. To be sure, such stalwarts had not invented Eastern Europe's ambivalence about the market or the West, any more than Eastern Europe had begun to be distinguished from Western Europe only in 1948. From the fifteenth century onward, all of Eastern Europe had been incorporated into the Ottoman, Habsburg, Russian, and (late-coming) German empires, emerging as independent national states in the nineteenth and especially twentieth centuries. In the process, many Eastern European public figures urged their countryfolk to follow a special path instead of an inevitably weaker imitation of the West. The Communists took up the challenge. They conceded that Western borrowings might be necessary but had to be limited. The idea of permitting some market mechanisms had come under discussion early in the revolutionary regimes, but always only as a way to have profit-and-loss calculations assist administrative methods, not as a displacement of planning. Even Hungary's János Kádár, considered perhaps the most flexible Communist leader on economic experimentation, pointedly remarked during a visit to a large factory in 1986, "It must be understood that the foundation of Hungary's people's economy is socialist, that the means of production are 96–97 percent in social property and that our future will be decided in the socialist factories. Everything else can be a useful supplement to this, but nothing else."[70]

China's Tiananmen crackdown resounded throughout the East bloc in summer and fall 1989, but the incipient market success of the Chinese Communists mostly escaped the Eastern Europeans. Károly Grósz—the fifty-seven-year-old who had emerged as Kádár's prime minister in 1987 and then shunted Kádár aside as party chief in 1988—supported a number of long-contemplated economic reforms: capitalist-style banking, majority foreign private ownership. Grósz also showed intransigence over relinquishing the party's monopoly and explored the possibility of martial law. This desperate, crisis-ridden groping appears to have been inspired not by Communist China's example, however, but by the high-growth authoritarianism of 1980s South Korea. Be that as it may, in October 1989 Grósz was definitively eclipsed by Hungary's Communist-party *political* reformers who sought survival in a Western-style multiparty system.[71] The possible exception of Grósz aside—the evidence is ambiguous and the time period short—the Eastern European ruling circles insistent on retaining one-party rule ruled out embracing the market. For them, it was tantamount to treason. Indeed, in East Germany, which faced a hugely successful market-economy Germany right across the barbed wire, "capitulation" to the market appeared to entail the end of the country. Would East German uncivil society risk suicide? Would the Soviets accept the "loss" of East Germany, paid for with 27 million Soviet lives? Here, most prominently, ideology meshed with geopolitics.

A reversion to capitalism under Communist rule—something like China's market Leninism—seemed out of the question. Socialism had been a promise to transcend all problems, but the accumulated entrenched interests of socialism, its uncivil society, would not countenance an attempt to transcend socialism's problems, only "more socialism." The Soviets, in other words, were not alone in keeping Eastern Europe locked on its fatal trajectory, in the teeth of the radically altered circumstances of the postwar capitalist world. Still, there were nearly 600,000 troops in the bloc, contributing to the what-me-worry stance. But everything changed with Gorbachev's repeal of the Brezhnev-Andropov Doctrine to use force to maintain the satellite regimes and his insistence that the bloc leaders not use force on their own. In 1989, the scholar Mark Kramer has argued, had the East European uncivil societies been left *entirely* to their own devices, the endgame would likely have been bloody.[72] This is a point we shall explore. What happened to the Eastern European establishments in 1989? What did they do, or not do, and why? "The fundamental question," the Hungarian intellectual György Konrád had written in 1984, "is: can an ossified, conservative elite absorb ideas that are foreign to it? Can it distribute and devolve power so as to exercise it more skillfully, so that the danger of collapse will no longer threaten it? Our not altogether reassuring experience has been that communism will break before it will bend."[73] In fact, the uncivil societies set themselves up for the equivalent of political bank runs.

II

NO EXIT

Walter Ulbricht, the first Communist leader of East Germany, is sitting in a restaurant. One of the waitresses flirts with him, and the responsive Ulbricht coos, "I will grant you one wish."

She thinks and says, "Open the wall for just one day."

"Ah," says Ulbricht with a wink, "you want to be alone with me."

Born in 1949 following mass rapes by the Soviet army and almost toppled in its fourth year of existence by mass popular revolt, the German Democratic Republic, a rump abutting another German state, lasted four decades. That was not quite as long as Wilhelmine Germany (1870–1918) but longer than the Weimar Republic (1918–33) or the Third Reich (1933–45). Over time, the GDR's Leninist technocratic image—as a "Red Prussia"—developed a wide following both inside and outside the Soviet bloc. In 1980, the World Bank judged East Germany to be tenth highest in the world in per capita income, above Great Britain.[1] But in the period after World War II, particularly from the 1970s, the formula of Communist-party monopoly and state planning failed to maintain competitive economies, including in the supposed great success, the GDR, as Jeffrey Kopstein has pointed out.[2] East Germany's infamous State Security Service (Stasi) managed to produce files on 6 million people, more than one third of the country's total population (16.4 million). But the political police had no answer for a prosperous West Germany, which, in the 1950s, took off on a multidecade economic miracle to become, after the United States and Japan, the world's third most powerful economy.

East Germany's populace, no less than the regime, understood that comparisons with West Germany were the basis of the GDR's legitimacy. Either socialism was superior to capitalism, or it had no reason for being. This logic—starkly evident in the case of the two Germanys—held for the entire bloc. And the bloc being a bloc, the fate of each national Communist regime depended on the fate of the others. When it announced its second Five-Year Plan (1956–60), the GDR committed itself to overtaking West Germany in per capita consumption of key food products and consumer goods by 1961. Rash? Announced or not, some form of a consumer competition was inescapable. In 1961, however, rather than outconsuming West Germans, East Germans were completely enclosed: on top of the already existing 857-mile inner German-German border, a new wire fence was hastily erected some 90 miles across Berlin. The next year, a second, inner fence went up, creating a no-man's-land, "the death strip," patrolled by self-firing machine guns triggered by movement. These barriers were soon concretized. Still, East Germans could continue to make direct comparisons with life in West Germany from their own living rooms—just by watching West German television. In Albania the populace could watch Italian TV and in Estonia Finnish TV—rare windows. But in the GDR, Western TV was accessible in the inhabitants' native tongue (except in a poor-reception area around Dresden, dubbed "the valley of the clueless").[3] North Koreans have never had anything like that vis-à-vis South Korea. West German TV offered East Germans a "nightly emigration"—and a frustrating tease.

Samizdat (self-publication) in the GDR was virtually unknown, and antisocialist dissidents were relatively few, a circumstance often attributed to the supposed lack of a strong sense of nation and nationalism.[4] (As we shall see in the next chapter, Communist Romania is said to have lacked dissent because of a too-powerful sense of nation.) In fact, even when they were critical, intellectuals in East Germany exhibited a high degree of loyalty. The East German novelist Christa Wolf (born Christa Ihlenfeld in 1929), who after a brief stint as an informer fell under extended Stasi surveillance, openly criticized the East German leadership, but like most East German intellectuals, she hoped not to undo but to revivify the antifascist, anticapitalist cause. There was no anomaly in an intelligentsia committed to the socialist cause. True, many East German intellectuals were apolitical. And repression was omnipresent. "We were always afraid of being denounced," recalled one person critical of the regime.[5] But for most, West German consumerism was not their idea of better socialism. Even the hideous Wall was accepted by some of them. "I took it to be an evil, but a necessary evil for the existence of the GDR," said one socialist intellectual, adding that "whoever wants to tear down the Wall must also be clear that he is at the same time tearing down the basis of the existence of the GDR."[6] Those deemed antisocialist could apply to leave or be expelled, blunting opposition domestically. As for intellectuals who refused to leave, in many cases they also refused to campaign for freedom of movement (human rights)—if leaving was betrayal, why defend the right to betrayal?[7]

This dynamic—leave or stay—turned out to be the crucial mobilizer in 1989, when the GDR was suddenly struck by mass demonstrations, to near-universal shock, in Leipzig.[8] As throngs of East Germans—eligible for automatic citizenship upon arrival in West Germany—clamored for exit, others massed to voice the sentiment "We're staying." The period from the time this agitation erupted, in autumn 1989, to the time the regime disappeared was astonishingly brief. Before a momentous peaceful demonstration on October 9 in Leipzig, the country counted fewer than 100,000 total protesters at all events, but the total would rise to 4 million by November 9, when the Berlin Wall was breached. And yet, this was mass mobilization without mass organization. The best-known organized social movement outside the regime, New Forum, was announced only in late September 1989. Though loyalist, New Forum was immediately declared "hostile to the state" and illegal by the Stasi and found no counterpart inside the ruling party—such as the reform Communists in Hungary—to negotiate with and to bolster its fledgling organization. New Forum's activists had no offices or telephones. Its name was sometimes evoked at marches, but it was overwhelmed by events. "Social movements in the GDR evolved largely spontaneously," argues the scholar Steven Pfaff, adding that "detestable, poorly performing authoritarian states are commonplace; it is revolutions that are unusual."[9] When does popular acquiescence to dictatorship vanish? When does the uncivil society lose its nerve?[10]

The Communist establishment could not emigrate: it had no exit. In 1987, dismissing suggestions that East Germany would have to emulate Mikhail Gorbachev's reforms, Kurt Hager, the GDR's ideology chief, remarked, "If your neighbor put up new wallpaper in his home, would you feel obliged to put up new wallpaper in your own?" But the Soviet changeover to perestroika and glasnost from Brezhnevism was game-changing for all of Eastern Europe's uncivil societies. Gorbachev (despite lobbying by his advisers) did remarkably little to nudge East Germany's lingering Stalinists out. Still more remarkably, however he acquiesced when the entire socialist Germany suddenly started disintegrating under the pressure of street protests. The precipitous collapse of the GDR cannot be explained by citing some quest to fulfill German identity, a generational change, or "civil society."[11] The GDR collapsed because the Soviet Union let it. More fundamentally, though, East Germany was crushed by its West German counterpart, before being abandoned by its Soviet backstop as well as by fellow bloc members. On August 18, 1989, prior to the dramatic eruptions in the GDR, a non-Communist government took office in Poland, demonstrating the power of organized, implacable opposition and the system's vulnerability. In 1989, the Communists in Hungary voluntarily promised elections in a multiparty system, a jump from Kádárism's supposed gradual transcendence from within. Erich Honecker, the GDR's orthodox leader, refused to emulate Poland or Hungary. But confidentially he conceded that East Germany could not "go the Romanian way either"—that is, a total refusal to reform—because "the situation vis-à-vis [West Germany] will not allow that."[12] In sum, the GDR crystallized the options, or lack thereof, of uncivil society.

HITLER AND STALIN'S JOINT VENTURE

Not for nothing was 1945 called Zero Hour in Germany. Defeat was total. The ovens and mass graves were fully revealed. The country was a physical ruin, too, its infrastructure destroyed, its factories and farms inoperable, its medieval-era cities flattened. Dresden, the target of infamous firebombing of civilians, lost 65 percent of its dwellings. Millions of German refugees flooded in from points east, creating further strain. Food and medicines were in short supply. Above all, the German state evaporated—the executive branch, the civil service, the judiciary, the education system, the police. Into the vacuum stepped the occupiers: the United States, the United Kingdom, and the Soviet Union. (France was soon added.) Soviet revenge for the war of extermination consisted of mass violation of German women, looting and trophy collection, and wholesale dismantling and eastward shipment of German industrial equipment. "You liberate us from everything, from cars and machines," went the German ditty. "We cry for joy. How good you are to us."[13] Whereas back in 1923 wild Bolshevik schemes to help German Communists seize power in a coup had ended in a debacle, Adolf Hitler had managed at unprecedented cost to implant Soviet overlords in Berlin.

None of the Big Three initially sought what they got: two German states. In late 1943 and early 1944, they had agreed that, once defeated, Germany would be carved into occupation zones. But then what? The United States initially shared with the Soviets a determination to avoid a revival of the German colossus. In 1944, Henry Morgenthau Jr., Treasury secretary from 1934 until 1945, proposed that Germany be dismembered into many states (Bavaria, the Rhineland), denuded of its heavy industry, and forced back to an agrarian condition. A reluctant Winston Churchill, mindful of ongoing Lend-Lease deliberations, signed on to this "pastoral" scheme at Franklin Roosevelt's urging, but the plan was never implemented.[14] The United States was mindful of instability and Communist subversion in Western Europe. But policy was still not fully settled in 1948, when George Kennan, then head of policy planning at the State Department, advised capitalizing on "the Tito defection"—actually, Stalin broke from Tito—by uniting Germany and eroding the Soviet domination of Eastern Europe. The Soviets, Kennan felt, were not ready for war. True, and neither was the United States. There was also the risk that a united Germany would not align with the Americans. That, in fact, was Stalin's vision—a united but "neutral" Germany, which the dictator expected to fall under Soviet sway.

A big sticking point to unification, however, was Stalin's insistence on maintaining Soviet troops on German soil indefinitely, even though he believed U.S. troops would be withdrawn from Europe. What Stalin feared was that a separate West German state—possessing most of German industry, resources, and population—would become a rebuilt, powerful member of an Anglo-American-led bloc. He was prescient but utterly maladroit in acting to prevent this outcome. Stalin implemented what Franklin Roosevelt and Harry Truman would not—a Morgenthau-like "pastoralization" in his occupation zone, hauling off much of the industrial plant and even half the zone's railroad track to the Soviet Union as reparations. Following that as well as the Communist takeovers throughout Eastern Europe in 1947–48, on top of a German economic malaise and Soviet fiscal excess (printing marks), the Americans, British, and French, in their unified occupation zone, invalidated the existing currency (reichsmark) and introduced a new one (deutsche mark) on June 20, 1948. The Soviets mounted a blockade of Berlin, which was eventually broken by airlift, but were compelled to create a separate new German currency for their zone. Each side had envisioned a united Germany under its sway. But each side had also feared such a united Germany. The upshot was formalization of the wartime exigency—occupation-zone division.[15] By May 1949, the Americans proclaimed a separate, Western Federal Republic of Germany (FRG). On October 7, the Soviet zone, accounting for around 40 percent of German territory, became the German Democratic Republic (GDR).

Sovietization on the ground, however, had been under way from the get-go. "Soviet officers Bolshevized the zone," the scholar Norman Naimark wrote of the occupation, "not because there was a plan to do so, but because that was the only way they knew how to organize society."[16] The initial aim was establishing control—after all, it was a big zone and full of former Nazis. And although the number of German Communists (KPD) shot up—from 100,000 in July 1945 to 600,000 by spring 1946, double the size they had been during the Weimar Republic—they were still outnumbered by the Social Democrats. In April 1946, under heavy Soviet pressure, Communists and Socialist Democrats in the Soviet zone merged into the so-called Social Unity Party (SED). This was accomplished by organizing relentlessly at the grass roots, especially in factories, blackmailing resistant Social Democrats with compromising material and prodding compliant ones with special rations (chocolates, cigarettes). Socialists and Communists remained wary of each other, but both desired an antifascist alternative on German soil. "We are sacrificing our party for the freedom of Germany," remarked one Social Democrat about the "merger."[17] In this way, the Communists expropriated much idealism and much of the long-standing attachment to the labor movement. Forcing through a Soviet-style party, however, did not mean that Stalin initially sought a fully Soviet-style system. It was the East German Communists, against their Soviet overseers, who from the start had pushed zealously for a separate socialist German state. Privately, they whispered that they would do socialism better.[18]

Leading the way was Walter Ulbricht (1893–1973), known informally as "Goatee," one of essentially only two leaders the East German ruling party knew over four decades. The son of a Leipzig tailor, Ulbricht had joined the Social Democratic Party in 1912, then after World War I split off with its left wing to found the German Communists in 1918–19. During the Nazi period, he fled to Paris and Prague (1933–38), then Moscow (1938–45). The day Hitler committed suicide, he returned with the Soviet army—and with the clenched-fist intransigence that had conditioned the German Communists from inception, in hostility to the nonrevolutionary Social Democrats.[19] Hitler and especially Stalin had killed off much of Ulbricht's competition for the top party post (60 percent of German Communists who had sought refuge from the Nazis in the Soviet Union perished). Ulbricht ruled the GDR from 1950, yet even then Stalin contemplated cashing in the German Communists for a "neutral" unification on his terms, and thus he allowed pan-German radio and TV. Only in spring 1952 did Stalin finally accede to Ulbricht's insistent lobbying for a "systematic implementation of socialism." Launched in July, the drive resulted in a crisis. Collectivization pushed nearly half of the GDR's wealthier farmers to West Germany by spring 1953, worsening food shortages. The clampdown on the private sector emptied store shelves. That, in turn, precipitated steep price increases—in effect, wage cuts. After Stalin died (on March 5, 1953), his Kremlin successors browbeat Ulbricht to ease up, but the East German leader refused to rescind the 10 percent increases in production output quotas.

A general strike and riots on June 17, 1953, blindsided East Germany's rulers. Around 600,000 protesters—by some accounts, up to 10 percent of the GDR's adult population—massed in almost every city of the country, stoning Stalin monuments, freeing prisoners, and shouting "Death to communism!" The East German Politburo fled to the Soviet military base at Karlhorst. Rumors circulated that Ulbricht had been arrested and that former landowners, along with the Americans and British, were arriving. In fact, on the night of June 17 the Soviet military massed T-34 tanks and special troops to institute martial law, killing hundreds of people, arresting thousands, and saving the East German regime.[20] Ulbricht's personal rule survived the uprising too (as it had Stalin's death), thanks to Moscow. But in 1971, with Moscow's connivance, he was toppled by his protégé Erich Honecker (1912–94), the son of a coal miner and himself a roofer. Under Ulbricht, Honecker had overseen the construction of the Berlin Wall, which was called the "antifascist protection rampart." (In January 1989, he would defiantly insist that "the Wall will remain so long as the conditions that led to its erection are not changed. It will be standing even in fifty and even in a hundred years, if the necessary conditions are not removed.") Honecker, too, embodied German communism's clenched-fist intransigence—which, in his case, had been instilled by studying in the Soviet Union during Stalin's heady First Five-Year Plan and then nearly a decade in Hitler's prisons.

East German Communists repeatedly stressed that in free elections in 1932, 10 million Germans had voted for Hitler. The purported antidote, Communist civic values, was inculcated in East German schools, workplaces, poster art, festivals, parades. One component was a cultivated association with German *Kultur*—Goethe, Schiller, Bach, Beethoven—and the provision of cultural enrichment opportunities, such as the GDR's more than fifty classical symphony orchestras. Another facet was the mooring of the GDR in German national history, connecting to Frederick the Great, the nineteenth-century wars of liberation (prior to Otto von Bismarck's unification), the labor movement. Third, the GDR promoted the Soviet Union and its purported historic achievements as a superpower and a friend. Fourth was the heroic role, often with tragic sacrifices, that Communists had undertaken in the antifascist struggle, a struggle that had carried over into the GDR's mission.[21] Fifth, the regime appealed to a yearning for social justice and world peace, which were said to be attributes that distinguished socialism. Finally, holding it all together was a promise of material advance. "In the GDR there are no capitalist corporations or private banks. The working class rules supreme," explained a regime pamphlet issued as East Germany approached its thirtieth anniversary. "Socialism means permanently rising living and cultural standards."[22]

Amid such hopes, as well as the lying and spying, many East Germans led what they saw as normal lives.[23] For the politically reliable, normal included being able to buy Western goods (at Intershops) and even traveling to the West. For the majority, normal involved some measure of cheap food and housing, job security, child care, health care, sports, culture, friends, and family. The East German state invested in education and training in the 1950s and '60s, and it opened pathways for the offspring of people of modest circumstances to rise up. To many of the upwardly mobile—in an economy that was wholly owned and managed by the state and growing, so that the ranks of middle management kept expanding—this really was a "workers' and peasants' state." Around 2.3 million people—one in five adults—belonged to the Communist party, which honeycombed every workplace and neighborhood. Party members were often university-educated, rather than peasants (as in Romania) or blue-collar (as in Czechoslovakia). At the same time, the mass of the GDR's inhabitants—party members or not—belonged to the official trade unions, the youth groups, women's organizations, the Society for German-Soviet Friendship. They also flooded the corridors of power and the media with petitions seeking redress for this or that problem. Most engaged in arts of evasion, many (including officials) told biting jokes about the system, and a few formed socioethical subcultures associated with Protestantism. But the GDR developed a shared socialist way of life, as satirized in the film *Good Bye, Lenin!* (2003) about a bedridden East German woman emerging from a coma after 1989 whose son, hoping to avoid shocking her frail system, re-creates the GDR in their apartment, knowing exactly what it takes, materially and mentally, to do so.[24] Right next door, Poland (as we shall see in part III) was engulfed by mass strikes and demonstrations in 1956, 1968, 1970, 1976, and 1980, which enabled the legalization of mass independent trade unions. And yet communism in the GDR fell, too. It was undermined by its own uncivil society.

BANKRUPTCY, DEPENDENCY, PARALYSIS

Planning was socialism's supposed advantage. But East Germany's
first planners had no idea how a planned economy should function in
practice. Until 1954, no standard text on a planned economy existed,
not even in the Soviet Union. Planners could, of course, study the
Soviet Union in action, but many wondered whether a model based
on vaulting a peasant country to modernity was appropriate for an
already highly industrialized country like East Germany. In fact,
after Stalin's death a handful of East German economists questioned
the Soviet model as outdated, comparing its hypercentralization
with the Prussian-style wartime economy, a comparison, as everyone
knew, that could also have been made with the Nazis. These economists, in permitted public debates, used highly technical studies fo-
cused on the firm to advocate for market mechanisms to address
planning's cost inflexibility, the disincentives for technological development, and the evasion of responsibility. They envisioned a socialism in which planning would entail general decisions on investments,
not day-to-day oversight. But a 1956 statistical yearbook the economists put together—the first in the GDR—showed East German
workers' real income lagging behind that of West German workers,
and party conservatives pounced on the experts for undermining socialism.[25]

Ulbricht ping-ponged in the debates. Having encouraged the
economists to plump for decentralization and self-regulation within
planning, in 1957 he suddenly joined the venomous attacks against
them. Six years later, however, the East German boss—then age seventy—pushed through these very measures, overriding conservative
resistance, in what was called East Germany's New Economic System. The changes made everyone's job harder. If production associations were independent, how did one implement financial planning?
Would not central ministries and the Politburo lose control over investment strategy? "In some respects the conservatives were right,"
Jeffrey Kopstein points out. "Enterprises left to their own devices
would not necessarily invest in projects that served the long-term

goals of the planners." And what if reforms spilled over into the cultural and even political spheres? Ulbricht switched sides again. In 1968, during the Prague Spring, Anton Ackermann, Ulrich's rehabilitated old rival, denounced the "socialist market" and championed orthodox planning in a private letter to Ulbricht, who had the letter circulated internally. "In the present situation," Ackerman pointedly wrote, "when the class enemy concentrates from outside on discrediting the socialist planned economy, on stimulating 'convergence theory' and the change from a socialist economy to a so-called socialist market economy, must we not wage a struggle not only against the open but also against hidden forms of this ideological diversion?"[26]

Resurgent orthodox types could prevail in internal power struggles, bucking Moscow's wishes for greater liberalization in the East German showcase, yet German hard-liners still faced an insurmountable challenge. The Soviets had radically suppressed consumption in building socialism, but that was back when the capitalist world had been mired in the 1930s Great Depression. In the 1950s, West Germany's yearly growth rates were *in the double digits*. In July 1960, Ulbricht had written to Khrushchev that "you can be sure that we are doing everything in our powers. But West Germany has turned out to be economically powerful." The GDR, he said, was being subverted by "hostile-negative forces"—that is, by Western daily life. "In the final analysis, we cannot choose against whom we would like to compete," Ulbricht added. "We are simply forced to square off against West Germany. However, the GDR does not have enough economic power to do this alone." Ulbricht begged for more hard currency (and even laborers). Moscow refused. In January 1961, Ulbricht wrote, "The booming economy in West Germany, which is visible to every citizen of the GDR, is the main reason that over ten years about two million people have left our republic."[27] The runaways included entrepreneurs and skilled professionals (one day the entire Mathematics Department of the University of Leipzig defected). In August of that year, Moscow finally relented to Ulbricht's insistent requests over many years to wall in East Germans. But the living-standard differential could not be walled out.[28]

Supplication before the Soviets never ceased, but Ulbricht turned to the enemy, too. In 1970, the year before his ouster in a palace coup, he told the head of the USSR Council of Ministers that because the Soviets would not underwrite the GDR to the extent necessary, the GDR would have to borrow from the capitalist West. "We know the plan will be upset by it," he admitted.[29] The GDR would seek hard currency to make an industrial leap and, in theory, pay the debt back with a range of new manufactured goods for export. This, however, presupposed a Western demand for East German goods—as well as no competition from other low-price exporters. It also required expensive imports of components and raw materials, on top of the consumer imports necessary to placate a populace aware of West German lifestyles. And unless the GDR's export earnings kept ahead of these import expenditures, the country would suffer a trade imbalance and be unable to pay back the hard-currency loans. Poland had already embarked on this gamble. But Brezhnev and the comrades in Moscow suspected that in turning westward for loans, Ulbricht was ready to sell out the Soviet Union in a deal to resolve the German question. Ulbricht, though, remained a dreamer. The same year he told the Soviets about the need to go cup in hand to the imperialists, Ulbricht assured his chief planner that within five years the GDR would be selling computers to the West.

Ulbricht's replacement, Honecker, redoubled the efforts to build up a socially oriented consumer society under the banner of socialist orthodoxy. In 1971, the GDR's semiprivate and private sector still employed nearly half a million people and accounted for 11.3 percent of output, but Honecker nationalized these mostly small, flexible private enterprises, whose profits were deemed political anathema. Ironically, they had manufactured specialty machines and other goods for Western export (one East German efficiency expert had dubbed them the country's "secret weapon"). At the same time as he thus reduced foreign currency revenues, Honecker also ratcheted up outlays for consumer and housing subsidies, which leapt nearly sevenfold between the onset of his rule and 1989. "The people need cheap bread, a dry flat, and a job," the former roofer remarked. "If these three things are in order, nothing can happen to socialism."[30] The subsidies, however, came on top of the pensions, hospitals, and schools, and the East German regime could not increase productivity enough to pay for the lifestyle that it promised and the populace had come to expect. The almighty uncivil society walked on eggshells for fear of triggering a repeat of the June 1953 uprising (when the regime collapsed and had to be restored by the Soviets). But the locked-in low productivity also derived from the inherent nature of central planning, which through the unlimited demand for labor gave workers the power to shirk, especially in the emigration-depleted GDR.[31] The supposed ace in the hole was the big bet on technology, which Honecker increased—just as the limits of the GDR's Fordist, big-batch production model were being felt globally, thanks to rising energy costs. In the international political economy, socialist East Germany was not capitalist East Asia—as would soon be poignantly demonstrated when East Asian goods, produced under market discipline, trounced East German goods on global export markets.

The Soviets, who had egged on Honecker in his putsch against Ulbricht and his total eradication of private enterprise, balked at underwriting his rule. After the first oil shock hit in 1973, the Soviets announced price rises for their oil, and the GDR found itself needing to export 20 percent more goods to the West just to stay even in hard currency. But amid the capitalist world's first major post–World War II contraction, East German economic growth began to taper off (either from more than 7 percent on average to around 4 percent or from around 4 percent to not much more than 1 percent, depending on how one assesses Eastern European data). Honecker had been re-exporting some of the cheap Soviet oil at world prices, but in August 1981, Brezhnev informed his pal that following three consecutive poor harvests in the Soviet Union, Moscow would have to shrink its oil deliveries to the GDR. East German State Planning Chairman Gerhard Schürer told his Soviet counterpart, Nikolai Baibakov, "I assume that a healthy, stable, socialist GDR plays an important role in the strategic thinking of the USSR. Imperialism stands right at the door of our house with its hate on three television channels." In addition, Schürer said, complaining of the independent trade union

Solidarity, "now we have counterrevolution in Poland at our backs." He begged for 3.1 million tons more fuel. "Should I cut back on oil to Poland?" Baibakov asked rhetorically. "Vietnam is starving...should we just give away South East Asia? Angola, Mozambique, Ethiopia, Yemen...we carry them all. And our standard of living is extraordinarily low."[32] This was in 1981—so much for the oil-fueled uplift experienced by the Soviets in the 1970s.

So Honecker, too, found himself going to the imperialists, cup in hand. He had blasted Ulbricht for running up the foreign debt, then himself had ballooned it beyond anything previously seen. The GDR's increasing dependency on the imperialists, especially West Germany, struck a psychological blow among the leadership. It was embarrassing enough that East German schoolbooks taught that the goods of the West—for which the GDR was sinking into debt and which the regime doled out as rewards—were produced by exploitation. But Honecker forbade even internal discussion of the debt issue. When in November 1973 the regime's chief finance expert had warned the party chief that by 1980 the GDR's foreign debt would soar by a factor of ten, from DM 2 billion to DM 20 billion, Honecker had instructed him to cease making the calculations. (The debt in 1980 turned out to be DM 25 billion.) Gerhard Schürer, the chief planner, strove again and again to convey the dangerousness of the situation, but he was told to avoid taking action, lest he magnify the troubles! By 1989, East German foreign debt reached DM 49 billion, or $26.5 billion. The annual cost of servicing this obligation was $4.5 billion, nearly 60 percent of export earnings. Merely stabilizing the debt by imposition of austerity measures would lower living standards by nearly a third—and that was only provided that buyers could be found for East German exports. In other words, there was no end in sight to more hard-currency borrowing. All this was revealed, finally, by Schürer to the rest of the East German leadership in October 1989. By then there was no way out, except for Western debt forgiveness. Living well beyond its means, the GDR had essentially lost its sovereignty.[33]

"The economy is our destiny," the ill-fated Weimar industrialist and politician Walther Rathenau had once said. The GDR's state-owned and state-managed economy had failed the test of competition, and the people began to feel it by the 1980s, when a consumer pinch and an end to the vaunted social mobility became evident, as detailed in oral histories of the baby-boom generation conducted before the GDR's end, as well as in the subsequent avalanche of memoirs.[34] But the GDR had not sat still. Günter Mittag (1926–94), a former railway inspector who ran the Central Committee's Economics Department from 1962 through 1989 (with only a brief "Mittags-Pause" from 1973 to 1976), oversaw large-scale administrative reorganizations and experiments to perfect planning. At one point the GDR dismantled its "industrial associations" (the links between enterprises and ministries) in favor of "combines" (vertical and horizontal integration of enterprises). The aim was to improve communication, curtail conflicts in planning jurisdiction, and achieve economies of scale in production, research and design, and marketing. Still, prices remained fixed, and plants were just placed under the thumb of their sector's parent firms—combines averaged 24 enterprises (some had more than 150) and 25,000 employees.[35] Beyond the reshufflings, the massive investment in technology, especially microelectronics—not just the dream of Ulbricht and then Honecker but a global competitive imperative—produced colossal waste, even by East German standards. Yet the GDR's industrial decay may not have seemed so threatening to the party leaders; they had survived both Hitler and Stalin, after all. Crisis management, meanwhile, afforded both authority and reward to regional and lower-level party apparatchiks. The ceaseless campaigns to enhance efficiency and productivity did little for the economy, but they did enhance political careers.[36]

The bad policies were structural, not personal, even if they were enacted by persons. Still, many people were fooled. Every night on East German newscasts, factories were featured surpassing their output quotas, and even authoritative outside observers insisted that the East German party of utopian revolution was becoming a party of technocrats and managers. Expertise, even an "institutionalized counterelite," some analysts imagined, had come to the fore in the supposedly increasingly autonomous state apparatus. Such a view was hugely influential—and exactly wrong.[37] The GDR's 149 large industrial combines were run mostly by managers with higher degrees in technical and economic sciences, but these "superdirectors" were "kings of improvisation" in the often self-defeating socialist economy. For them nothing was impossible—most kept managerial positions in the reunited Germany—but the obstacles they overcame were often simply planned-economy absurdities.[38] True, at the middle and lower levels, the initially half-trained proletarian scions who had risen up in the GDR system in the 1950s, promoted for their political loyalty, were being replaced by much better educated types—that is, by their own children and other offspring of the GDR's technocratic stratum. But despite the improved qualifications, political criteria still remained uppermost in advancing careers. In short, the East German state was as full of incompetence, corruption, and informality as any other Communist system.[39] The common Leninist structures, not some distinctly efficient German culture ("Red Prussia"), ensured that East Germany had no more created a sustained economic-development trajectory than had Romania.[40]

The GDR's uncivil society became immobilized by its own advance. By 1989, Honecker, who had begun his party career as a youth league agitator, was seventy-seven. Willi Stoph (1914–99), East German prime minister since 1964 (except for a brief interlude when he was head of state), was seventy-five. Erich Mielke (1907–2000), the head of the Stasi since 1957, was eighty-one. This ruling echelon, which had first settled in the villas of the northern Berlin suburb of Pankow, near Soviet military headquarters, moved farther out in 1960 to the more easily guarded, isolated Wandlitz woods (near Hermann Göring's old hunting lodge). There they enjoyed Western food, fashion, jewelry, and electronics imported for them by the Stasi. Their uncivil-society compound became known as "Volvo-grad" for their chauffeur-driven imported vehicles (they could not bear to follow global elite practice and import West German Mercedeses). But despite herding together, the East German elites and their families mostly refrained from socializing—Mielke's men were not supposed to keep a watchful eye on the private lives of party officialdom, but maybe they did? Decision making was a mystery even for high officials. "One of the most interesting findings is how little most policy-makers, including many members of the SED's highest circles, knew," explained one scholar of East German ruling circles. "At Politburo meetings leaders discussed very little of substance. Two or three individuals walking in the woods on a weekend frequently made important decisions, and expertise rarely played a major role."[41]

What about the vaunted Stasi? The Stasi possessed an immense fortresslike complex in East Berlin and more than two thousand buildings, homes, bunkers, shelters, hospitals, and resorts throughout the GDR. Its staff, which numbered 5,000 in its early days, exploded to 45,000 by 1970 and 91,000 by 1989—meaning that Ulbricht and especially Honecker had built up a security ministry larger than Hitler's Gestapo (7,000 in 1937).[42] And that was for an East German population one quarter as large as that of Nazi Germany (66 million). In the Communist bloc, too, the Stasi stood out. Whereas the massive Brezhnev-era Soviet KGB counted one staff person for every 600 inhabitants and Poland's equivalent SB had one for every 1,574 inhabitants, full-time Stasi personnel numbered one for every 180 East Germans. (Officially, the GDR bragged that it had one medical practitioner per 400 people.)[43] The Stasi also developed an informant network estimated at seven times the per capita density of that of the Third Reich. Of course, for all the beatings they administered, the Stasi left behind not millions of corpses but millions of files. Its surveillance was overkill: some 6 million files, even though as late as 1989 the Stasi enumerated just 2,500 individuals as opposition activists, with only 60 deemed "hard core" (comparable to Czechoslovakia, though absurdly fewer than in Poland).[44] That year alone the Stasi compiled 500 situation reports (each of 60 pages)—more than one per day. But the dictatorship proved incapable of using this vast reportage. As Karl Marx had written in 1842, often a "government hears only its own voice. It knows it hears only its own voice and yet it deceives itself that it hears the people's voice."[45] The East German regime was out of touch, but partly for that very reason the paragons of uncivil society were in no mind to capitulate.

THE EAST GERMAN TIANANMEN SQUARE

Leipzig, whose name derives from a Slavic word (*lipsk*) meaning a settlement by linden trees, was an ancient market town. By 1989, its trade fair—"Open to the World"—was 824 years old, having become a biannual (March and September) showcase that attracted Western media. The city's St. Nicholas Church, named for the patron saint of merchants, had been built in the twelfth century and rebuilt in the sixteenth, when the inhabitants had gone over to Martin Luther's Protestant cause. Leipzig's university, where the physicist Werner Heisenberg taught, dated from 1409, its opera house from 1693. Johann Sebastian Bach was the city music director from 1723 until his death in 1750 (he is buried in a Leipzig church). Felix Mendelssohn once directed the city's symphony orchestra, and Richard Wagner was born in Leipzig in 1813, the year Napoleon Bonaparte went down to decisive defeat at the city gates in the "battle of the nations." Leipzig was also the birthplace of Karl Liebknecht, the radical German Social Democrat martyred in 1919. For the revolutionary wing of the Social Democratic Party (SPD), Leipzig's leftist newspaper had been the most important (it had published Vladimir Lenin), and during World War I strikes in Leipzig had helped dethrone the kaiser. Leipzig's anti-Nazi underground was the strongest in Germany. In 1945, Leipzig was liberated by the Americans, but they pulled back and ceded it to the Soviet army. It became an industrial city of 530,000, the GDR's second largest. Between its leftist traditions—it was even the hometown of Walter Ulbricht—and the German high culture, Leipzig could not have been a more quintessential East German showcase. It also turned out to be where the bank run on the East German regime began.

"Peace" was the official policy of the GDR. Beginning in September 1982, at the St. Nicholas Church in the Leipzig urban center, near Karl-Marx Square, a few theology students and church workers took part in "peace prayers" (*Friedensgebete*) under the guidance of the new pastor, Christian Führer (1943–), a product of Leipzig's university. Their self-organized regular candlelit vigils, for years thereafter, remained sparsely attended. But by 1987–88, with change afoot in the Soviet Union, many East German environmentalists and others seeking a more humane socialism, as well as applicants for immigration to West Germany, joined the peace prayers. Suddenly, it was not the same old isolated small circle—and the agenda had widened, too. The Stasi knew, of course, that groups used the sanctuary, typewriters, and telephones (with intercity lines) of churches, but the police were content to contain activists there.[46] Now, however, the churches were becoming a platform. By May and June 1989, attendance at the peace vigils approached a thousand—not a stampede, to be sure, but this was the GDR. (Others gathered at Leipzig's polluted rivers.) The participants remained disciplined and peaceful, and Stasi violence against them brought the protesters sympathy and publicity. During the March 1989 Leipzig trade fair, foreign media had captured on camera brutal dispersals of peaceful marchers chanting "Let us out!" "We want to leave!"[47]

Applications for exodus were spiking. Back in September 1971, legal emigration had become possible, though this involved years of waiting, with an uncertain outcome and, in the meantime, harassment (about 25,000 people did depart annually, but mostly due to expulsion). Now, the Stasi complained, "every permitted exit generates, as a rule, one or two new applicants"—applicants had taken to sharing information and advice.[48] Still, the GDR seemed in control of the flow. After all, Communist bloc member countries had signed protocols not to permit inhabitants from other "fraternal" nations to leave for a "third" country—say, from Hungary to Austria (leading on to West Germany). But on May 2, 1989, Hungary announced that it was "demilitarizing" its border with Austria, news that West German television broadcast and East Germans heard. East Germans did not need a visa to enter Hungary, a popular vacation spot for its many lakes and rentable cabins; also, car ownership in the GDR— celebrated as an achievement of socialism—had shot up to 57 per 100 households by 1989, from 17 per 100 households in 1971. All summer, people piled into their smoky, boxy, two-cylinder plastic Trabants ("satellites") and drove for Hungary, where many then made for the border on foot through the woods. Getting caught crossing without exit documents had always meant being returned with a menacing stamp in one's passport, but Hungary announced that it would stop this practice, which infuriated the East German Politburo. "How can we allow ourselves to be kicked around?" one East German official recounted of conversations among party members. "More and more people are asking: how is socialism going to survive at all?"[49]

Budapest's flamboyant border "opening" was not meant for non-Hungarians—or even for Hungarians, who were already free to travel to Austria (their former partner in the Habsburg Empire before 1918). Rather, Hungary was making a virtue of necessity, shutting down the frontier's obsolete electronic alarm system to save precious hard currency and to curry Western favor.[50] On June 27, 1989, just before U.S. President George H. W. Bush was due to visit Budapest, the Hungarians sought more good publicity: Gyula Horn (1932–), the foreign minister, made a symbolic cut of the barbed-wire border fence along with his Austrian counterpart. Freedom? Hungary was broke, owing Western creditors, especially West Germany, a fortune in hard currency, and the Hungarian prime minister, Miklós Németh, and Horn had flown secretly to confer with the West German leadership near Bonn. Németh later confessed that the West Germans had asked him what the Hungarians wanted and that they had agreed on a credit of DM 1 billion (which was announced only on October 1, well after the secret meeting, so it would not look like the bribe it was).[51] For the clipping ceremony on the Austrian border, Horn had selected the very spot—Sopron/Klingenbach—through which thousands of fleeing Hungarians had sought refuge in Austria in 1956 during the Soviet crackdown. Back then, Horn had been in the Hungarian "padded-jacket" units that had helped the Soviets "restore order." Never mind. In 1989, many fell for his "border opening" stunt, including desperate East Germans, tantalized by West Germany and locked in by a ruling party that refused to reform.[52]

West Germany, by lubricating the Hungarians—and by not expelling GDR refugees thronging at West German embassies in Budapest and Prague (on the way to Hungary)—was ceasing to prop up the GDR. What incensed the GDR's leadership, though, was that

Hungary (!) could infringe on East Germany's sovereignty. "Hungary is betraying socialism," fumed Stasi chief Mielke. In fact, Budapest had at first sought to fulfill its treaty obligations with East Germany, turning East German travelers back over to the GDR. But on September 10, the Hungarian government announced that it would no longer try to restrict access to its Austrian frontier for East Germans. East Germans, increasingly frustrated at their ruling "cement heads" (*Betonköpfe*) and afraid that the domestic changes in Hungary and Poland would completely pass their country by, took notice. Back in Leipzig, however, the exit hysteria that had been fomented by the Hungarians since May now began to elicit a different reaction. On September 4—Fair Monday—the peace prayers and marches had resumed after a summer hiatus, with around 1,200 people, under the banner "For an open country with free people." (Arrests were avoided in the presence of many foreign journalists.) But by September 11 and especially September 25, several thousands gathered, breaking through police cordons and even drumming on police cars, with a new slogan. As usual, they sang the Latin hymn "Dona nobis pacem" ("Lord, Grant Us Peace"), along with the "Internationale" and the American spiritual "We Shall Overcome." But now, with a daily average of two thousand East Germans departing for the West, the Leipzig peace marchers chanted "We are the people" and "We're staying!"[53]

The regime appeared equally resolute. Beatings and arrests had been constant at gatherings in Leipzig, and for October 2, the Stasi arranged for extra water cannon, dogs, and truncheon-wielding troops—everything except dialogue. To reduce the scope of the vigils, the authorities pressured Superintendent Friedrich Magirius (1930–), the ordained minister who headed one of the two Lutheran dioceses in Leipzig. (He answered that "It concerns me very deeply that neither Party nor State has responded to the question I put forth again and again, 'What must we do so that people will gladly live and remain in our land?' ")[54] Some 20,000 marchers were disrupted by the heavily armed riot police. The next day, the regime suspended visa-free travel with Czechoslovakia, the route to Hungary. On October 4 and 5, demonstrations of 30,000 in Dresden, sixty miles from

Leipzig, were met with repression. The specter of civil war gripped the country. The next day, however, Mikhail Gorbachev arrived on a state visit to East Berlin in connection with the GDR's fortieth anniversary. On October 7, the GDR staged its customary torchlight parade with 100,000 people, sending tanks and missiles rolling down Karl-Marx-Allee (the old Stalin Allee). Several thousand counter-demonstrators, chanting "Gorby" and "Stasi state!," were beaten. Gorbachev stated that "matters affecting the GDR are decided not in Moscow but in Berlin"—signaling that there would be no Soviet military intervention. But for the upcoming October 9 prayer night in Leipzig, Mielke promised, "I will now once and for all deploy my special troops, and will show that our authority still has teeth."[55]

Looming over Leipzig was a "Chinese solution"—that is, a bloody domestic crackdown against peaceful protesters, as had happened in Tiananmen ("Gate of Heavenly Peace") the preceding June, eliciting plaudits from the GDR's leadership. Large containers of tear gas were unloaded at the Leipzig freight yard. Extra hospital beds and blood plasma were readied, and Honecker conspicuously received the Chinese deputy premier in East Berlin. On October 9, 3,000 riot police with loaded pistols, 3,000 regular army troops with automatic weapons, and 500 "party militia" surrounded Leipzig's churches and boulevards. More than 7,000 celebrants (Stasi plainclothes included) overflowed Leipzig's four downtown churches, three of which were newly opened to the peace prayers; a total of 70,000 people assembled for the postservices procession—almost one of every seven Leipzigers. It was the largest unofficial gathering in the GDR since June 1953. "Comrades, from today it's class war," a commander supposedly told the riot squads in Leipzig. "Today it will be decided, either them or us ... If sticks aren't good enough, use firearms." Unexpectedly, however, the police removed the chains blocking the marchers, who, as per usual, traveled along the city's Ringstrasse, reached the Round Corner, the local Stasi headquarters, and made a full circuit back to Karl-Marx Square before dispersing on their own after 9:00 P.M.[56] The crackdown never materialized. The main reason was that even though GDR party boss Erich Honecker advocated using force to hold the line against "counterrevolution," he

had failed to give an unequivocal order. That way, he may have cal-
culated, local officials could be blamed for any bloodshed.[57] Had
Honecker given an explicit order to disperse the marchers by force,
it is unclear if local officials would have summoned the courage to
resist it.[58]

On October 8, a conference of 150 Leipzig party and police officials had failed to agree on a strategy for the next day. Some Leipzig
officials, however, learned that on October 8 in Dresden—the only
other East German city with mass demonstrations—the district
party chief, Hans Modrow, had negotiated with clergymen and activists. A group of Leipzig officials were emboldened to do the same,
on the spot, on October 9. Security officials in Leipzig began to see
that local party officials were distancing themselves from possible repression. Moreover, even though the national Stasi chief, Mielke, had
called his subordinate, Leipzig Stasi head Manfred Hummitzsch,
twice on the morning of October 9, Mielke, following Honecker,
did not *explicitly* order a crackdown. Troops were to shoot only if
provoked. "We expected provocations would come, stones would fly
or Molotov cocktails," recalled one militia commander. But the
marchers provided no such pretext: not even a single shop window
was smashed.[59] In that regard, a major role was played by Kurt Masur
(1927–), Leipzig's internationally renowned philharmonic director.
On the morning of October 9, Masur met at home with a theologian,
a cabaret performer, and three midrank party officials to hammer out
a call for nonviolence. Their completely unauthorized "Appeal of the
Leipzig Six" was read out at the church services, on the radio, and
over public loudspeakers throughout the city.[60] At St. Nicholas, the
sermon also stressed that "the spirit of peace must go forth from
these walls. See to it that men in uniform are not antagonized." At all
four churches, the bishop's blessing carried a similar message—heard
by the numerous Stasi officers and party stalwarts who had occupied
the pews.[61] Later, one Stasi officer recalled that, although they had
been told to anticipate a mob, "we saw that they were entirely normal
people shouting '*Wir sind das Volk*' [We are the people]," adding "and
we belonged to them too."[62]

The Stasi part of "the people"? Would Germans no longer kill columns of Germans in the name of defending an ideology or even their own sinecures? At the local level, apparently, many police and decision-making elites had come to value the lives of their conational demonstrators more than the Honecker regime (which even Moscow wanted changed). No less significant, though, the usual repressive devices themselves came up short. Against Solidarity in December 1981, Poland's General Wojciech Jaruzelski had shown that a domestic crackdown could succeed via mass targeted arrests, and the Stasi had prepared plans to take ringleaders and others into custody.[63] But in Leipzig, the Stasi could not readily identify "ringleaders." Essentially, because of the nature of the prayer marches, there were no ringleaders. Leipzigers were already familiar with assembling on Karl-Marx Square—after all, it was the site of official regime rituals such as May Day. And the peace vigils always took place on the same day, Monday, at the same place, the St. Nicholas Church, and at the same time— 5:00 P.M. for church services, 6:00 P.M. for the march. "Our evaluation of the situation," the Leipzig Stasi head, Hummitzsch, had informed Mielke in Berlin already in August, "is that the 'Peace Prayers' no longer need to be organized.... They have no need of leaflets or any other activities. The people go there completely of their own accord."[64] No one had to join an organization to take part, but there was hidden organization. Two thirds of those who joined the marches claimed to have done so through friends and associates—what were called "niches."[65] The latter term had been popularized by Günter Grass, the West German writer, who saw in East Germany "a slower pace of life" and "more time for conversations."[66] Grass's romanticism aside, niches in the GDR did form as refuges from the surveillance— small circles of mutual aid (amid shortages) and solidarity.[67] At private dachas and state workplaces, friends gathered to complain, smoke, share meals, and exchange gossip. Whereas the GDR's tiny "opposition" was concentrated, subject to division, and easily infiltrated, the niches were ubiquitous, dispersed, and tightly knit.[68]

Asked to explain what happened, West German president Richard von Weizsäcker replied, "Gorbachev and the churches."[69] Throughout the peace marches, Soviet troops—the saviors of the East German regime in 1953—remained confined to their barracks by Moscow. At the same time, students at Leipzig's venerable university were not conspicuous in the protests. Nor did the still more numerous factory workers come out en masse. True, workplaces were important in that people who attended the peace prayers, once back at work the next day, often relayed what they had seen and heard, spurring discussions. Another factor that extended the demonstrations' makeup beyond the small peace and ecology subcultures was the combined Hungarian–West German encouragement of flight from the GDR.[70] A further contribution came from the GDR's own strong emphasis on German high culture, embodied by the prominent role of the conductor Kurt Masur. But in the end, the innumerable small niches coalesced around the physical space and moral authority of St. Nicholas Church. "There was no head of the revolution," recalled the cabaret singer who signed the Leipzig Six appeal along with Masur. "The head was the Nicholas Church and the body the center of the city. There was only one leadership: Monday, 5 P.M., the Nicholas Church."[71] The Lutheran Church enabled a moral, nonviolent resistance that perplexed and stymied the regime with prayer, candles, and collective song and managed to break the Stasi's spell. "The city of Leipzig," recalled St. Nicholas pastor Reverend Christian Führer, referring to October 9, "was literally circled by a massive cordon of peacemakers." Leipzig's urban heart had indeed become a "Tiananmen Square"—not a bloodbath but a "Gate of Heavenly Peace."[72]

THE IMPOSSIBILITY OF A CHINESE SOLUTION

The GDR was a Ponzi scheme that fell in a bank run. After the dictatorship failed to suppress the Leipzig peace marchers, Egon Krenz (1937–), Erich Honecker's "crown prince" in waiting, deposed his mentor, but the next Monday, October 23, in Leipzig, more than 200,000 marchers turned out to denounce the undemocratic process of Krenz's elevation. By then the Stasi had ceased reporting to the Politburo on the crisis.[73] On November 4, upwards of 1 million people rallied in East Berlin, demanding an end to the party's monopoly. Amid murmuring that there might be free elections (the last ones had taken place in 1933), on November 9, 1989—the seventy-first anniversary of the proclamation of a German republic during World War I, the sixty-fifth of Hitler's failed Beer Hall Putsch, and the fifty-first of the Nazi Kristallnacht—Günter Schabowski, the East German propaganda chief and Politburo member, faced scores of journalists. The proceedings, in the International Press Center in East Berlin, were broadcast live. The embattled regime planned to announce a new policy allowing people to apply for visas to travel to West Germany the next day. But near the end of the press conference, in response to an Italian journalist's question on the travel issue, Schabowski, looking uncertainly at colleagues, blurted out, "Um, we have decided today, um, to implement a regulation that allows every citizen of the German Democratic Republic (um) to (um) leave the GDR through any of the border crossings." Could it be? Asked when the new travel policy would go into effect, Schabowski, who had not even been at the Politburo meeting on the new travel policy, shuffled through his papers, finding a memorandum, which was marked not to be announced until the next day, and said, "That comes into effect, according to my information, immediately, without delay."[74]

Just like that: 27 million Soviet lives lost to defeat the invading Germans and take Berlin, and then some apparatchik misspeaks at a press conference, and gone! The prematurely revealed travel plan was not meant to remove the Wall, only to permit visits to the West in an orderly fashion. The GDR did not even have the legal authority to make decisions for Berlin without the four powers, including the Soviets. But Schabowski's startling open-ended announcement was quickly relayed on the East German evening news, and people began massing at the Berlin Wall checkpoint, near the remains of Hitler's bunker. The East German border guards, who as recently as February had shot someone trying to cross, were telephoning furiously for instructions. But just as the Leipzig Stasi had not received a clear order to use force that they could have implemented against the demonstrators, so now the Berlin border guards received no firm directives. The GDR was a state that utterly depended upon but could no longer give unequivocal commands. At 10:30 P.M., with 20,000 massed and surging, the guards finally just...opened the gates.

Within a week, between 2 million and 3 million people had crossed into West Berlin, most to shop (many received free gifts in West German department stores). Hammers and chisels, meanwhile, were taken to the Wall. By this point, more than a quarter of the party—at least 500,000 members—had quit. Way back at the ruling party's founding, in 1948, one official had thundered, "We, as Marxists, must know: if we establish a government, we can never give up power either through elections or through other means."[75] On December 1, however, the party relinquished its monopoly. Krenz, the new leader, was gone two days later. It was all over but the shouting.

That shouting—"Helmut! Helmut!" for West Germany's chancellor—took place in the selfsame streets, Leipzig's included, where East German crowds had only recently chanted "Gorby! Gorby!"[76] New Forum—legalized the day the Wall fell—issued a statement warning East Germans not to become "rent slaves to Western capitalism."[77] This summons by East German intellectuals to get socialism right on the second try fell on deaf ears. Stasi chief Mielke put it well: confronted at an internal meeting back in late August 1989 with reports on the situation, he had insisted that "socialism is so good, but they demand more and more."[78] Indeed they did. The GDR was not mired in the dire poverty of the Third World, but it was not the First World either. It had achieved second-rate citizenship in a world that already had a first-rate Germany. China alone had discovered a stable and secure path for Communist-party survival—namely, enhance the Leninist party's political control but accept a market economy, including new family-run private businesses and insider privatization of major state assets. But Deng Xiaoping's acquiescence to capitalism ("socialism with Chinese characteristics"), which was roughly coincident with his historic visit to the United States in 1979, constituted a step that the East German establishment, conservative or reformist, would not undertake.[79] In the United States, Deng discovered a capitalist superpower, when China was on its knees. The East German ruling clique, as the scholar Eric Weitz has noted, were all Weimarera Communists—that is, lifelong intransigents who had refused in the late 1930s to join a wider leftist "popular front" with the German Social Democratic Party (SPD) against the Nazis. For these lifers, "capitalism" meant the hated Social Democrats right across the border as well as Nazism. Anyway, even had the GDR's uncivil society wanted to relent ideologically, West Germany took a Chinese-style market embrace off the table. "What right to exist would a capitalist GDR have alongside a capitalist Federal Republic?" warned Otto Reinhold, the director of the East German Central Committee's Academy of Social Sciences, in summer 1989. "In other words, what justification would there be for two German states once ideology no longer separated them?" His answer: "none."[80]

China's transformation flowed from a government-led as well as a spontaneous move toward real prices and forms of private ownership, but even a so-called mixed economy (mostly planned, with some market mechanisms) remained anathema for the GDR's ideologues, as it did for other uncivil societies elsewhere in the bloc.[81] Consider Kádár's Hungary. His reforms had involved a degree of enterprise autonomy, the replacement of central distribution by marketing, investments that followed not central directives but company profits (which were heavily taxed), and limited private enterprise in services. Many prices were freed, though a good deal remained fixed. Above all, no labor or capital markets were permitted. Still, there was a notable impact on daily life. Roughly 75 percent of Hungarians resided in privately owned family homes or owned a holiday home. Noticing the absence of shortages and queues during a visit, Nikita Khrushchev had spoken approvingly of this "goulash communism." But Hungary's reforms remained cautious, in order not to spook the Soviets *and* to remain within socialism. Even then, part of the Hungarian Communist establishment rebelled. "How can there be a planned economy if there is no compulsory plan for companies?" some officials asked. They also questioned the limited private retail shops, small restaurants, and independent artisans. In the 1970s, Kádár maneuvered to preserve the earlier reforms, but a second stage was aborted. Instead, orthodox planners forced through an economic recentralization. By the 1980s, however, Hungary, too, was mired in unpayable debt—needing a surplus in hard currency from trade of more than $1 billion annually just to pay off the interest. Come 1989, Hungary's Communists gave up on the mixed-economy quest and blessed major privatization. They did not face an already existing capitalist "West Hungary."[82]

For the GDR, which could not just go capitalist (and survive), the only option that had remained was conservative modernization—that is, still more "discipline," still more investment thrown at heavy industry. This last-ditch roll of the dice in high tech had failed, too. Perhaps, hoped the GDR's uncivil society, West Germany would succumb to some profound crisis (even as the Federal Republic kept outperforming). That is how East Germany found itself on the very same path of no-reform paralysis as Romania, despite Honecker's warning that West Germany's existence precluded the GDR doing nothing. In the meantime, East Germany kept on taking Western loans to avoid the pain of lowering living standards. Many suspected that West Germany had deliberately ensnared East Germany in debt to gain leverage over its behavior. But even the West Germans did not fathom the full failure of the East. Something so small as the 1976–77 rise in the world price of coffee—a staple beverage in East German society—could spark an existential crisis, quadrupling the commodity's cost in hard currency. The GDR appeared to have a future only insofar as foreigners (Soviets and Western) agreed to underwrite it. By the late 1980s, however, the Soviet pillar had instead suddenly become a battering ram. And Western banks were approaching the end of their eager lending. It was a pincers. Still, the regime's capitulation had to be compelled. And it was compelled, by the peace vigils of Leipzig. In the end, the GDR's uncivil society produced fewer "heroes of retreat" (in the words of the poet Hans Magnus Enzensberger) than woolly "mammoths with rigor mortis" (as one insider called them), who, no thanks to themselves, were retired on West German state pensions. West Germany also assumed responsibility not only for East Germany's state debt, some $26.5 billion, but for infrastructure and economic overhaul, at a cost estimated at more than $2 trillion.

III

BREAKTHROUGH

A man is hopping across Palace Square in Bucharest.
"Have you lost a shoe?" someone shouts. "No," says the
man, "I found one!"

In late 1981, Communist Romania's foreign debt hit $10.2 billion (in 1977 it had stood at $3.6 billion). Per capita, this liability was one third less than East Germany's. Nonetheless, Romania found itself becoming the second East bloc country, after Poland—which faced the Solidarity crisis—to seek rescheduling of its external borrowing. Indeed, alarmed at the foreign leverage over Romanian affairs, Nicolae Ceauşescu, Romania's dictator, determined to pay off the country's hard-currency obligations within the decade. The "Genius of the Carpathians," as he was known, ordered planners to import as little as possible and export whatever they could for dollars, essentially immiserating and freezing the country. State expenditures on housing, education, and health care dropped precipitously. Amid ceaseless propaganda about Romania's "golden epoch," not only villages but many cities went pitch black at night. During the polar-style winter of 1984–85, when ice claimed Bucharest's unlit streets, the regime banned all automobile traffic, except for the tyrant's cortege, to conserve fuel. By then, household energy consumption stood at a mere 20 percent of the 1979 level. Rationing, even for bread, returned to Romania's major cities, except the capital, after twenty-seven years. Full repayment of the debt that was crushing the socialist economies of Eastern Europe produced, in 1980s Romania, involution.[1]

Communist Romania suffered the highest maternal mortality rate in Europe. A 1966 pronatalism law had driven abortions underground, and an estimated 11,000 mothers died of illegal abortions in the period 1966–89. As of 1984, doctors were supposed to inspect females on the job to see if they were pregnant and, if so, to make sure they did not have abortions—and if they were not, to demand an explanation.[2] ("Breed, comrade women," Ceauşescu exhorted, "it is your patriotic duty.") As Romania went cold and dim, as its people queued for life's necessities, and as its women especially suffered, much of central Bucharest was gutted for a Boulevard of the Victory of Socialism. At one end of it arose a gargantuan marble "House of the People"—that is, new offices and amphitheaters for the regime. Meanwhile, across the country's highest mountain a new highway was laid, which was perennially blocked by rockfalls. Villages with less than 2,000 population were slated to be "systematized"—that is, bulldozed to make way for concrete agroindustrial complexes. Anger seethed. ("What's small, dark, and knocking at the door?" went the bitter Romanian joke. Answer: "The future.") Incredibly, even though Romania paid off almost its entire hard-currency debt by March 1989, Ceauşescu insisted that the grueling, economizing austerity measures be retained! The populace was not up in arms. Neither was the establishment. On November 24, 1989, at Romania's Fourteenth Party Congress in Bucharest—a long-scheduled event enabling all manner of scheming preparations— the seventy-one-year-old Romanian dictator was "reelected" general secretary by the 3,308 delegates to rhythmic chants of "Ceauşescu and the people."[3]

Romania seemed impervious even to the fall of the Berlin Wall in November 1989. But then, on December 15, 1989, at church services in provincial Timişoara, a Calvinist pastor and member of the Hungarian ethnic minority, László Tőkés (1952–), summoned his parishioners to protest his upcoming eviction from his residence on church-owned land. Within a week, Ceauşescu, together with his wife, Elena, would flee Bucharest from the roof of the Romanian Central Committee building by helicopter. En route, the pilot may have warned they were being tracked by radar and could be shot down, or he may have been ordered by the military to say that. Be that as it may, the helicopter was brought to a landing, and Ceauşescu had his bodyguards hijack one car (of a village doctor), then another (of a bicycle repair man). But the fugitives were captured and held by the police, then by the military. On December 25, after some reported attempts to spring the dictator, as well as sniper attacks and a bizarre disinformation campaign in the capital, a kangaroo court was hastily convened at the provincial garrison. That day, the Ceauşescus were convicted of genocide and sentenced to death. So many members of the garrison wanted to be in the firing squad, it is said, that lots were drawn. In the end, all eighty were allowed to take part and pumped the deposed couple with more than a hundred bullets.

"The Antichrist has been executed on Christmas Day," exulted the announcer on state radio. The shock at what many came to call Romania's "miracle of December" was incalculable. How in the world could one disaffected pastor, gathering a few score supporters, spark protests that would abruptly topple the latest Romanian dictator in his twenty-fourth year of absolute power? Timişoara, located in the Banat region, part of Austria-Hungary before 1918 and Romania's westernmost city, was sometimes known as "little Vienna." It stood closer to Budapest and Belgrade than to Bucharest, and information about events around the bloc—such as the fall of the Berlin Wall on November 9—passed readily into the town over Romania's western border (and then on to the rest of the country via the rail network). In turn, Pastor Tőkés and his battles in Timişoara were featured on Hungarian radio and television, which broadcast into Romania and was accessible to anyone with the right antenna. (Belgrade Television, also accessible, was running taped CNN broadcasts at night with reportage about events throughout Eastern Europe and the Soviet Union.) Still, as late as October 1989, the Securitate—Romania's Department of State Security, i.e., the political police of the Interior Ministry—had judged the Timişoara region to be "quiet."[4] It probably was. Romania's 1989 revolution seems highly distinct—each country's was, in its own way—yet Romania, too, fits a pattern of uncivil-society paralysis and nonorganized mass mobilization.

CUL-DE-SAC

For centuries, Romanian speakers had lived mostly under Ottoman as well as Habsburg or Russian imperial rule, but Romanians in the territories of Wallachia and Moldavia gained an independent state in the nineteenth century. This core was greatly enlarged as a result of World War I, which gave Romania the Banat, Transylvania, Bessarabia, southern Dobruja, and Bukovina. Thus did Greater Romania, as it was known, take shape with a plethora of national minorities (28 percent), some of whom (Hungarians and Germans) indulged feelings of superiority toward ethnic Romanians. Many of the latter, meanwhile, were thrown together for the first time. The upshot was the crystallization of a nasty illiberal political culture even before Romania's fragile liberal order was overturned for one-party rule in 1938.[5] In fact, Romania's homegrown fascist movement—known by the name of its youth wing (the Iron Guard) and reminiscent of the Falangists in Spain—was the strongest in interwar Eastern Europe. In World War II, ever conscious to outdo Hungary in currying favor, Greater Romania contributed more troops to fight the Soviets than all other Nazi allies combined. Romanians cobutchered their way to Stalingrad, where, however, they suffered immense losses. By summer 1944, the advancing Soviets crossed Romania's frontier. On August 23, 1944, Romania's King Mihai ousted Marshal Ion Antonescu (1882–1946), the country's pro-Nazi military dictator, in a coup, deftly switching the country to the winning side. The Soviet army, pushing out the genocidal Germans, fought, plundered, and raped its way westward, but the Romanian state was intact.

By this time, late 1944, Romania's Communist party, after twenty-three years of existence, most of it while banned, numbered fewer than 1,000 members, including 80 in Bucharest.[6] Stalin had toyed with sparing Antonescu for use as a Soviet puppet and with endorsing an independent Transylvania. Instead, in February 1945, with the war still raging, Andrei Vyshinsky—the prosecutor at Stalin's 1930s show trials—arrived to blackmail King Mihai. Vyshinsky threatened annexation, slamming a palace door hard enough to send plaster crashing down; the dynast acceded to a Communist-dominated coalition government under the guise of a "National Democratic Front." The king also got back Transylvania, and tried and executed Antonescu (who according to the official transcript went down shouting, "Scumbags, scumbags!"). But Romanian Communists connived to control key ministries, such as the police, as well as the press, and they employed "salami tactics" (the immortal phrase of the Hungarian Stalinist leader Mátyás Rákosi) to reduce their opponents by slicing them off, one by one. Romanian Communist-party member-ship shot up above 250,000 by the end of 1945 and to 800,000 by December 1947, when the king abdicated under pressure (and was permitted to go into exile). Thus did the Communists take over. Peasants lost their land, urbanites lost their businesses, and political figures who had smoothed the Communists' path to power lost their freedom.[7] Such is totalitarianism: people serve as agents in the destruction of their own agency.

Romania's Communist police state would know only two leaders. Both were ethnic Romanians, in stark contrast to the party's interwar composition, which had been drawn from the many persecuted minorities incorporated into Greater Romania.[8] Gheorghe Gheorghiu-Dej (1901–65) was a worker's son with minimal education, who had been incarcerated for eleven years in prisons and camps and who operated from 1947 as the party's *primus inter pares.* He consolidated his unitary rule in a 1952 purge that removed Hannah Rabinsohn, a Jew, better known as Ana Pauker (1893–1960), and László Luka, an ethnic Hungarian better known as Vasile Luca (1898–1963), who, unlike the "homegrown" Dej, had spent the war years in Moscow.[9] Dej, like East Germany's Walter Ulbricht (and Albania's Enver Hoxha), would out-last Stalin. In 1956, following the shock of Khrushchev's secret speech, Dej massed Romania's top three thousand Communists at a sports hall to make the party complicit in his refusal to de-Stalinize. He also carefully pursued contacts with China.[10] One leading scholar characterized Dej as "an unscrupulous, gregarious criminal whose cruelty and cunning remain unsurpassed in twentieth-century Romania."[11] In 1965, Dej suddenly died of cancer (his entourage suspected radiation poisoning by the Soviets). He was succeeded by the diminutive Nicolae Ceaușescu, a pitiable orator but a canny operative.[12]

Ceaușescu (1918–89), the third of ten children, came from poor peasant stock, signed on as a shoemaker's apprentice at age eleven, and joined the Communists as a teenager. As a "person dangerous to the public order," he spent much of his youth in Romania's Doftana Prison—the "Marxist University"—where he met Dej. Following the late-1947 Communist takeover, Ceaușescu was eventually put in charge of personnel. When he became general secretary at age forty-seven in 1965, he was not only the youngest Romanian Politburo member but the youngest party chieftain in Eastern Europe. Six years later, during the Sino-Soviet split, he provoked Soviet military maneuvers on Romania's border by undertaking a bold state visit to China. Ceauşescu aimed to study what could be adapted from Mao's Cultural Revolution to forestall "socialism with a human face" in Romania. On the same trip he visited Kim Il Sung's North Korea, and liked what he saw there, too.[13] Back in Romania, as Ceauşescu's mini–cultural revolution and maximal cult unfolded, at least twenty-seven members of his extended clan got high posts. Most prominently, and unusually for Communist regimes, his wife, Elena (1916–89), who had dropped out of grade school but suddenly held a doctorate in chemistry, became coruler. Their debauched son Nicu (1951–1996), the minister of youth, became the heir apparent. The patriarch himself, who had completed only the four-year elementary school in his village, became a god. He bore the same title as had Antonescu (and Dej): Conducător.[14]

Samizdat was virtually unknown in Communist Romania, and dissidents there always seemed fewer than even the small numbers elsewhere in the bloc. "Romanian dissent," went the saying, "lives in Paris, and his name is Paul Goma" (the Romanian writer [1935–]).[15] One reason was that unlike dissenters under other Communist regimes, those in Romania elicited indifference or even scorn from the West, where Ceauşescu was lauded as the great "maverick" willing to buck Moscow. As one analyst noted, "three presidents of the United States, three presidents of France, the Emperor of Japan, the Queen of England and a lot of other important people expressed their admiration" for Romania's supposed "independent course."[16] In 1968, Ceauşescu, alone among East bloc leaders, refused to join the Warsaw Pact invasion of Czechoslovakia. In fact, on August 23, a holiday in Romania commemorating the anniversary of the 1944 coup against the pro-Nazi regime, he publicly condemned the operation against the Prague Spring. The West was not alone in going bananas with approval: the overjoyed Goma *joined* the Romanian Communist party. In 1973, however, he was expelled from the party and in 1977 exiled for supporting the Czechoslovak Charter 77 human rights movement and writing two letters to Ceauşescu denouncing the Securitate, making Goma an international cause célèbre. Still, that such a nonparty critic could have joined the Romanian Communist party, even if only briefly, showed that many Romanians strongly identified with the regime's gestures to distance Romanian communism from Soviet tutelage, while aiming for a special Romanian mission within the Communist world.

Leaving aside the few pro-Western critical types, such as Goma abroad and, at home, Doina Cornea (1929–), a professor of French literature at Cluj and advocate for human rights, the émigré historian Vladimir Tismăneanu has observed that "many Romanians despised, even hated Ceauşescu and his tyranny, but did not like liberal, Western-style democratic values either."[17] Communism drew upon and deepened this illiberal side of Romania's political culture, while also spawning a new elite—Romania's uncivil society.[18] Around 10,000 made up the central establishment and 200,000 the regional one.[19] This elite, largely provincial and undereducated, by design had become far more Romanian and far less Jewish, Hungarian, or German than any previous elite in Romania. Its grateful members shared career paths and life experiences—to a point. Officials "regularly attended party meetings and courses for ideological indoctrination and in this way were molded and shaped in a certain spirit and acquired a certain behavior in society," explained Silviu Brucan (1916–2006), a onetime protégé of Dej. "The cohesion of this social group sprang from the status of its members and the special relations among them, from their position in the structure of power, from their high salaries, and particularly from their access to a wide range of restricted benefits and privileges." Brucan—a Jew who had been born Saul Bruckner—was uncivil society's ambassador to Washington (1956–9) and to the United Nations (1959–62), and then head of Romanian TV.

Elite perquisites varied greatly, however, within and across state agencies. Ion Mihai Pacepa, a former deputy chief of Romanian intelligence who defected in 1978—one of the highest-ranking intelligence defectors ever from the bloc—described the lavish Interior

Ministry "club." It was just outside Bucharest, "spread over some ten acres and tucked away between a kolkhoz and a forest," its gated entrance further shielded by a simulacrum of the Versailles gardens. Behind "artificial lakes, artesian fountains, graceful gazebos" stood villas for overnight stays, as well as riding stables, a bowling alley, a screening room, and an indoor firing range stocked with Johnnie Walker Black Label. The candlelit restaurant offered caviar, goose-liver paté, truffles, and two musical ensembles. The waitresses and female musicians evidently performed double duty (for the male officers).[20] But whatever the merriment among the top echelon, any potential elite solidarity was punctured by hierarchies. Most members of the Central Committee had initially taken residences in the early 1950s in Bucharest's Primăverii district, where Brucan and his wife "were neighbors on the same street with the Ceaușescus... and other communist leaders." That was before Ceaușescu had ascended to general secretary. Nonetheless, encounters with him were limited to exchanging greetings. "Social life unfolded in keeping with party hierarchy," Brucan wrote. "My wife and I belonged to the second echelon."[21] Additional barriers arose from the surveillance, snitching, fear of provocations, and Ceaușescu's fastidious practice of cadre "rotation." Communism in Romania, as elsewhere, provided common bonds among, but also control over, elites.

The regime also succeeded in getting the intellectual class that Ceaușescu despised to work for it. A combination of surgical arrests and manipulated perquisites certainly did most of the trick, but the regime also appealed to convictions and egos. This intellectual subservience in Eastern Europe has puzzled some observers. Czesław Miłosz dubbed it "the captive mind," and Norman Manea (1936–), the émigré Romanian writer, labeled it "the profession of self-abasement." Whereas Miłosz analyzed mental gymnastics, which he called "Ketman," Manea argued that in a world in which everything was absurd, the truth teller, too, looked ridiculous. Above all, Manea concluded, "anyone who did not want to give in to the Terror's lies and travesties suffered not only fear but often a deep sense of uselessness."[22] *That was the key.* Feelings of impotence in Romania were widespread, but so was a sense of usefulness, even empowerment.

Romanian intellectuals frequently attained status within the dictatorial regime by engaging questions of national identity, motivated by the need to please the political authorities, but also by their own sense of mission. Nationalism was a deeply felt preoccupation stretching across intelligentsia and party.

The Romanian Communist party indulged in national-origin myths, especially after the Kremlin—impressed at how Romania had walled off its 1.5 million ethnic Hungarians during Hungary's uprising of 1956—had acceded to Romania's urgings for a Soviet troop withdrawal in 1958.[23] The preoccupation with myths has given rise to a scholarly myth about nationalism's eclipse of communism in Romania. No such thing happened. From the 1,000 members in 1944 the party had mushroomed to 3.7 million by the 1980s, giving Romania the most Communists per capita of any country—about one quarter of its adult population and one third of its workforce.[24] Still, many observers insisted that Romania had the fewest Communists, at least in terms of sincerity.[25] To be sure, people used party membership to manage practical issues—the party's Romanian initials, PCR, were mocked as "*pile, cunoștinte și relatii*" (connections, acquaintances, and relations). And the Romanian Institute of Party History failed to issue a single volume of party history during its entire existence. But in 1971, Ceaușescu ordered a surge in ideological training in Marxist terms, with a second such push in 1976. These campaigns partly targeted the younger generation and its supposed susceptibility to "decadent Western values." The campaigns also coincided with the launching of new five-year plans with ambitious targets and sought to mobilize the party and Communist ideology to attain miracles in the planned economy.[26] Romania flirted with tweaks of the planned economy, such as so-called enterprise autonomy, but as in Poland the ministries retained tight control. Romania's Leninist party never gave up the fixation on heavy industry or, most important, anticapitalism. There was never a reversal of the nationalization of industry and banking, never a reversal of collectivization—in short, no resemblance to China after 1978.[27]

Despite cultural differences, all East bloc countries shared remarkably similar Soviet-style institutions. At the same time, all East bloc countries were national Communist, to a greater or lesser degree. What set Romania apart was not the nationalism per se but the absence of a reform wing inside the Leninist structures, which placed Bucharest closer to Pyongyang. To explain this absence, the émigré Tismăneanu—who was born to ardent Romanian Communist veterans of the Spanish Civil War International Brigades and who went to lycée with Nicu Ceaușescu—has characterized Romanian communism as a peculiar amalgam of Byzantium and Marxism-Leninism. Of course, that could also be said of the Soviet Union, whence emanated a Communist reform movement that took down the whole Communist world. More to the point, Tismăneanu argues that in Romania the nationalism, rather than reinforcing a reform inclination as elsewhere in Eastern Europe, nourished resistance to reform, since reform came from colonial Moscow (first under Khrushchev, then under Gorbachev).[28] Romania's various individual reformist Communists could never overcome this barrier, or the special attention of the Securitate, to coalesce into a movement. True, in March 1989, a "Letter of the Six" was broadcast over the BBC urging "President Ceaușescu" to redress his mistakes and expressing grave concern that "the very idea of socialism, for which we have fought, is discredited by your policy." But six signatories is not exactly a groundswell. (The letter writers, career Communists, were placed under house arrest.)[29] Because it had no liberal wing to combat, the Romanian party did not really develop a fully articulated conservative wing either. This structurelessness facilitated, and in turn was reinforced by, the regime's extreme personalization.

But there was method to the madness. In the 1940s, Romania's Leninist-style party had "broken through" politically, in the words of the scholar Kenneth Jowitt, and established a monopoly.[30] And in such a peasant country, the Soviet example resonated as a magic wand for this new political avant-garde—many, like Ceaușescu, from the peasantry—to "break through" economically as well, thereby avoiding dependence on (subservience to) Western Europe. The attraction of this aspiration was brought out by the scholar Henry Roberts, who had been in Romania during the post–World War II Soviet occupation and who in 1951 placed Romania in the broad framework of a modernizing agrarian society living in a world of powerful industrial states. Roberts shrewdly pointed out that Romania's interwar liberal parties had wanted industrialization but were perceived as being for an oligarchy, while the interwar National Peasants' Party had been egalitarian yet hardly proindustry. The fascist Iron Guard, he added, had had nothing to offer, while the Social Democrats had lacked the means to achieve their plans for either industrialization or social peace. Enter Leninism, which provided the apparent answer: emphasis on industry, on the social, and on a backward country bootstrapping itself.[31] That was precisely why Romanian elites roundly rejected a proposed role as agricultural and raw materials supplier to the East bloc in the specialization scheme that accompanied Moscow's 1961–62 revival of the bloc's economic organization, the Council for Mutual Economic Assistance, or COMECON. (COMECON, founded by Stalin in January 1949, turned out to be less a socialist "common market" than multiple bilateralisms.)[32] Hitler, too, had mused (in 1941) that "Romania would do well to give up . . . the idea of having her own industry."

Instead of making the country an agricultural supplier à la Khrushchev or Hitler, Romanian uncivil society embraced even greater heavy industrialization (for which they completed the collectivization of agriculture in 1962). They also shifted away from the East German and Czechoslovak machinery they had been importing to Western European equipment, so that Communist Romania's trade with the Soviet Union and the socialist bloc COMECON declined, while its trade with the West expanded. But the larger goal was industrial self-sufficiency, and the 1960s and early '70s did seem to vindicate this strategy. The Dacia, a Romanian version of a low-end Renault, began production at a newly built factory, and car sales took off from around 9,000 in 1965 to 45,000 in 1975. Sales of Romanian-made television sets—fatefully, as we will see—shot up into the hundreds of thousands. Of course, Romania's hastily erected industrial plants were producing second-rate goods. All the while, the country remained the bloc's second agricultural producer after the Soviet Union, but its neglected agriculture had the bloc's lowest productivity per cultivated area. The country was falling further behind Spain, Greece, and Portugal—other predominantly rural European countries whose dictatorships had yielded to democracies. Romania's supposed special path to modernity was looking more and more like a cul-de-sac. A 7.4 magnitude earthquake in 1977 exacted a toll, especially in Bucharest, but the biggest blow was self-inflicted. Ceauşescu had overzealously expanded Romania's oil-refining capacity. Utilization of the plants—to pay for the staggering investment—compelled the country, though a big oil producer, to begin importing crude in the 1970s. That was right when world oil prices skyrocketed. Iran, Romania's main foreign oil supplier, cut off the spigot in 1979 after Ceauşescu's ally the shah was deposed. All this was the background to Romania's hard-currency debt binge and the imposition in 1982 of suffocating austerity measures. Like the owner of a company beset by declining revenues, the regime forced down wages and overhead, though it kept claiming greater success than ever, committing what in business would qualify as fraud.[33]

Romania had to beg from Moscow as well. Thus did the aspirations for a great industrial leap and a defiant autonomy result in a two-front dependency. Romania's uncivil society did not feel the pinch, but it was aware of the misery outside the elite enclaves. From 1986, the head of the Securitate's economics division evidently spilled his bile to local Securitate chiefs at the "imbecility" of the economic program of Ceauşescu and his wife.[34] Such expressions of frustration among the powerful, however, were generally overwhelmed in the Ceauşescu cult. As late as December 20, 1989, Patriarch Teocist, the head of the Romanian Orthodox Church, telegrammed to congratulate Ceauşescu on his "wise and far-seeing guidance." The patriarch sang the praises of Romania's "golden epoch, which justifiably bears your names, and its achievements, which will endure for thousands of years."[35] By then, its actual future would be counted in days. Romania's Leninist breakthrough had been no breakthrough at all, and it would take a different kind of breakthrough to overcome it.

"What?" "Shut Up!"

László Tőkés had a history of conflict with Romania's Reformed (Calvinist) Church authorities as well as with the political authorities; that's how the pastor had ended up in Timişoara. At previous postings in Braşov and Dej, both in Transylvania (which has a large ethnic Hungarian minority), Tőkés had spoken out against the leadership of the Reformed Church, whose congregation in Romania was entirely ethnic Hungarian, and the condition of Romania's Hungarians. This had provoked his relocation to Cluj—where his father had been dismissed as deputy bishop—and then, in 1986, to Timişoara (outside Transylvania), a predominantly Romanian Orthodox yet cosmopolitan city of about 350,000. What major trouble could the Hungarian pastor possibly cause there? In Timişoara, Tőkés set about reviving the small local Reformed church with his charisma. He allowed students to recite poetry at services, which was expressly forbidden, and spoke out against Ceauşescu's unpopular "systematization" (destruction) of villages and their Orthodox churches. The Timişoaran authorities, faced with the prospect of organized dissent, pressured the Reformed Church bishop to remove Tőkés as pastor, which he did in March 1989. On that ground, the authorities set eviction proceedings in motion. Tőkés appealed. At Timişoara's Reformed church building—three modest stories of grimy brick and stone, lacking even a cross or spire—every window of the pastor's flat was smashed. In November, Tőkés was slashed in a knife assault by thugs during a break-in; police who were posted outside to keep him under house arrest did nothing. Finally, losing his official appeals, Tőkés appealed to parishioners at Sunday Mass to witness his scheduled "illegal" eviction on the coming Friday, December 15. That's right: the authorities had informed the pastor of the precise date.[36]

Around forty parishioners, mostly elderly, formed a human chain outside the pastor's residence. They benefited from a sudden unseasonably warm winter stretch, following a brutal cold snap, but, more important, they defied the conspicuous Securitate. When the Securitate did not disperse the small crowd, more people beyond the pastor's supporters joined, including ethnic Romanians, Germans,

Serbs, Greeks, and, some have said, a few Gypsies. The Hungarian pastor spoke from his windows to the crowd outside in Romanian.[37] Some who joined were from other Protestant denominations, such as the Baptists and Pentecostals, religious minorities that were similarly harassed. Others came from an adjacent stop for the tram that ferried workers to the city's outlying industrial plants and students to the big local universities. The tram also facilitated the spread of information about the confrontation throughout the town. Timișoara's inhabitants that winter, as previously, had no electricity for most of the day and often for much of the evening, including during the interval from 6:00 until 9:00 P.M., when people needed it most. Elevators were avoided, since the blackouts, coming without warning, trapped people in them. The strongest lightbulbs sold were only 40 watts. The temperature inside homes was no more than 55 degrees Fahrenheit in winter, and hot water usually came on just once a week.

People in Timișoara, as elsewhere in Romania, were given coupons to buy a few kilos of meat and fifty grams of butter—a month. They queued for hours, and sometimes even the meager allotments their coupons permitted ran out. Meanwhile, as everyone in Timișoara knew, on the outskirts lay one of Europe's largest pork-processing plants. The town also had large local bread factories and other major food production facilities. Many Timișoarans labored in these plants, and they doubtless told others what was made in them and in what quantities. But much of this locally produced food, like everything else, was being exported for hard currency. The furious townsfolk, spending years shoulder to shoulder in queues, were united in their deprivation.[38] But they could call upon no forms of social organization other than their churches, which were under Securitate surveillance. Their workplaces belonged to the regime. Furthermore, crowds on the streets were permitted only in connection with scripted holidays and soccer matches. In fact, back on November 15, following Romania's defeat of Denmark in a World Cup qualifier in Bucharest, Timișoara's streets had filled with elated fans, some of whom had apparently chanted "Down with Ceaușescu!"[39] This unpublicized incident had indicated the potential for a wider conflagration if something set it off. That is exactly what the pastor's principled, stubborn defiance had triggered on December 15.

On December 16, Timişoara's mayor, summoned to intervene by the Securitate, arrived at the Reformed church with workmen to replace the shattered windows and with doctors to examine the pastor's pregnant wife. In turn, the mayor requested that Tőkés instruct the crowd to disperse. In order to avoid bloodshed, the pastor agreed. But the crowd, by then much beyond his congregation, was in no mood to go home; some began accusing Tőkés of collaboration. Others assumed that his dispersal request resulted from pressure by the Securitate. Tőkés discovered himself a "prisoner" of the people's anger. But "in that street," recalled one eyewitness, "was a tension and a feeling of power that you could almost touch."[40] Both joyous and apprehensive, the gathering crowd began to relocate from the small church toward the city center, Opera Square, several blocks away. Having initially assembled to defend the ethnic Hungarian pastor, the crowd began singing the 1848 nationalist anthem, "Awake, Romanians." Shop windows were smashed—the regime's blackouts enabled some people to hurl rocks without being seen—and some chanted "Down with Ceauşescu!" "Down with tyranny!" "Freedom!" This lightning escalation—precisely what the appearance of the mayor had sought to preempt—had transpired in a single day.

It was the beginning of a political bank run. Jets from water cannon sent protesters scrambling, but the commotion also brought others out. "At first," recalled one inhabitant, "we thought it was a football [soccer] match . . . then it dawned on us. A demonstration!" In the wee small hours of the next day, December 17, Tőkés—by then protected only by seven associates—was brutally beaten, forced to sign a blank sheet of paper, and removed to an isolated village, as if he were still the root cause of the protest. But even without the pastor, that day some two thousand people faced down mounted bayonets and marched in columns, many carrying the banners of their factories, toward the gray granite party headquarters on Timişoara's Boulevard of August 23. Drenched once again by cold water from a fire truck, the infuriated crowd rushed the vehicle, broke it apart, and drowned it in the river. Then they ransacked the party building, tossing books by Ceauşescu onto a bonfire. They also captured five tanks loaded with a few hundred shells.

Ceauşescu had already berated his interior minister on the night of December 16 on the need to show the regime's teeth to subdue the Timişoaran hooligans—after all, the Conducător insisted, it was just a "Hungarian" stirring trouble. But this harangue had led, on the morning of December 17, to an absurd military parade (!) through the Timişoara town center, replete with buglers. Far from intimidating people, the parade drew onlookers and mockery. It was a Sunday, and the townsfolk had idle time. It was then that the major vandalism and the tank capture took place, which were duly reported to Bucharest. The reaction was ferocious. That afternoon, a conclave of the regime's Political Executive Committee in the capital was held, followed by a closed-circuit teleconference with officials around the country. Ceauşescu railed at a conspiracy involving West and East (Moscow), voiced suspicions of his own Securitate, demanded restoration of order, and threatened anyone who failed to use the requisite force. "I've given the order to shoot," said the Conducător, according to an official transcript. "They'll get a warning," he added of the demonstrators, "and if they don't submit, they'll have to be shot. It was a mistake to turn the other cheek.... In an hour order should be reestablished in Timişoara."

That very afternoon, December 17, Army Chief of Staff and First Deputy Defense Minister Major General Ştefan Guşă (1940–94), under the watchful eye of a party hard-liner, arrived in Timişoara, as did armored and motorized columns. Guşă claimed he found hundreds of shops damaged, looting, wild shooting, and rumors of possible assaults on munitions depots. That evening, armed forces, using newly distributed live ammunition, set about recapturing the city. Several score civilians were massacred, and several hundred were wounded and arrested. "The number of victims is not known yet, but there is no doubt that the [Romanian] authorities used force with exceptional brutality," one foreign body would soon note in a condemnatory statement about the Timişoara crackdown. That foreign body was Poland's lower house of parliament. Despite Poland's by then Solidarity-led government, its legislature was still full of Communists, but it passed the resolution censuring the Romanian regime unanimously. Lech Wałęsa (1943–), the Solidarity leader, responded to a letter from Reverend Tőkés, writing "I appeal to all people...to take up a common action in defense of clergyman Tőkés, to express solidarity by exercising international pressure on Romanian authorities."[41] Poland was still technically in the Warsaw Pact, too, so the tables had been turned on Ceauşescu, the man who had condemned the Warsaw Pact's Prague crackdown in 1968.

On Monday, December 18, Ceauşescu flew to Tehran for a previously scheduled three-day state visit with the ayatollahs, with whom Romania had worked out a modus vivendi (arms for oil). In Timişoara, more civilian casualties were inflicted, including at the Romanian Orthodox cathedral, a place of sanctuary. Still more fatefully, the Timişoara authorities, in typical regime fashion, convened a series of workplace meetings to impart the "right" interpretation to events. Only now did many workers learn of the scope of the bloodshed from party officials, who proffered ludicrous explanations about legions of "fascists" run amok in their city. Above all, these meetings, as the former local party chief said, "essentially enabled them [the workers] to organize." Workers at the city's Electrobanat (ELBA) factory—a prerevolutionary enterprise that had been nationalized in 1948—laid down their tools, formed ad hoc strike committees, and issued demands to Guşă of the General Staff. Rumors of shootings at the factory, which manufactured lighting equipment, further shifted the spotlight from a single priest, Tőkés, to the working class in a workers' state. On the nineteenth, General Guşă later claimed, he had been called to rescue the city party secretary at Electrobanat, which had a predominantly female workforce, but was himself greeted with shouts of "Criminals, you murdered our children!" Before fleeing in the confusion, the local party boss had recorded the irate women's demands: "We want heat.... We want chocolate for our children...socks, underwear, cocoa, and cotton."[42]

Timişoarans were withdrawing their fear. General Guşă later asserted that close up, he belatedly discovered that the protesters he had been violently suppressing were not hooligans but people.[43] Perhaps, but the next day, December 20, the Conducător returned from Iran and appeared on state television, pugnaciously denouncing the demonstrators in Timişoara as "hooligans," "fascists," and "foreign agents." He thereby confirmed—for the first time in Romania's official media—the fact of the much-rumored protests. In Timişoara, meanwhile, more workers declared stoppages, in effect creating a general strike (only the two bread factories seem to have continued operation). General Guşă blinked. Already on the night of the nineteenth, he appears to have ordered the military withdrawn from around the Electrobanat plant; now, on the twentieth, he seems to have ordered the army's heavy vehicles and troops withdrawn from the city center, where at least forty thousand people were massed on Opera Square. Protesters began embracing soldiers and chanting "The army is with us!" Indeed, one of the reasons for the pullback may have been that the troops were fraternizing. On the balcony of the opera house, loudspeakers had been set up for the prime minister, who was expected to arrive that day. Instead, at 2:00 a forty-one-year-old professor from the Technical University of Timişoara, Lorin Fortuna, announced himself. He delivered a speech proclaiming the formation of a "Romanian Democratic Front." Suddenly, local authorities started looking to the professor to negotiate on behalf of "the opposition."

The central regime, however, was in no mind to capitulate. But it only dug itself a deeper hole. The Bucharest authorities ordered in workers with clubs and "patriotic guard" uniforms from other regions to Timişoara by train. The working class, Ceauşescu appears to have imagined, could be "trusted" to put down the "hooligans." Yet it was precisely the working class that posed the principal challenge in Timişoara. And when the famished, club-wielding outside workers finally arrived in the city on December 21, they were not met at the train station or given directions. They went home. Others turned around still en route. In the meantime, however, the central authorities continued their forceful response. For the same day, December 21, Ceauşescu also ordered a mass rally in Bucharest to support the regime against "foreign interference" (meaning the supposedly orchestrated protests in Timişoara). That meant that the Communist-party apparatus worked overtime to bring tens of thousands of workers from the big factories on buses to the heart of the capital, the old Palace Square. The crowd was given the usual placards. "To begin with," the dictator said to those below from the second-story balcony of the Central Committee building, whence he had harangued the country so many times before, "I would like to extend to you...warm revolutionary greetings." Revolution it would be.

The run on the bank was broadcast to the entire nation. As Ceauşescu spoke, some people apparently sought to penetrate the cordon around the official rally; there were jostling and a thud, perhaps from a falling lamppost. Whatever the source of the noise, tear gas grenades were fired, which sowed greater confusion. Some members of the crowd, perhaps fearing another massacre, or perhaps being assertive, shouted "Timişoara! Timişoara!" Soon TV viewers and radio listeners, instead of "Ceauşescu and the people" (*Ceauşescu şi poporul*), began hearing "Ceauşescu the dictator" (*Ceauşescu dictatorul*). Before censors cut the live broadcast—it took three minutes to do so—Romanians saw a startled, frightened tyrant, angrily flailing his hands, and heard pathetic cries of "What?" and "Shut up!" It was a crucial moment. Security forces around the country had been instructed to watch the speech on television to buttress their fighting spirit, and they, too, witnessed the regime's vulnerability. Emboldened, a mostly young crowd swelled that night, December 21, on the nearby University Square, which the demonstrators declared a "zone free of communism." But security forces assaulted them with tank and machine-gun fire. News of the carnage spread by telephone and word of mouth. On the morning of the twenty-second, at 10:58, the regime declared a state of emergency, deeming illegal any grouping of more than five people. But hundreds of thousands of people had already lined the capital's streets and reassembled in front of the eight-pillared Central Committee fortress. They were on the verge of Romania's biggest breakthrough of all.

Hundreds of thousands of Romanians massing in the heart of Bucharest against the express orders of a well-armed dictatorship was astonishing enough. But then state radio and television declared that Defense Minister Colonel General Vasile Milea had shot himself and was "a traitor." Rumors flew that Milea had been executed for refusing to fire on the crowd. Whether a suicide or execution, the regime's announcement—entirely voluntary—of his death and the linking of it to treason had the unintended but predictable effect of calling into question the army's loyalty. That day, Ceauşescu was expected to make another television address. Instead, at 11:30 A.M. he again stepped onto the Central Committee building balcony. The crowd jeered him with the slogan "The army is with us." Shoes, stones, and other projectiles were hurled, and the dictator was hustled inside. The crowd began storming the party sanctuary. From the roof, an overloaded French-built helicopter staggered off, making Ceauşescu a fugitive—and one soon announced to the whole country, on TV. Rather than flee abroad, however, to an Arab country such as Libya, as expected, Ceauşescu and his retinue went to one of the provincial Romanian cities that they thought would be calm (apparently having called around first). Indeed, the vast majority of Romania—Timişoara, Cluj, and Bucharest notably excepted—was not up in arms. But the establishment (such as it was) had frozen. Many top central functionaries were not even in Bucharest, having been ordered to the provinces by Ceauşescu to keep order locally. At this point, the key lay in the hands of the military and security commanders.

Nondefection Defection

Prior to December 1989, the only serious challenge to the Ceauşescu regime had taken place two years before in Braşov, a medieval Saxon town that was Romania's second largest industrial center, situated in southeastern Transylvania. Back on November 15, 1987, fresh wage cuts for "unfulfilled production quotas" (in fact, demand was down) came on top of continued food rationing and further heat and electricity reductions, and a revolt erupted at the Red Flag truck factory. Several thousand workers at the 22,000-strong plant, upon finishing the night shift, gathered to vote in the Sunday municipal elections taking place across Romania. They marched, but toward the city center, an hour away. Along the way they were joined by counterparts from Braşov's 25,000-strong Tractor Plant, which had had some work stoppages the previous week, as well as by townspeople. Estimates of the crowd on the main square range from 5,000 to 20,000, perhaps reflecting its growth over time. They sang the forbidden anthem of the 1848 revolution, "Awake, Romanians," and chanted "We want bread" but also "Down with the dictatorship." Some protesters forcibly entered the party building, discovering ample food stocks laid out for local bigwigs to celebrate the predetermined election results. Overturning the furniture, the crowd tossed the food as well as portraits of Ceauşescu into the square and lit a bonfire that was visible far around. After some delay, troops arrived with truncheons and armored personnel carriers and cleared the square. Three people were killed and five score arrested.[44]

In Braşov, after a very brief sudden increase following the strikes, supplies of publicly available foodstuffs and electricity declined even further, and many workers were forcibly moved to other regions. The regime also managed a media blackout over the events in Braşov. But it had no answer for the distress arising from its economic mismanagement and the potential mobilization of those in whose name it ruled.[45] Everywhere in Eastern Europe, even in already industrialized Czechoslovakia, the Communists had created their own proletariat, drawn predominantly from the peasantry. Romania in 1948 had had a mere 3.8 million urbanites, but by 1980 its urban population was 11 to 12 million, meaning that several million people had moved to the cities, most joining the industrial labor force. In Braşov three fifths of the labor force worked in industry, often in factories that produced goods for export, so they were among Romania's better paid, with good schools for their children. But as elsewhere around the country, these proletarians had begun to sit idle in the absence of raw materials and other inputs. Then the regime not only sliced their wages, it started announcing the need for mass layoffs. There was no "market" to blame; the workers blamed the party-state. Braşov in 1987—absent the Hungarian pastor catalyst—presented the same scenario as Timişoara would in 1989: defiant workers, many of them rampaging, joined by young people, in anger but also in shame over what the regime had done to them.[46]

"Events, dear boy, events," the British prime minister Harold Macmillan once said when asked what could blow a government off course. True enough, but also context. The big difference between Braşov in 1987 and Timişoara (as well as Bucharest) in 1989 was the turn of events *outside* Romania. Gorbachev—who had visited Bucharest in May 1987, the first visit by a Soviet leader since Brezhnev in 1976, and returned in July 1989 for a meeting of the Warsaw Pact—had mostly avoided publicly pressuring Ceauşescu. But Gorbachev's own reforms ipso facto discredited Romania's long-cultivated standing in the West as the supposed heroic defier of Moscow. Now Bucharest was still defiant but in the guise of antireform and repression. In addition, Hungary, which had stopped returning Romanian travelers without valid travel documents in late 1987, accepted nearly 25,000 refugees from Romania by 1989. That was an average of 300 or so per week, and about a quarter of them were ethnic Romanians. And while circumstances outside Romania had helped transform the situation inside, it also bears underscoring the enhanced role of the media, both foreign and—what was unprecedented—domestic.[47] Not just "the voices" (such as the BBC, Radio Free Europe, and Deutsche Welle), but media of other East bloc countries now pierced Romania's isolation. The upshot was that whereas repression and censorship had essentially quelled the 1987 Braşov protests, the bloody crackdown in Timişoara—news of which was transmitted into Romania—sparked further protests and riots, in Cluj (Transylvania) and even in the capital.[48]

Romania's Communist regime would not negotiate itself out of existence, as in Poland, but rather had to be, and was, given a forceful shove, as in East Germany. Yet for all the courage shown by those who risked their lives, Romania's military would prove decisive—precisely because it was not decisive. The all-important Romanian high command had played a major part in the crackdowns in Timişoara, Cluj, and Bucharest, but the military finally ceased defending the regime, first in Timişoara, then in the capital. Defense Minister Milea may have sent a telex on the morning of December 22 to the regional commander in Braşov to withhold firing on civilians, just as Guşă had, belatedly, done on his own in Timişoara.[49] But Milea was dead before the order to pull back tanks and troops in the capital could have been given. On the morning of December 22, Ceauşescu named Lieutenant General Victor Stănculescu as the new defense minister. Stănculescu, the army's liaison with the Securitate, had been in Timişoara during both the massacre and the subsequent troop withdrawal from the city center; he had returned to Bucharest only the morning he was named the new minister (Guşă returned a bit later the same day). Stănculescu admitted that he had gone to a hospital and had a cast placed on his leg, feigning injury to escape being around to implement orders to shoot civilians. But he was still summoned by Ceauşescu. Stănculescu may have been the one who ended up ordering the more than one thousand army and Securitate troops defending the central party headquarters to be withdrawn. He organized Ceauşescu's helicopter flight (which he presumably tracked) and three days later was in the room at Ceauşescu's "trial."[50]

Had the army defected? There was as yet no one for the army to defect to. Romania did not have an organized opposition, let alone a Wałęsa or Havel or Boris Yeltsin. In the meantime, though, some lower-level commanders, on learning of Milea's suspicious death, or just reacting to rapidly moving events, had stopped blocking the routes into the capital's central square from the outskirts. Authority was eroding. To be sure, the top command, remaining faithful to its service oaths, had taken part in vicious repressions in Bucharest as late as the night of December 21. And Milea's death may have made some even more panicky for their own lives if they disobeyed. Still, the uncertainty resulting from Milea's death apparently provided a chance to confer collectively.[51] On the twenty-second, some commanders were trying to regroup their forces on or near Palace Square, perhaps with a mind to calling up reinforcements or at least to protecting the army's cohesion: the troops were fraternizing and beginning to merge with the protesting crowds.[52] We may never learn the sequence of decision making, the precise motivations, and who gave the key order to pull back from defending the Central Committee building, essentially countermanding Ceauşescu's repeated orders. But this we do know: the Romanian high command shrank from a "Chinese solution" (à la Tiananmen Square).[53]

Where was the infamous Securitate? The Securitate was directly subordinate to Ceauşescu. In 1964, Dej, uniquely in the East bloc, had succeeded in getting Moscow to withdraw the KGB advisers from inside the Securitate, meaning that during perestroika lacked direct levers over Romania's security police. By 1989, Romania's KGB equivalent appears to have numbered some 38,000 personnel, including around 23,000 troops. Add in the Ministry of Interior's militia, numbering around 30,000, and the so-called patriotic guard, another 12,000 core ruffians, and that made for around 65,000 total riot forces and goons. But at any given time, substantial numbers of these troops were actually employed in construction, and they, too, had to queue for foodstuffs and other scarce goods alongside civilians. The Securitate's troops did receive better rations, but the bulk of its troops, like the army's 140,000 troops, were conscripts.[54] Genuinely crack troops were few. Still, these forces were massed and ready inside and around the Central Committee building. To these loyalists with truncheons and automatic weapons, Romania's ideology of antifascism and anti-imperialism (U.S. and Soviet), as well as the constant talk of foreign interventionist plots and of a higher calling to defend the homeland, was mother's milk. By December 1989, however, it was too late.

Certainly the security police were a ubiquitous, intimidating aspect of life in Romania right through 1989 (and beyond). Popular fear of them was a force multiplier, and countless informants also enhanced the Securitate's reach. But since the early days of mass terror and the implanting of the regime, the Securitate had become an agency primarily of prevention or prophylaxis. The registry of all typewriters, the inventory of handwriting samples for a huge proportion of the population, the enormous capacity to listen in on telephone conversations and perlustrate mail, the criminalization of any failure to report contacts with foreigners, the psychiatric incarcerations—all this, in the face of a populace on the march, suddenly proved of diminished practical value. Recall that the East German Stasi had numbered 91,000, including 16,000 troops, and thus was more than double the size of the Securitate—for a much smaller population (East Germany 16.4 million, Romania almost 23 million)—but the Stasi, too, had not been able to halt the regime's collapse. "The Securitate," the leading scholar of it has written, was "a state of mind," meaning that its power worked if people believed it worked. By definition, then, the Securitate was less effective once enormous crowds had formed, especially after the army had stood down, and the "Genius of the Carpathians" had flown the coop.[55]

CIVIL SOCIETY, FINALLY POSSIBLE

"Olé, olé, olé, olé, Ceaușescu nu mai e" (Ceaușescu is no more)—so chanted Romanians, soccer-match style, after the tyrant fled. Still, his immediate whereabouts and intentions remained subject to wild rumor. Sniper shootings and even pitched battles between various groupings of uniformed men intensified in the capital's streets for days. More than 900 of the 1,100 deaths recorded during the Romanian revolution took place after December 22. That was one motivation for Ceaușescu's trial and summary execution on December 25: no one should think he might come back to power. Even then, however, the country remained mystified about what had happened, who had done what, when, and what would happen next. Tismăneanu has aptly called Romanian communism "an endless succession of plots, vendettas, and assassinations."[56] Adding to the atmosphere of intrigue, the salacious memoirs of the defector Ion Mihai Pacepa, the former deputy head of Romanian foreign intelligence, were serialized in 1989 on Radio Free Europe in Romanian and implicated Ceaușescu in blackmail, kidnapping, drug smuggling, terrorism, and murder. Phantasmagorical rumors spread of the discovery of 4,630 corpses in Timișoara; the actual number of deaths was about 75, but the regime had fed the rumors by sealing the local morgue to hide the carnage and relocating some 40 corpses to Bucharest for cremation. There were also stories of secret labyrinths under the capital, and of a long-planned coup d'état.

There was, however, no planned coup in 1989, and no counter-coup either.[57] Romania's uncivil society was unworthy of staging a coup. Some Securitate officers put on army uniforms (the two organizations' uniforms were, in any case, similar); many snipers in the mayhem wore no uniforms. Some shooters may have been freelancing, fulfilling an imagined mission, in the name of the "patriotic guards." The regime had had weapons stashed in the event of an emergency, and many arms were passed out during the events. Amid the chaos, military school cadets were dispatched to take Bucharest airport, but it was already in the army's hands and forty-eight cadets were mowed down. A special forces unit was sent to take the Defense Ministry, but troops were already there and they perceived the newcomers as attackers and slaughtered them.[58] In other words, the Romanian Communist police state disintegrated. One day everything had been apparently solid, like a bank's granite facade. The next, people lined up and said they wanted to withdraw, immediately. And when others saw this, they too wanted out, creating a spiral. It was not random, but it was unorganized. It was largely unexpected and then seemingly inevitable. The revolution in Romania had taken the form, as in East Germany, of a bank run on the regime. Timişoara had done to Ceauşescu's regime what Leipzig had done to Honecker's.

A breakthrough to mass participatory revolution had occurred in Romania even though right into 1989 the country had had almost no independent organizations, let alone some kind of "incipient civil society." Romanians under communism evinced little trust in organizations—for good reason. Organizations were oppressive: they relentlessly coerced people to do and say things according to the regime's dictates. And yet, in this land of the Securitate, large demonstrations had broken out and been sustained. During the revolution, nothing was organized—except the churches, like the small congregation in Timişoara, and the big factories in that and other industrial cities. In other words, workers did not have independent trade unions, but they did have their workplaces. "The only place the protesters could gather beforehand," wrote the scholar Peter Siani-Davies, in reference to Timişoara in 1989, "was their place of work." It was from there that protesters had taken to the streets. "Thus, with some irony," he concluded, "it can be said that Ceauşescu was toppled by mass protests that stemmed from an organizational form, the factory, that communism had elevated to be both the actual and also the mythical heart of the state."[59] A few dress rehearsals, including for vandalism, had been provided during soccer matches. To put the matter another way, Romania had a society, just not a civil society. You go to revolution with the society you have.

The new government announced itself as the National Salvation Front at the state television offices. The motley Front, despite some ambiguous pre-1989 antecedents, was a postcollapse formation—essentially the Romanian Communist reformed party wing that never was (while there had been a party), joined by some dissidents and others.[60] But as in the case of East Germany's New Forum, which may have provided Romanians with a model, the National Salvation Front's initial vague mutterings about a better socialism were forgotten posthaste. But rather than an Anschluss or takeover, as of East Germany by West Germany, in Romania the top layers of uncivil society were cast aside by fast-rising second- and third-power echelons in what became a drive for order and state continuity without the ruling dynasty. Elena Ceauşescu's couture collection was donated to Europe's last remaining leper colony.[61] The new revolutionary flag was the old Romanian tricolor flag (blue, yellow, and red), but with a hole cut in the middle where the Communist insignia had been. On state television on December 22, Mircea Dinescu (1950–), nicknamed "the Jester Poet," had appeared and exclaimed, "God has turned his face to Romania again." Some months before, Dinescu, the son of factory workers, had told the French leftist newspaper *Libération* that God had turned his face away from Romania, for which he had been expelled from the party and fired from his position at the main literary magazine.[62] With the revolution, the Jester Poet was elected head of Romania's Writers' Union (1990–96)—which, like so much else, survived into the new era.

Violence and rioting continued into 1990, as workers armed with clubs and crowbars—Ceauşescu's hoped-for shock troops—materialized belatedly, bused in to bash protesters who opposed the new regime for its conspicuous surfeit of former Communist-party members. Ceauşescu and his wife were among the very few prosecuted for what happened during the Communist era. (Their son Nicu, the onetime heir apparent, died in 1996, age forty-five, from bleeding of the esophagus as a result of liver cirrhosis.) But the violence and the accusations about neocommunism—predictable in terms of personnel—obscured the crucial fact that the planned economy had been terminated. The legalization of private property and the market fundamentally changed the possibilities for Romanian society. In 1990, the activist Gabriel Andreescu (1952–)—who beginning in 1984 had courageously written letters to foreign human rights organizations on behalf of jailed Romanians and who himself had been jailed for treason in 1987—told an American correspondent that "the most important thing at this moment is to create a civil society." By that he meant "free trade unions, free mass media, lots of different structures," which should accompany the new electoral democracy. "Until Romania has a civil society, elections are of no significance," he concluded, adding that political parties might proclaim freedom, but "only a civil society can assure it."[63] After the breakthrough of 1989, Andreescu did his part, establishing a legal human rights organization in Romania that has not been short of work. A liberal state cannot be taken for granted.

IV

A͟S I͟F

Among the local Communist-party bosses in Poland who boasted to higher-ups that their drives to instill communism had succeeded, one functionary was particularly proud. "In my district," he reported, "the number of people who attend church regularly is down to 85 percent."

Bronisław Geremek, a Solidarity adviser, said a book he had written on medieval France could not be published because Polish Communist authorities had objected to just a single word in the whole work. Asked what the word was, he replied, "Geremek."

Was there or was there not a revolution in 1989? Characters in the Romanian film *12:08 East of Bucharest* (2006) trying to recall.

Prague Spring, in the ornate castle, 1968. Above: Vasil Bilak (left), the Czechoslovak party conservative, conferring with another conservative, Gustáv Husák. Bilak signed a letter requesting Soviet intervention. Below: Zdeněk Mlynář (right), ideologue of the party's "socialism with a human face" reforms, talking with party chief Alexander Dubček.

Above: Władysław Gomułka (left), Poland's party chief, normally a teetotaler, and animated comrades offer New Year's toasts, 1970. Below: Training for the regime's police, October 1969.

The 1973 "oil shock" clobbered Eastern Europe. In 1974, the Soviets were still accepting 800 units of the Ikarus bus, Hungary's prized export, in exchange for 1 million tons of oil (roughly 7.3 million barrels), but before long payment for that same quantity of oil required 4,000 buses.

Uncivil society at play, January 1965: East German party chief Walter Ulbricht (right), Erich Honecker, and their spouses. Honecker, who had overseen construction of the Berlin Wall, pushed Ulbricht aside six years later.

East German Robotron computers, 1987. The regime's big wager on high tech failed.

Peace processional, downtown Leipzig, October 23, 1989. The nonviolent marches proceeded from the St. Nicholas Church after the 5:00 P.M. Mass on the same day (Monday) and at the same time (6:00 P.M.) every week, requiring no special organization. As the marches grew and the authorities failed to crack down, the regime began to disintegrate.

Berlin Wall breached. Above: Politburo member Günter Schabowski at an international press conference bungling the announcement of a new East German travel policy, November 9, 1989. Below: That same night, an East German–West German embrace, after a westward crossing through the suddenly opened checkpoint.

FPG, Getty Images

Doftana Prison, dubbed the "Marxist University" under Romania's right-wing dictatorship, 1930s. It was here that a young Nicolae Ceauşescu (below right) met Romania's soon-to-be Communist dictator Gheorghe Gheorghiu-Dej (below left). When Dej died in 1965, Ceauşescu took over.

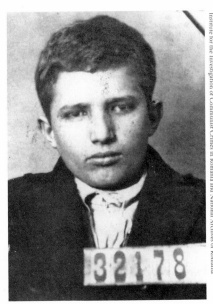

Mark Caror, Alamy Images

Institute for the Investigation of Communist Crimes in Romania and National Archives of Romania

Services in the Reformed (Calvinist) church, Timişoara, Romania. Below: The determined pastor László Tőkés at home with his wife, Edit. Exterior of the building (housing both the church and the apartment) where the authorities' attempt to evict Tőkés was blocked by approximately forty parishioners, an incident that helped set off the revolution.

Fundatia General Ştefan Guşă

Romanian Generals Ştefan Guşă (left) and Vasile Milea. In Timişoara, Guşă initially bloodied demonstrators, then pulled the troops back, ceding the provincial city to protesters. Defense Minister Milea's suicide, announced the morning of December 22, 1989, broke the regime.

General Guşă hustled onto Romanian state television, as evidence that the army backed "the revolution," December 22, 1989. It was from TV that day that the entire country learned "the dictator has fled."

Mircea Hudek, Agerpres, Romania

Above: Uncivil society, led by Ceauşescu (standing), partying on "international workers' day," May 1, 1966. Romanian elites would not suffer the severe austerity imposed by the regime. Below: Long queues to the bitter end: outside a Romanian dairy store, November 21, 1989.

Above: Striking workers at Poland's Gdańsk shipyard, where Solidarity was established, August 1980. Below: A shipyard fence painted with the slogans "Long live free and independent trade unions and world peace" (upper left) and "Only Solidarity" (right). Underneath the Polish national flag is a portrait of Mary, mother of God.

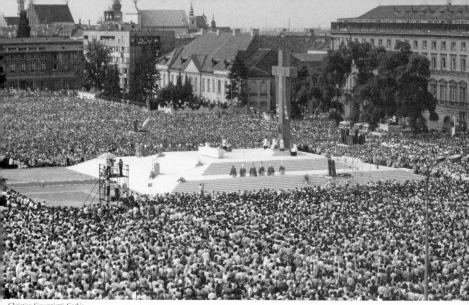

Christian Simonpietri, Corbis

Above: John Paul II, the first ever Polish pope, celebrating an open-air Mass on his return to his hometown of Krakow, March 1979. Below: The Black Madonna of Częstochowa in procession, trailed by Stefan Cardinal Wyszyński (in headgear), May 4, 1966. Wyszyński's ten-year "Great Novena" celebrations mobilized millions to commemorate the thousandth anniversary of Christianity in Poland.

Edmund Uchymiak, Polish Press Agency (PAP)

Self-confident Alfred Miodowicz (left), the leader of Poland's Communist trade unions, preparing to debate Lech Wałęsa, the leader of Solidarity (right), in front of a live TV audience estimated at 25 million (in a country of 35 million), November 1988. It was Wałęsa's first permitted appearance on national TV. He reduced Miodowicz to mincemeat.

This is the way it ends: "roundtable" negotiations between Poland's Communist rulers (uncivil society) and opposition (civil society), April 5, 1989.

Polish and Romanian Communist leaders Edward Gierek and Nicolae Ceaușescu (center, both in hats) bear hunting in the Carpathians, October 1976. Not long after Soviet leader Mikhail Gorbachev formally renounced the "Brezhnev Doctrine" (the use of force to uphold communism in Eastern Europe), the regimes imploded.

Defense of Poland's freedom precipitated the Second World War in Europe in 1939, but as a result of agreements among the Big Three at conferences in Tehran (1943) and Yalta (1945), the country fell into a Soviet sphere of influence. Poland's western border was extended into what had been German territory, while its eastern regions—more or less what the Soviets had seized in connection with the Hitler-Stalin Pact in 1939—were incorporated into the USSR (in contravention of the Atlantic Charter that Winston Churchill and Franklin Roosevelt had announced in 1941). Free postwar elections in Poland, as specified in the Yalta Agreements, did not happen. Władysław Gomułka (1905–82), the first secretary of the Polish United Workers' Party—as the Communist party was known—had some blunt words for Stanisław Mikolajczyk (1901–66), the Polish Peasant Party leader and onetime prime minister of the government in exile who returned from London to Warsaw and joined what was called the Provisional Government of National Unity. "You can shout all you want that blood of the Polish nation is being spilled, that the NKVD rules Poland," Gomułka confided to Mikolajczyk during a break in negotiations, "but this will not turn us back from our path— once we have taken power, we will never give it up."[1] Yet that is exactly what transpired in the spring of 1989 as a result of roundtable negotiations that took place between the Communist establishment and the Polish opposition.

Poland was different.[2] Even though peasants fiercely resisted the collectivization of agriculture everywhere, only in Poland did the party abandon the process (in 1956), so that the overwhelming majority of Polish farmland (80 percent) reverted to individual households, with only 1 percent organized as collective farms (and the rest as state farms).[3] Such an independent peasantry was unique in the East bloc (and matched only by China when it disbanded its communes beginning in the 1970s). Further, as a result of Hitler's murderous war and Stalin's border shifts, Poland had become an almost universally Catholic country, and most people were churchgoers, including—often on the sly—party members. By 1977, after three decades of continuous administrative and fiscal pressure against it, the Church in Poland counted 20,000 priests and 27,600 nuns—many thousands more than during the pre-Communist interwar period. Communist Poland was organized into nearly 7,000 parishes, as well as 27 dioceses supervised by 77 bishops, with some 10,000 churches along with 4,000 chapels. Almost 5,000 students were enrolled in 44 higher Catholic seminaries, while another 1,400 studied at the Catholic Theological Academy and 2,500 at the Catholic University in Lublin—the only such Catholic institution of higher learning in the Communist world.[4] In 1978, the archbishop of Kraków, Karol Józef Wojtyła (1920–2005), became the first non-Italian pope in 455 years and the first-ever Polish pope.

No less distinctive was Poland's militant working class (which Communist industrialization had greatly enlarged). Unlike the one-off explosions in East Germany (1953), Hungary (1956), Czechoslovakia (1968), and (on a smaller scale) Romania (1977), eruptions in Poland recurred. In Poznań in 1956, a strike at the gigantic Josef Stalin Metallurgical Complex against a new system for calculating wages prompted more than 100,000 people (out of the city's 380,000) to march to Adam Mickiewicz Square, where, in front of Poznań's old royal castle, they chanted "We are hungry," "Down with the Red bourgeoisie." Around seventy were killed and many hundreds wounded when Poland's uncivil society unleashed one of the bloodiest repressions in the East bloc's history that did not involve Soviet troops.[5] But more strike waves and demonstrations followed in 1968, 1970, 1976, and 1980 like jolts on an uncivil-society electrocardiogram. Poland's workers developed powerful organizational forms—above all, elected interfactory strike committees—that would culminate in an independent (non-Communist) trade union known as Solidarity.[6] In a parallel breakthrough in fall 1976, fourteen members of the intelligentsia established a Workers' Defense Committee (Komitet Obrony Robotników, or KOR). These were men and women of different generations and different political biographies: a well-known elderly writer, a famous actress, a young and an old university professor, two retired attorneys, two officers of the wartime Home Army, a priest, some student activists, and a few hard-core dissidents. Making public their names, addresses, and telephone numbers, they invited victimized workers and their families to contact them for help.[7] "Do not burn down committees," exclaimed KOR's Jacek Kuroń (1934–2004) in the aftermath of the 1976 strikes and riots, "set up your own!"[8]

Lifted from a penumbra of semilegality, an array of activities coalesced. KOR combined its citizen-provided welfare with public accounting of acts of injustice via uncensored publications, *KOR's Communiqué* and *Information Bulletin*. This samizdat lastingly breached the uncivil society's monopoly on the circulation of ideas and information, helping open the floodgates. Nationalistically minded oppositionists created the Movement to Defend Citizens' and Human Rights, while Catholic conservatives founded the Movement for Young Poland. Highbrow alternative journals—*Res Publica, Zapis, Krytyka*—appeared, as did practical ones, such as *Robotnik* (The Worker), in which the Charter of Workers' Rights was printed in 1979; signed by more than one hundred activists from around the country and circulated in more than 100,000 copies, it would have a direct impact on Solidarity.[9] The most successful independent publishing house, launched by Mirosław Chojecki (1949–) and known by its acronym NOWa ("new"), placed in circulation more than sixty works and reprints of eminent but banned Polish authors—Czesław Miłosz, Witold Gombrowicz, Aleksander Wat, Leszek Kołakowski—in print runs of several thousand copies. By late 1977, a so-called Flying University (soon known as the Society of Scientific Courses) arose. Meetings in apartments or church facilities provided by sympathetic priests featured major thinkers in disfavor, such as Tadeusz Mazowiecki (1927–), the editor of the Warsaw Catholic monthly *Więź* (Link), and Bronisław Geremek (1932–2008), who offered non-Communist Polish history and civic lessons.

Poland's unique opposition became the bloc's only counterelite and comprised not just intellectuals and clerics but also workers. It drew upon a uniquely strong tradition of resisting Russia, including the 1830–31 and 1863 unsuccessful uprisings against tsarist rule—

which had led to peaceful, stateless nation building known as "organic work"—and a 1919–20 successful war for national independence against the Bolsheviks.[10] (Marx had called Poland "indigestible.") On top of it all, the opposition discovered a remarkable strategy: acting "as if" Poland were already a free country. "As soon as they started to act 'as if,' the 'as if' started to melt away," observed the American writer Jonathan Schell. "Then they really *were* defending the worker (and often with success), or giving the lecture, or publishing a book. It wasn't 'as if' it were a book, it *was* a book, and soon people were really reading it." To be sure, conceded Schell, "in the country at large the 'as if' did not melt away. That became clear when the book was confiscated, or the lecture was broken up by the government goon squad, or the innocent worker was sent off to prison." All the same, "in the immediate vicinity of the action—and that vicinity expanded steadily as the movement grew—the 'as if' was no pretense."[11] This project for societal self-emancipation would be called, by its proponents, "civil society." Miraculously, it seemed a reality when the strike waves and religious pageants converged, beginning in August 1980, and the nation experienced sixteen unprecedented months of an independent national union, Solidarity, chaired by an electrician, Lech Wałęsa, with tens of thousands of other new leaders at grassroots and intermediate levels. But the antitotalitarian strategy of "as if" was possible only because the opposition had come to reject the idea of reform ("socialism with a human face") and instead to see the system as "totalitarian." At the same time, the actual Communist system they were challenging was the *least* totalitarian country in the bloc, with non-Communist values, public spaces, and even institutions.

For all that, Communist rule in Poland lasted four decades and without needing a single instance of Soviet armed intervention. Moreover, throughout most of 1989, neither the establishment nor the opposition had a clue that the end was nigh. In December 1981, uncivil society had successfully imposed martial law, driving Solidarity and the "as if" civil society into prison or underground. Communist monopoly was restored. Yet the country remained economically broke because of its crack cocaine–style borrowing from the West to try to mollify the restive populace and its inability to win export markets for its goods. In November 1987, the uncivil society staged a referendum seeking to legitimize harsh economic measures by asking the populace if it wanted economic and political reform. But if fewer than 51 percent of *eligible* voters said yes, the effort would be invalidated. The call for a total boycott by Solidarity (then illegal) went unheeded, yet those who voted "no" combined with those who did stay home to form a bare majority; uncivil society lost its own plebiscite.[12] Then came a renewed strike wave in spring 1988. Geremek, the medieval historian and Solidarity adviser, publicly suggested to the regime that it enter discussions to reach an "anticrisis pact." After more strikes in August, General Wojciech Jaruzelski, the first secretary of the party and chairman of the State Council, manipulated the Politburo into agreeing to a "dialogue" intended to manipulate the opposition.

The Polish roundtable was transformative for the entire country (and for others in the East bloc—Hungary's roundtable, which followed, would produce far freer elections). But Poland's civil society–uncivil society roundtable of February–April 1989—thirteen working groups, ninety-four sessions—was neither initiated nor used as an end to the system. Uncivil society sought a miracle exit out of the economic catastrophe; Solidarity ("civil society") sought relegalization and, though mindful of the need to address Poland's baleful economic state, remained wary of taking responsibility. The wild, tense negotiations produced a blueprint for limited free elections to take place in June, whereby the trade union became legal and uncivil society was guaranteed to keep its hold on power. Nonetheless, because of a complicated procedural design, the vote produced a negative referendum on party rule. Solidarity, in effect, won. The establishment prime movers in the roundtable and aftermath, Generals Jaruzelski and Czesław Kiszczak, the interior minister, retained full operational control of a formidable repressive apparatus, but they refrained from trying to reimpose martial law. The circumstance of having cracked down in 1981 only to find themselves in the same predicament eight years later may have given them pause. On August 19, 1989, Jaruzelski asked the Solidarity official Tadeusz Mazowiecki to form an opposition-led government. Both sets of protagonists, civil and uncivil, were repeatedly stunned by the results of the steps they had each been taking in order to avoid what actually happened: the Communist establishment had not wanted to give up power; the opposition had not wanted to claim it. How and why did it come to pass that a still-armed uncivil society yielded control of state institutions to an opposition claiming to be civil society?

TOTALITARIANISM

By the end of World War II, more than one third of Poland's urban residents were dead. The country had lost more than half its lawyers, two fifths of its medical doctors, and one third of its university professors and Roman Catholic clergy. Gone, too, were many of the country's civil servants, army officers, sportsmen, artists, high school teachers, journalists, and engineers. These losses included a broad stratum of well-educated assimilated Polish Jews who had been killed in the Holocaust: 500,000 Jews had lived in Warsaw alone. Despite Nazi ruthlessness—or perhaps because of it—the Poles mounted the most impressive resistance movement in occupied Europe. In addition to an underground military organization, the Home Army, which at its peak counted some 300,000 sworn-in adherents, an elaborate network of institutions was set up in occupied Poland and known collectively as the underground state. This clandestine "state" included political parties, a shadow administration headed by a representative of the legal Polish government in exile, which resided in London, a press (more than two thousand titles have been enumerated), a school system, and a welfare distribution network.[13]

The Nazi despoliation was complemented by the Soviets. Sixteen days after Hitler had invaded Poland on September 1, 1939, Stalin and the Red Army invaded Poland from the east. In March 1940, the Soviet Politburo issued an execution order for 21,857 Polish detainees and POWs; 4,421 of them were buried in mass graves at a place called Katyń, not far from Smolensk. Most of the victims were reserve officers mobilized only in time of war, that is, professionals with university degrees. After Hitler invaded the Soviet Union in

June 1941, the Soviets reversed course and allowed the Poles to out-fit military units to fight against the Germans. But no one could locate the thousands of officers who had been taken prisoner by the Soviets and in spring 1940 vanished without a trace. Early in 1943 a German communications unit stationed in a former Soviet security police (NKVD) compound disinterred the remains of executed Polish officers from mass graves. They had been buried in uniform, many with bullet holes in the back of their skulls, letters from home still in their pockets. The Soviets bald-facedly denied responsibility for the mass murder, blaming it on the Nazis.[14] Lies about Katyń throughout the Communist period denied uncivil society a persuasive, legitimizing narrative about the war.

Under double occupation on and off from 1939, the Polish population directly experienced comparisons of the Nazis and Soviets many years before professors at Harvard and elsewhere institutionalized the paradigm of "totalitarianism" that linked the Soviet and Nazi regimes. A quarter-million Poles perished in August–September 1944 during the Warsaw Uprising, when the Polish anti-Nazi underground sought to liberate the country from the Germans before the Soviets arrived. Retreating Nazis returned and expended considerable resources to annihilate the Poles and reduce the Polish capital to a pile of rubble, while the vast Soviet army was encamped across the Vistula River. Another 30,000 lives were claimed by a low-intensity civil war between leftists and rightists that continued in Poland for several years after the Third Reich was defeated—right through the December 1948 "unification" congress of the Communist and Socialist parties that formed the so-called Polish United Workers' Party, under whose banner the Communists would rule. Mass terror against perceived political enemies and the brutality of collectivization ensued. The scale of violent social engineering in Poland during and immediately after World War II was incomparable, even by Nazi and Soviet standards.

At the same time, millions of Poles were beneficiaries of state-driven economic expansion and the opening up of the higher education system to all who had not been able to afford it in the past. Roughly one million peasants moved from the countryside to the cities from 1947 to 1950, and between 1949 and 1955 industrial employment went up from 1.8 million to 2.8 million. The favored model of industrialization was to construct huge factories on the outskirts of big cities. Joining the working class was a step up on the social ladder for poor peasant youths, but the construction of apartment buildings never caught up with demand and young proletarians were often confined for years to communal dormitories, with little opportunity to start a family life or find decent entertainment. Alcoholism became not only a public health problem but an impediment to safety and adequate job performance. The ranks of the party, in the usual indecipherable mix of enthusiasts and opportunists, shot up from 20,000 in July 1944 to 555,000 at the beginning of 1947. Eventually, the party in Poland would enroll more than 3 million members, some 8 percent of the population.

Poland's uncivil society viciously targeted the influence of the Catholic Church. The authorities confiscated church property, assumed control over the Church's welfare organization, Caritas, and sowed discord in Church ranks by sponsoring a "movement of patriotic priests." (At the height of Stalinism, one of every ten Catholic clergy, many blackmailed by the security police, partook in this Communist-sponsored "movement.") The Communists also promoted a lay Catholic organization, Pax (Peace), headed by Poland's foremost prewar fascist youth, now a Communist collaborator. It became almost impossible to obtain permission to renovate or build a church (local residents would often construct sanctuaries on their own, without building permits). Stalin's death in 1953 unexpectedly defanged the offensive against the Church (and against the peasantry), but even so a show trial of a bishop on trumped-up charges was staged in September 1953 (he got twelve years in prison). Stefan Cardinal Wyszyński (1901–81), an organist's son and the primate of the Catholic Church since late 1948 in Poland, was placed under "house arrest" in a remote mountain cloister. Still, a broad political démarche was precipitated by the escape to the West of a colonel of the security police in December 1953. Józef Światło (1915–75) was the deputy head of the Ministry of Public Security department that kept tabs on high party officials, and he had personally arrested the party's first secretary, Władysław Gomułka, in 1951. The colonel was privy to state secrets, including the private affairs of the elite, and his broadcasts over Radio Free Europe, which began in September 1954, were avidly followed in Poland and shook the confidence of an establishment used to conducting its business behind a veil of total secrecy.

Poland began an early de-Stalinization. In 1954, the Stalinist security apparatus was broken up and several of its most notorious functionaries were arrested; some political prisoners were released. In December 1954, Gomułka—jailed under Stalinism for "nationalist deviation"—was released. From 1955, discussion clubs of the intelligentsia sprouted in many cities, most famously the Crooked Circle in Warsaw, where several leading oppositionists of future decades cut their teeth. A political weekly of the young intelligentsia called *Po Prostu* (Speaking Simply) became a forum for critical reportage and commentary. Then came Nikita Khrushchev's secret speech denouncing Stalin's "mistakes and distortions" at a closed session of the Soviet Union's Twentieth Party Congress in February 1956, which was followed by the sudden death by heart attack of Poland's Stalin-era party leader Bolesław Bierut (1892–1956). In connection with Bierut's funeral and succession, Khrushchev delivered a second extemporaneous secret speech in Warsaw on March 20, 1956, at a gathering of the Polish party.[15] The Poles resolved to circulate Khrushchev's speech widely, a decision unique in the East bloc, and throughout late March and early April, thousands of party meetings took place all over Poland that probed previously taboo subjects in Polish-Soviet relations (the Hitler-Stalin Pact, the Katyń massacre). Would-be Polish reformers backed off a plan to have nonparty discussions of the secret speech even before June 1956, when the industrial city of Poznań erupted in strikes and food riots.

The uncivil society cracked down mercilessly on the workers, but it also retreated on a wide front. Collectivization was halted by the party and then abruptly reversed by the peasants, far faster than the party had anticipated. Church building permits began to be issued liberally (token Catholic representation was also invited to sit in the rubber-stamp parliament, or Sejm).[16] Cardinal Wyszyński—who in

April 1956 had refused a deal to return to Warsaw while other bishops remained cut off from their dioceses, saying "I could return as the last but never as the first"[17]—was released along with others in October. That same month, Gomułka was reinstalled as first secretary, to popular acclaim. Khrushchev and a retinue of Soviet Politburo heavies had flown unannounced to Warsaw on the eve of the decisive Polish party plenum, swearing at Gomułka and his colleagues right on the airport tarmac. (News of their rough treatment, witnessed by drivers and others casually present, immediately spread through Warsaw.) After the visit, though, the Soviets left reassured that the new Polish leader was a faithful Communist (rather than a Polish patriot), and Khrushchev ordered the Soviet army units already moving toward Warsaw to return to their barracks. "Those who are against socialism," Gomułka said, "are against Poland." Moscow's bet on Gomułka in 1956 may have been dictated by the Soviets' perceived need to intervene militarily against Imre Nagy in Hungary; or the reliance on a Polish figure in the crisis year enabled the Soviets to intervene in Hungary. Either way, Poland escaped a crackdown.

But Gomułka's triumphant return in 1956 (the "Polish October") proved to be an era not of reforms but of "tightening the vise." The intelligentsia's Crooked Circle would be shuttered after seven years' existence.[18] The Polish party's reformist wing would be confined mostly to the pages of the party periodical *Polityka*, founded in 1957 and edited for more than two decades by Mieczysław Rakowski (1926–2008), a disarming peasant's son (and future first secretary). The Catholic Church was especially targeted, but it proved resilient against the uncivil society. "In the popular consciousness," Jakub Berman (1901–84), the chief ideologue to Bierut in the 1950s, had complained, the Church "is the bulwark of Polish tradition and culture, the most complete expression of 'Polishness.' "[19] Indeed, in 1956, after his release, Cardinal Wyszyński—who had become a Marian mystic during his confinement—embarked on a renewal of the country's faith by reconsecrating the nation to Mary, mother of God, as queen of Poland (reprising the vow of King Jan II Kazimierz from three centuries earlier). In anticipation of the 1966 millennium of Poland's conversion to Christianity, the primate organized a nine-year "Great Novena" that engaged millions in meditation on Poland's moral values and its sins. A replica of the country's most important religious symbol, the Black Madonna (also known as Our Lady of Częstochowa) of the monastery in Jasna Góra (Clear Mountain), visited every single parish. Pilgrimages to the actual holy icon brought hundreds of thousands of believers to the monastery every year; then, in 1966, the genuine painting was taken on the road, commencing from the cathedral of the ancient Polish capital Gniezno. Despite panicky, shifting prohibitions by the uncivil society, the Black Madonna drew throngs to enormous Catholic Masses along its route across the country.[20]

Wyszyński ended up leading the Church in Poland for thirty-three years, far longer than any first secretary led the Polish party. His nonviolent "Great Novena" pastoral mobilization was unprecedented in the history of modern Christianity. It also borrowed from a familiar Polish strategy—dating back to nineteenth-century struggles under foreign rulers—of political accommodation combined with nation building; in this case, ever more peasants and workers living under communism but worshiping Christ. The largest, and sometimes newest, buildings in many towns became churches, and the country's connecting roads were lined with shrines to the Virgin Mary, usually with offerings of fresh flowers. The primate also nurtured lay clubs of the Catholic intelligentsia, as well as Lublin's Catholic University. His efforts helped yield a dynamic conciliar laity and a highly educated younger clergy, including Karol Wojtyła.[21] The Church in Poland came to speak with ever greater insistence not just about social justice and the dignity of labor—the regime's nominal values, too—but about absolute, universal moral values, the inviolability of individual conscience, and faith in God's incarnation in Christ as the foundation of genuine humanism. (These would be the themes of Wojtyła's sermons on his first visit home as Pope John Paul II.) During the severe repressions against workers in 1976 that had given birth to KOR, Wyszyński wrote a letter to the regime urging that "the workers who partook in the protests should have their rights and their social and professional positions restored; the injuries they have suffered should be compensated; and those who have been sentenced should be amnestied."[22] The next year, Adam Michnik authored an important book, published in Polish by the emigration in Paris, entitled *The Church, the Left: A Dialogue.*[23]

Michnik, born in 1946 into a family of Jewish prewar Communists, was a student activist who joined neither the Socialist Youth Organization nor the Communist party, spent some six years in Communist jails altogether, and became the most influential essayist of the opposition. In 1966, he and other Warsaw University students had organized a commemorative meeting for the tenth anniversary of October 1956 and its reform socialist hopes. They invited as a speaker the then-iconic representative of open Marxism, Leszek Kołakowski (1927–), their philosophy professor, who criticized Gomułka's abandonment of the "October 1956 ideals." The meeting was surreptitiously taped by the security police, and Kołakowski was thrown out of the party.[24] Michnik was suspended, but a letter protesting this decision was signed by more than a thousand students and 150 teaching staff in the university. Several eminent humanists turned in their party membership cards in a gesture of solidarity with dismissed colleagues. The uncivil society responded by stepping up the campaign to root out Marxist "revisionism" and resorting to a vicious anti-Semitic campaign (part of an internal regime power grab).[25] In 1968, thousands of university students were expelled, followed by their call-up for military service as well as by a wave of arrests (2,700 all over the country).[26] And then it dawned on them: democratizing the system was a delusion. By the outbreak of the Prague Spring's "socialism with a human face" in Czechoslovakia, Poland's substantial left-wing intelligentsia had turned away from striving for a better socialism and begun reflecting on the phenomenon of "totalitarianism."[27] This signified that Soviet-style socialism was unredeemable, equivalent to Nazism.

SECOND BAPTISM

The upper ranks of Poland's uncivil society counted some 270,000 functionaries, who, with their dependents, amounted to more than

1 million people (around 3 percent of the population). They controlled the country's industry. They also awarded themselves and their families privileged access to educational institutions, cash bonuses, and hidden special stores as well as weekly "packages" of prized goods. At their disposal were also the security police, the SB (Służba Bezpieczeństwa), Poland's equivalent of the KGB. With more than 20,000 agents (one for every 1,574 inhabitants), the SB was tasked with penetrating Polish émigré communities—among the strongest of any bloc country—manipulating Poland's Catholic Church, and minutely observing and neutralizing the opposition. Uncivil society could further dial up the ZOMO (Motorized Reserves of the Citizens' Militia), paramilitaries who rode in armored personnel carriers, threw tear gas, and wielded Plexiglas riot shields and truncheons. Established during the unrest of 1956 for "the protection of the nation" and derisively known and feared as the "beating heart of the party" (for all the beatings they administered), the ZOMO grew to more than 12,000 goons. But the greatest binding substances of Poland's uncivil society were vast patronage and a widely shared belief that it represented the lesser evil, the buffer against a Soviet intervention—in short, that they were patriots of Poland's "national road" to communism.

In December 1970, however, workers again undermined the party's grasping for the national mantle. In Gdańsk, on Poland's Baltic coast, the Lenin Shipyard struck over a sudden jump in food prices. It was ten days before Christmas. Around one half of workers' income was allotted to food purchases. When local authorities used the factory PA system to initiate a discussion, workers used it to address a crowd in front of the factory administration building and call for the regime's "resignation." Singing the "Internationale," they marched on and attacked the party building in the city center. Workers in Szczecin struck "in solidarity with Gdańsk," establishing a three-day "workers' republic" as the party-state melted away. Uncivil society, in a sign of desperation, encouraged the workers to form committees to put forth their demands in an orderly fashion. This was the beginning in Poland of the interfactory strike committee, with elected representatives. A twenty-seven-year-old electrician named Lech Wałęsa was among the Gdańsk strike leaders. After months of talks and continuing strikes, the food price increases were rescinded. But according to official records, forty-four shipyard workers had been shot dead during the food riots. Once again, the self-proclaimed vanguard of the working class was shooting workers. But the massacre forced a change in the leadership of uncivil society: Gomułka was replaced by Edward Gierek (1913–2001).

A former miner, Gierek had been in charge of a heavily industrialized coal mining region, Silesia, prided himself on being a real manager, and, unusually, had lived abroad (in Belgium) and spoke French. Under Gierek, uncivil society expanded—party membership rose from 2 million to 3 million over the decade of the 1970s—and power became more centralized. He installed his "Silesian mafia" in Warsaw and broke up the country's seventeen voivodeships (the largest administrative units) into forty-nine smaller ones, eliminating any chance that someone could accumulate the power to challenge the authority of the first secretary in Warsaw (the way he had done as an overlord in Silesia). Gierek also hit upon the idea of borrowing hard currency from the West to increase consumption in Poland and turbocharge the economy, with a plan to pay back the debts out of anticipated export earnings. GDP grew at a stunning annual clip of nearly 10 percent during the first half of the decade, and salaries leapt accordingly. In 1970, there were 450,000 private cars in Poland, but by the end of the decade, thanks to local production of the "small Fiat" from 1974, more than 2 million private cars were on the roads. Still, Polish products failed to find many buyers in the West, and the hard-currency loans were eaten up: by 1979, up to one half of the raw materials and basic inputs necessary to keep production going in Polish factories had to be imported for hard currency. Foreign debt, nearly $4 billion in 1974, doubled the next year and reached $20 billion by decade's end.

Centralizing power, Gierek loosened the autarky, exposing the system far more to the world economy.[28] He also entered into long-term agreements linking Poland to Soviet-sponsored projects through COMECON, the Soviet economic bloc, which guaranteed access to Soviet raw materials, particularly oil and natural gas, but led to shortages of capital goods (such as locomotives) because COMECON obligations required Poland to export such products to other members of the bloc. All this, on top of the 1973 oil shock, as well as central planning's inherent wastefulness and nonmarket rigidity, bludgeoned the borrowing strategy, leading Gierek, again, to try to lower the costly subsidies for food. In June 1976, price hikes—69 percent for meat and fish, 100 percent for sugar, 60 percent for butter—provoked 130 factories to strike. (The atmosphere had been inflamed the preceding year by attempts to insert the "leading role" of the party as well as "special friendship" with the USSR into the country's Constitution.) The workers again humiliated uncivil society—the ashen prime minister went on television and revoked the "price adjustment" for meat products *one day* after having introduced it and belatedly promised consultations with unspecified "representatives of society." Imagine a state with monopoly control over everything—economy, education, media, cultural institutions, unions, police, the military, entertainment—that could not raise the price of sausage without risking mass social protests. Such was the price of price hikes in Poland. It was at this point that a group of individuals formed KOR, offering a recourse to beaten and incarcerated workers and their families—efforts that were supported by the strengthened post-1968 political emigration. Suddenly, every provincial party secretary had to reckon with the fact that if anything untoward happened to a member of the opposition, it would be publicized on Radio Free Europe and might affect Poland's standing with Western creditors.

By the late 1970s, Gierek's consumption-led boom strategy had stalled in growth fatigue, and Poland's current-accounts balance had sunk to $25 billion in the red. Communist-system labor productivity could not support Communist-promised lifestyles, and the price of the compensatory foreign loans was not only economic dependence on the West but also a certain independence of maneuver for Poland's opposition. To be sure, uncivil society and party members possessed the career paths, apartments, vacations, choice schools, and everything else craved by individuals and families. Poland was still a police state, with abundant police. Opposition members were tailed, jailed, and sometimes killed. But the more KOR somehow managed to exist, the more its existence was possible—the simple yet remark-able strategy of "as if." The opposition had discovered that because totalitarianism entailed an aspiration to control all aspects of life and politicize everything, it left itself oddly vulnerable on the terrain of the everyday. The insight had been arrived at by Kołakowski—the former Stalin-era Communist, then reform Communist, and by now ex-Communist—whose theses "Hope and Hopelessness," published in 1971 in the Paris-based émigré journal *Kultura*, drove a dagger through the (hopeless) attempts to reform the system. Kołakowski's hopeful part—a societal self-democratization—was amplified by Michnik in a prominent essay in 1976 entitled "A New Evolution-ism." Explaining that "what sets today's opposition apart is the belief that a program for evolution ought to be addressed to an indepen-dent public, not to totalitarian power," Michnik summoned society to cease being a "sack of potatoes" (Marx's dismissive phrase for peasants) and do something, *anything*, as long as it was in public life, and on one's own initiative.[29] Jonathan Schell, the American, summed up the approach succinctly: "Do you believe in freedom of speech? Then speak freely. Do you love the truth? Then tell it. Do you believe in an open society? Then act openly."[30] All this was under way before October 1978, when the white puffs of smoke emerged from St. Peter's in Rome, indicating the election of a new pope.

Kraków was Poland's ancient cultural center, and the Communists had conspicuously built their most colossal steel complex in its suburb Nowa Huta (New Mill), to dilute the influence of the Catholic intelli-gentsia with a new working class. But the workers went to church. And the old city—with its Gothic and Renaissance quarter, graced as well by much Habsburg baroque—remained a bastion of intellectual Catholi-cism. That was in no small measure thanks to its remarkable magazine, the Catholic weekly *Tygodnik Powszechny* (Universal Weekly), put out from 1945 by Jerzy Turowicz (1912–99). In 1953, perhaps uniquely in the East bloc, *Tygodnik Powszechny* refused to publish an obituary for Josef Stalin. Its entire editorial board was "replaced" by regime-sponsored "progressive" Catholics of the Pax organization (led by the interwar Polish fascists). It was only in late 1956 that de-Stalinization fi-nally enabled Turowicz and the original board to return. Thereafter, the influence of the periodical and its dialogue-promoting circle was enhanced by the patronage of Kraków's leading cleric, Karol Józef Wojtyła. He had been struck by a streetcar as a little boy and by a truck as a young man during the Nazi occupation (when the university was shuttered and he labored in a limestone quarry). In 1942, at the height of man's inhumanity to man, he gave up acting in the theater, his passion, and entered an underground seminary; four years later, he was ordained a priest. Sent to the renowned Saint Thomas Aquinas Pontifical University in Rome, known as the Angelicum, he wrote the first of two doctoral dissertations—"The Doctrine of Faith According to Saint John of the Cross"—which was approved at Jagiellonian University in Kraków. An intellectual and published poet, Wojtyła would openly support the illegal activities of the Flying University as well as KOR (he met several of its members, including Kuroń and Lipski, in the Warsaw apartment of a Catholic intellectual with KOR ties). Made cardinal in 1967—doctrinally orthodox and charismatic—he was made pope eleven years later, when just fifty-eight years old. The way had been opened when his predecessor, John Paul I, died after thirty-three days in office.

By custom, the Vatican cardinals knelt before the new pontiff to swear their vows and kiss his ring, but when the Polish prelate Cardinal Wyszyński started to kneel, Wojtyła, now John Paul II, stood him up and hugged him. Back in 1966, during the culmination of Wyszyński's "Great Novena," Poland's uncivil society had refused to grant a visa to the then pope, Paul VI, but how could they deny a return home by a native son? John Paul II's pilgrimage began on June 2, 1979. Upon deplaning, he knelt and kissed the ground before acknowledging the greeting party of uncivil-society dignitaries—transmitted on live TV—and then was driven into Warsaw in an open-top car past more than a million people. For nine days, the party-state virtually ceased to exist. Not the uncivil society but the Catholic laity handled the logistics of the papal visit. When the pope celebrated an open-air Mass in front of a forty-foot-high wooden cross for more than a quarter-million people on Warsaw's Victory Square, the assembled chanted, "We want God, we want God, we want God in the family, we want God in the schools, we want God in books." Uncivil society scripted television coverage to avoid showing the extent of the crowds. Still, texts of the pope's sermons were published with minimal censorship, and all of his Masses were shown on local television, while two were broadcast on national TV. Radio Free Europe's Polish service, meanwhile, ran thirteen hours of coverage each day. The pope in effect enacted and consolidated the wholly Catholic nation that Hitler and Stalin had engineered and that Wyszyński had painstakingly renewed.

John Paul II's visit home, in the words of the writer Julian Stryjkowski (1905–96), was akin to "Poland's second baptism" (exactly what the previous pope, Paul VI, had called Wyszyński's "Great Novena").[31] The hard work of thirty years of Communist propaganda, one high apparatchik was overheard complaining, was undone in a few days. Thirteen million Poles—more than a third of the nation—saw the pope in person. "We were hanging out as usual in the narrow streets of Warsaw's Old Town," recalled Andrzej Stasiuk (1960–), a nineteen-year-old and not easily impressionable hippie at the time who would become a distinguished writer of the younger generation. "The next day the first papal mass service in the country was to be celebrated in the Victory Square.... Usually around ten or eleven at night streets emptied, ... but now the area between the Castle Square and the Old Town Square was full of life, as if it were a corso of an Italian city." He added that this was his "first experience of collective freedom," camping out with others awaiting Mass the next day. "Even we—long-haired, shabbily dressed, in rebellion against the entire world—even we were convinced that all these people next to us, their resemblance to our fathers and mothers and detested teachers notwithstanding, were in some fundamental, bodily, physical way dear to us."[32] The pope's message—heard by almost every living Pole in person, on radio, or on TV—was "the inviolable right, in God's and man's order of things, for human beings to live in freedom and dignity."[33]

SOLIDARITY

Again the trigger was food price hikes, this time on July 1, 1980. Immediately, sporadic strikes took place in several cities, and then a mass work stoppage in Lublin that lasted eleven days. Rumors spread about how railway workers in Lublin—along the rail line connecting East Germany and the Soviet Union—had welded a train full of goods to its tracks to prevent it from leaving Polish territory for the USSR.[34] (It was the eve of the Summer Olympics in Moscow, and the Soviets were vacuuming the bloc to stock supplies for the attendees.) The Lublin strike was ended by a generous economic package. But in mid-August, the workers at the 17,000-strong Lenin Shipyard in Gdańsk, who had struck in 1970, seethed upon learning from thousands of illegal leaflets of the firing of Anna Walentynowicz (1929–), a respected female crane operator with thirty years' experience at the shipyard. She had been cashiered five months before she was due to retire with benefits, for distributing copies of a samizdat newspaper (*Coastal Worker*) at the factory gates and for belonging to the illegal Free Trade Unions of the Coast, founded in 1978. The organizer of the tiny underground union in Gdańsk, Bogdan Borusewicz (1949–), a graduate of Lublin's Catholic University and a member of KOR, had correctly surmised that the Walentynowicz firing could help transform the shipyard workers' plans for a work stoppage into a mass action. In Poland there was no theme deeper than martyrdom.

On August 10, when several Gdańsk oppositionists met for a social occasion, Borusewicz galvanized Lech Wałęsa, another member of the illegal Free Trade Union, who had been fired from the shipyard back in 1976. Four days later, with a strike by the workers ready to begin, Wałęsa was smuggled into his old workplace.[35] As the father of five children, Wałęsa had plenty at risk, and this would win over the many workers with families. He quickly established himself as leader of the strike committee, proving to be a brilliant speaker and entering negotiations with the shipyard director. By August 16, a Saturday, the director promised to raise wages substantially, covering the food price hike, and to reinstate Walentynowicz and Wałęsa. The local boss also pledged immunity to the strikers. Wałęsa proclaimed an end to the occupation strike over the shipyard PA system, and people began to go home for the remainder of the weekend. But representatives of smaller enterprises in Gdańsk, which had walked out after the shipyard, felt they had been left exposed and reproached Wałęsa for abandoning them. Wałęsa, sensing that he had made a mistake, ran over in the company of Walentynowicz and others to plead with workers at the gate to remain in the shipyard and continue the strike—now in "solidarity" with other enterprises. But just a few hundred workers remained inside through Sunday, unsure of the disposition of the full 17,000 workforce, which would return Monday morning. At this point, a local priest, Father Henryk Jankowski (1936–), celebrated Mass in front of the gates and after services helped worshipers mount a commemorative wooden cross on the spot where the striking workers had been killed in December 1970. It was this "loyalty to the memory of the dead" that would vivify the 1980 strike, as shipyard workers reprised the tactic of a disciplined sit-down, or "occupation strike."[36]

The Gdańsk strike proved extraordinarily disciplined and resolute. Those inside the locked gates over the weekend had reconstituted an Interfactory Strike Committee and hammered out twenty-one "postulates," including abolition of censorship, release of political prisoners, and the right to form "independent, self-governing" labor unions. The term "free" unions was avoided—in the knowledge that it would drive the uncivil society berserk—but the document clearly aimed at breaking the party's monopoly. Although phone lines to and from Gdańsk were cut, censorship was tightened, and disinformation was stepped up, samizdat newspapers (in print runs of 30,000) spread the word. Also, sympathizers from the Flying University and KOR passed news they heard from Gdańsk to Radio Free Europe and the BBC, whose broadcasts were widely listened to all over Poland. On August 18, shipyard workers in Szczecin struck. More factories followed suit and sent representatives to join the Interfactory Strike Committee in Gdańsk. In the capital on August 20, several prominent intellectuals including Kuroń and Michnik were arrested, but a number who eluded detention (including Geremek and Mazowiecki) reached

Gdańsk to support the workers in the negotiations. On August 23, a letter from the pope (dated six days earlier) to Cardinal Wyszyński was published, calling on bishops to help the nation "in its difficult struggle for daily bread, for social justice, and the safeguarding of its inviolable rights to its own life and development." On state television, Wyszyński called for peace and reason—until his death in May 1981, the primate would urge moderation—but the pontiff's words were taken as an endorsement of the strike.

As townsfolk brought food, warm clothes, and blankets to the workers inside, doctors and nurses provided medical attention, and priests led prayers, tanks and armed units were readied to take up positions outside the gates of the worker-occupied shipyards. But in the evening of the day the pope's supportive message was published, the official commission dispatched by uncivil society belatedly entered direct negotiations with the Interfactory Strike Committee that were broadcast live all over the Gdańsk shipyards. Within a week the Interfactory Strike Committee assembled representatives of 700 striking factories, employing 700,000 people. The Szczecin Accord of August 30, 1980, and the landmark Gdańsk Accord the next day contained fundamental regime concessions—not just substantial pay raises for the workers but, in Gdańsk, legalization of an independent union.[37] In early September, Gierek (ruled 1970–80) was ousted, the second leader in a row following Gomułka (ruled 1956–70) to fall victim to failed price hikes. The party leadership was assumed by Stanisław Kania, and then, in October 1981, by the defense minister since 1968, General Wojciech Jaruzelski (1923–). After much legal wrangling, in November 1980 a court registered Solidarity as a legal entity. In January 1981, Wałęsa, a devout Catholic, led a delegation to the Vatican. By that time, Solidarity's membership had risen to 10 million—nearly 80 percent of the workforce. Fully one third of the party joined Solidarity—up to a million Communists, 70 percent of them workers.

Communism brought industrialization everywhere in Eastern Europe—most of all in the Soviet Union—but Solidarity emerged only in Poland.[38] Of the strikes and organization, it is important but not enough to say that the workers did them.[39] Solidarity, the historian Martin Malia wrote, was "the eternal return, but in nonviolent form, of the classic Polish insurrectionary struggle for independence and democracy, or for the 'self-governing republic' as the union's program put it."[40] True, more Polish intellectuals did the regime's bidding than opposed it—after all, it meant their livelihoods—but a core from a wide spectrum of orientations risked life and limb to defend workers. No less consequentially, portraits of the Virgin Mary and crucifixes adorned Polish factories and Solidarity offices, while the nine years of "Great Novena" processionals as well as the papal visit offered carryover experience, an alternate symbolic universe, and a moral compass: the word "morality" can be found in just about every Solidarity document, hitting at communism's weakest point.[41] "We know that we will win," the character Birkut says to his son Maciej in Andrzej Wajda's *Man of Iron* (1981), a film about the 1980 Gdańsk shipyard strikes, "because the lie cannot last eternally." The Polish pope was a beacon of strength, having looked out over his compatriots and calmly instructed, "Be not afraid." In March 1981, when Poland's security police roughed up Solidarity activists in Bydgoszcz, Solidarity's charismatic leader, Wałęsa, called a four-hour warning strike, which brought the country to a standstill. It was the largest walkout in the history of the bloc, and the uncivil society felt compelled to announce an investigation into the Bydgoszcz beatings.

Wałęsa agreed to defer further strikes, but the same month Kania and Jaruzelski had already been summoned to an impatient Kremlin to present plans for martial law. The two Polish leaders met conspiratorially the next month (April), too, with Soviet KGB chief Yuri Andropov and the Soviet defense minister in a railway car in a Belarus forest, and again vowed "to restore order with our forces."[42] Pressure meetings and calls never relented. Polish regime sources, meanwhile, fomented anxiety-provoking rumors of an impending Soviet intervention. The country also suffered worsening scarcities of consumer goods—perhaps deliberately exacerbated so that uncivil society could blame Solidarity for "disorganization." But for many Poles, it was still a festive time of role reversal and hope. Solidarity was a movement of people armed with nothing but personal dignity and personally held opinions, which they debated in public. The country became a nationwide workshop in political liberty, an apprenticeship in exercising citizens' rights. It was a lasting experience, for the exercise of liberty is a fix that human beings find addictive. "People went to the town assemblies," wrote the political philosopher Hannah Arendt of the 1776 American Revolution, "neither exclusively because of duty nor, and even less, to serve their own interests but most of all because they enjoyed the discussions, the deliberations, and the making of decisions."[43]

Organizationally, Solidarity sought to remain a dues-funded labor union, declaring its lack of interest in political representation or government. It aimed, as Marxists would say, to overcome the "alienation of labor" and put employees in charge of their workplaces, or, as some in the opposition said, to be "civil society," and restore individuals' dignity by ensuring them control over their lives in public settings. By design, this was a circumscribed ambition vis-à-vis governing institutions and therefore a limited program for the exercise of citizens' rights. Solidarity did not seek to take over the state. It preferred, instead, to reinvent the public realm to break the state's monopolization. Solidarity even refrained from demanding free elections to parliament. But in its own ambit, Solidarity organized nationwide free elections for representatives to the First Solidarity Congress, a boisterous affair in Gdańsk from September 5 to 10, 1981. In stages, beginning at the shop floor, the elections had involved reviews of the ideas and leadership qualifications of thousands upon thousands of active citizens, a national immersion in open debate and multicandidate balloting, to find the best qualified to fulfill the expectations of the 10-million-strong electorate. Of the nine hundred delegates chosen for Solidarity's founding congress, several dozen were SB informants, but their reports (about six hundred would be filed) mattered little since the union carried on its business in the open.[44] The *practice* of liberty, under the umbrella of Solidarity's organization, helped structure something of a self-governed society.[45]

Workplaces remained state-owned and -supervised—private property (farms excepted) was not on either side's agenda—but within Solidarity, relationships of authority were based on consent, and the leaders who emerged, many of them in their twenties and thirties, commanded respect and loyalty. The union built up some 40,000 regular paid "cadres," disproportionately factory workers and devout Catholics, often elected in workplaces, where the opportunities for a social practice to structure society began, then extended through ever-larger territorial units of the union and to the National Coordinating Council chaired by Wałęsa.[46] Poland's Solidarity-enhanced counter-elite appeared studded with individuals of talent and charisma—a perverse consequence of the uncivil society's "negative selection" mechanism, which weeded out people with integrity, curiosity, and creative independence. The writer Marek Nowakowski was not alone in noticing the "nice-looking faces," *ładne twarze*, suddenly appearing in Polish public life, as if uncivil society attracted only dullness or fate had given many oppositionists what in comparison seemed not just smarts but also good looks. Something of a new generation—Zbigniew Bujak (1954–), Władysław Frasyniuk (1954–), Bogdan Lis (1952–), and dozens upon dozens of others—left their jobs as bus drivers, mechanics, or electricians and became leaders in the union and society. (At the end of the 1980s, the desperate uncivil society would know exactly whom to approach in order to negotiate a pact.)

Just as there were bruising, sometimes histrionic disagreements among the opposition over tactics and goals, turbulent debates took place within party forums, sometimes publicly, on how to respond to Solidarity.[47] There was, however, no way forward acceptable to both Solidarity and Moscow. Whatever the quixotic hopes arising from the formal Accords and the regime's promises of political and economic "reform" (again), uncivil societies excelled not at adaptation but at locking people up, shuttering organizations, censoring publications, disorganizing agriculture and industrial production, and scuttling reforms. Indeed, on December 13, 1981, General Jaruzelski pulled off an especially smooth imposition of a "state of war" using the ZOMO riot police and the army. (In Poland's Constitution legal provisions for martial law were lacking, hence the awkward terminology.) In an operation effectively against 10 million, involving five thousand (eventually ten thousand) arrests, fewer than two dozen were killed—exceptional military police work by any standard. "Our country stands at the edge of an abyss," the general proclaimed on the radio on that freezing winter dawn, adding "we desire a great Poland" and "the only road to this goal is Socialism."[48]

This was, however, the bloc's first indigenous resort to martial law, and the political impotence of the party was plain for all to see, both in Poland and abroad. Indeed, the Polish leader not only interned an entire countrywide network of oppositionists, grounded air traffic, halted intercity rail travel, and enforced an evening curfew, but he put martial music on the radio, dressed up TV newscasters in military uniforms, and placed military commissars in factories, universities, ministries, and other institutions. It was a turn to the military as supposed national savior. Poland's army was the largest in the Warsaw Pact after that of the Soviet Union, with some 320,000 soldiers and 64,000 officers (one for every five grunts), including more than 200 generals.[49] General Jaruzelski formed a temporary junta of sixteen generals and five colonels, the Military Council of National Salvation, or WRON (which derisively became *wrona,* or "crow"; the national symbol was an eagle). But Poland remained mired in debt, needing but lacking an economic upswing. And although Solidarity would be outlawed, it survived as a clandestine organization led by those who eluded capture. Poles had spent the sixteen electrifying months since August 1980 pouring out words in the workplace, at home, during social gatherings (as during every revolution), freely deliberating any and all issues they fancied, and deciding a few—*as if* they lived in a free society, now en masse. Many continued such acts in sermon, song, satire, and samizdat. "We've got all the symbols," one Polish worker said, "and they've got all the guns and tanks."[50]

ELECTORAL SURPRISE

Already on August 25, 1980, even before the Polish regime's concessions in the Szczecin and Gdansk Accords, the Soviet Politburo formed a special commission to monitor events in Poland chaired by Mikhail Suslov (1902–82), the number two under General Secretary Brezhnev. The "Suslov Commission" worked throughout the last decade of the Soviet Union's existence, and, as its chairmen kept dying off, it was named successively "the Andropov Commission," "the Chernenko Commission," and finally "the Gorbachev Commission."[51] But by then Poland was on its own. Gorbachev's glasnost and perestroika were followed with great hope by the selfsame figures in Poland who had imposed "the state of war" in December 1981: Jaruzelski and his associates. By 1988, these Polish Communist would-be reformers were anxious not to make things difficult for Gorbachev as he seemed to struggle with internal opposition. But the Polish Politburo had no magic wand for reversing the country's debilitating economic situation. In May 1988, a new strike wave was organized by a younger post-Solidarity generation of workers (around a third of Poland's industrial workers were under twenty-five). That same month a secret internal report noted that "the memory of martial law no longer holds people back" and that "profound changes in the USSR as well as the withdrawal of Soviet forces from Afghanistan are interpreted by the opposition and its international instigators as a sign of the limited danger of outside intervention in Poland."[52] But when queried by Jaruzelski about what needed to be done, Politburo members delivered memos full of "babble" (*bełkot*).[53]

Michnik and others in the "as if" civil society looked to Catholic Spain, which through evolutionary processes had managed, without bloodshed, to incubate a transcendence of dictatorship even before General Francisco Franco died in 1975. For Poland's "Franco," Jaruzelski, awareness began to register that "out of the box" measures were necessary to cope with the deteriorating socioeconomic and political circumstances. In August 1988 new strikes broke out in the Gdańsk shipyards, accompanied by demands for the relegalization of Solidarity. "We must square the circle of impossibility to reform socialism," Jaruzelski said in despair to the comrades. "How long can people's power hang on by just threatening workers with tanks and police truncheons?"[54] This was the point when conversations toward a roundtable began in earnest. On August 31, General Czesław Kiszczak met with Lech Wałęsa in the company of designated Church representatives. Kiszczak and Jaruzelski were themselves a bit "out of the box," professionals of a certain cast, not career apparatchiks: Jaruzelski, educated in Catholic schools, was a soldier; Kiszczak had made his career in military intelligence and counterintelligence before taking over—on the eve of martial law in 1981—the country's central police job of interior minister. But most of uncivil society found scandalous the proposal to recognize Wałęsa as an official interlocutor (for years the media had insultingly called him a mere "private person"). This recognition was now made against the howls of party conservatives and the functionaries of the regime-sponsored unions, which were directed by Politburo member Alfred Miodowicz (1929–).

The negotiations about whether there should be negotiations went in circles, deadlocked by the regime's refusal to allow Solidarity's return to legal status or to have the "radicals" Jacek Kuroń and Adam Michnik participate in any roundtable. But help came from an unlikely quarter: Solidarity's staunchest enemy, Miodowicz. A clever charmer, a self-made man who happened to have a high opinion of himself, he blurted out in an interview with the main party daily, *Trybuna Ludu,* that the official state labor unions under his leadership were doing a better job protecting workers than Solidarity ever would and that he could prove this by debating Wałęsa on television. The interview was printed on November 16, 1988, and the next day Wałęsa accepted the duel. Miodowicz's Politburo comrades were flummoxed. Without consulting them, he had created a major political event: Wałęsa's appearance on national television. It was Poland's Günter Schabowski moment (the East German Politburo member who would bungle a press conference and help bring down the Berlin Wall). But Miodowicz insisted he could handle Wałęsa, fourteen years his junior, and the uncivil society let the debate go forward on November 30. Many believed Wałęsa would melt under the klieg lights and be exposed as a myth. He was dismissed as a mere puppet of Geremek, not his own man. Solidarity, meanwhile, had been convinced the regime would never let the union on TV, and when Wałęsa was allowed to go live, some of his colleagues were worried what would happen and whether the regime had *something up its sleeve.*

Wałęsa made marmalade out of Miodowicz. While the representative of uncivil society delivered a harangue on the dangers of pluralism, the representative of civil society, in a folksy, humorous style, said, "Let's give pluralism a chance, I trust the people." Many Poles were seeing Wałęsa for the first time—and this was an audience of 25 million (in a country of 35 million). "As a result of the televised debate Miodowicz-Wałęsa we may have to deal with quite a radical change in the internal situation," Interior Minister Kiszczak warned the next day behind closed doors. "The stereotype of Wałęsa's personality, represented up to now by party propaganda, has been completely ruined.... Wałęsa presented himself as a politician of great stature, with a clear and convincing vision of the country's future. He turned out to be a man with a constructive attitude, motivated by a will toward real dialogue and understanding."[55] It no longer made sense to pretend that Solidarity was irrelevant, especially when Wałęsa was invited to France and on December 10–11 received like a head of state by President François Mitterrand. It was also evident that at Wałęsa's beckoning, Western economic assistance could be forthcoming.

Miodowicz's pridefulness had accidentally recatalyzed the stalled roundtable, but no one knew how it would go. Solidarity was not confident. The relegalized union regained about 1.5 million members, a sizable number but just 15 percent of its 1980 peak membership. Wałęsa had barely managed to cajole striking workers back to their benches as part of opening the negotiations. His handshake before the cameras with Interior Minister General Kiszczak at the opening plenary on February 6, 1989, was perceived as a potentially compromising gesture. Inside the regime some argued that the country needed not a roundtable but a table full of food. Still, those with reform-Communist inclinations, such as Prime Minister (and former *Polityka* editor) Mieczysław Rakowski, had joined Jaruzelski's faction in the strategy of coopting the opposition. But the Politburo proved able to launch the roundtable only after a tense internal fracas culminating in an announcement by Generals Jaruzelski, Kiszczak, and the defense minister, as well as Rakowski, that they would resign all offices if their initiative were voted down. Then they left the meeting. Their blackmail carried the day. Aleksander Kwaśniewski (1954–), the top negotiator for uncivil society (and later the president of post-Communist Poland), explained that the ruling party believed it was strong enough to retain power. "This illusion," Kwaśniewski argued, "saved us from the Romanian experience," meaning a violent attempt by the regime to try to hold on. "If the party leadership had realized how weak it was, there would never have been the roundtable talks and peaceful change."[56]

So overconfident was the uncivil society of its control over the process that, once again, it allowed live television coverage, but that only produced another ideological shock—recent prisoners on screen, Solidarity logos pinned to their lapels, negotiating with the establishment. Just as Wałęsa had won the Nobel Peace Prize in 1983 and been visited by U.S. congressmen while all the ZOMO could do was take surveillance photos, so the SB had spent three years combing the underground to arrest Zbigniew Bujak, another electrician and the chairman of Solidarity's Warsaw branch, and now he was right there on national TV. Names and faces supposedly consigned to history's dustbin were miraculously resurrected, brought into people's living rooms, and seen talking in normal language about the country's genuine problems. In fact, the same actors as at the beginning of the 1980s confronted each other—Jaruzelski, Kiszczak, Rakowski, *e tutti quanti* on one side; Wałęsa, Geremek, Bujak, Kuroń, Mazowiecki, and Michnik on the other. But each side had learned (painfully, in the case of many oppositionists who spent years in prison) that attempts at unilateral resolutions produce only stalemate. Still, the roundtable implied recognizing the opposition as a legitimate autonomous partner, and that meant that the party's historic claim to monopoly for incarnating the logic of historical progress and the working class was surrendered. But this appeared to be the only way out of the Ponzi scheme of seeking ever more Western loans to pay off the Western loans.

When sitting down to negotiate, both sides had an identical conception of what was at stake. Bronisław Geremek, whom Wałęsa empowered to head negotiations at the "little table" (*stolik*) of political reforms, put it thus: "At the roundtable the division of labor was clear—Mazowiecki was responsible for legal registration of Solidarity, that is, for what we were supposed to gain, and I was to oversee that part of the negotiations where we were to pay a political price." The price was ostensibly legitimizing the party's authority by participating in semisham elections that the party was guaranteed to win.[57] The establishment, for its part, in conceding legal status to the opposition, would implicate it in the affairs of state and do so without sharing power. It was a straight-up horse trade. But each side felt squeamish about the concessions it had to make. After the deal was done, Wałęsa did not stand for a seat in the parliament on the assumption that he must stay "clean," in case the whole business blew up in the face of the opposition. But everybody got it exactly wrong. The uncivil society had seemed to lose nothing by the legalization of Solidarity and the opposition to gain little. In fact, uncivil society lost everything as a result of the "nonconfrontational" elections it insisted on having, while the opposition gained everything as a result of those selfsame elections that it had not wanted to participate in.

For the lower house of parliament, the Sejm, comprising 425 seats, 65 percent of the mandates were reserved for the ruling "coalition," that is, the Communists and their traditional "allies," the United Peasant Party and the Democratic Party. These were organizations controlled by the Communist party since 1945, allowing it to pretend it was ruling in a coalition of "progressive forces." The remaining 35 percent of the lower house was to be contested freely—opposition candidates, too, could stand. Meanwhile, during the negotiations, the uncivil-society side had suddenly suggested adding a strongly empowered presidency, elected indirectly (by the parliament). This was to calm presumed Soviet concerns by ensuring that General Jaruzelski would remain the ultimate arbiter. The opposition refused to go along. But Kwaśniewski came up with a quid pro quo—a new 100-seat second chamber, the Senate. For this Senate—which the opposition had not requested—he proposed free elections, a suggestion that seems to have been made on the spur of the moment. The opposition agreed. Finally, there was also a "national list," 35 slots for prominent personages of the regime to be able to run unopposed. Pollsters for uncivil society had been doing surveys for years, and they estimated the regime could count on between a quarter and a third of the electorate. In any case, a majority of the seats seemed prearranged for them. The first round of elections was set for June 4, just two months after the conclusion of the roundtable, to leave as little time as possible for opposition campaigning.

The election turned out to be a single-issue referendum: Do you want the Communist system to continue in Poland? This was hinted at when the opposition discovered it did not need to promote its previously unknown candidates to the public. It ran the same electoral poster throughout the entire country: a photograph of its local candidate, whoever that was, shaking hands with Wałęsa, over a Solidarity logo. As Kwaśniewski later said in mocking complaint, even a cow running on a Solidarity ticket would have won. Furthermore, the electoral law adopted for this election stipulated a winner-take-all system, rather than proportional representation; that is, only a candidate who received an absolute majority of the votes cast (at least 50 percent plus one vote) would be elected in a first round. Absent such a result, in a second round, two weeks later, the winner of a plurality of votes cast would get the mandate. Back in March, Prime Minister Rakowski had been warned by a wizened and wise colleague that under such an electoral procedure the party would not win a single Senate seat. But the clairvoyant only passed the memo along, without doing anything about it, because electoral law was not his bailiwick.[58] In the first round, the opposition won 160 mandates out of the 161 it was allowed to contest in the Sejm and 92 of the 100 in the Senate. The ruling coalition, in the first round, took 3 seats in the Sejm—out of the 264 set aside for it—and zero Senate seats.

Two weeks after the debacle, Rakowski wrote in his *Diaries* that "to assume a candidate from the national list would get 50 percent plus one vote was a fundamental mistake. That the entire establishment of the state exposed itself to such a test is simply incomprehensible." Indeed it was, Mr. Prime Minister. He added that "another mistake was the method for Senate elections. If the proportional system had been adopted, we would have gained thirty to forty seats in the Senate."[59] Most embarrassing of all, thirty-three out of the thirty-five candidates from the special "national list"—the top establishment figures—although running unopposed, had nonetheless been crossed off by a majority of voters. General Kiszczak was beside himself that in Polish embassies all over the world—except Albania—the national list had been voted down by the diplomatic corps and staff.[60] "Somehow, in the depth of our brains, we were convinced that we would win the elections," wrote Rakowski, a party member since 1946, "because, after all, we had always won elections."[61] In the races that Solidarity had not been allowed to contest, there was still the second round to ensure victories for the candidates of uncivil society by a mere plurality of votes, thereby securing the original plan of a regime-dominated parliament, which in turn would elect Jaruzelski to the presidency. But there were no provisions to recuperate the establishment figures' completely unopposed thirty-five seats: against whom would they run in a second round? The opposition, wary of losing everything, left it to the party-state to fill these seats by post facto procedural sleight of hand. The generals still had command over the repressive apparatus, and while many people suspected (rightly) that Poland's uncivil society had lost the stomach to shed blood, again, for such a ruinous system, the Chinese launched a crackdown in Tiananmen Square on the very day of the Polish elections.

In Poland, all the political figures who profoundly mistrusted one another and who worked doggedly to ensure they were not outfoxed by the other side were dumbfounded by the results of their joint labors. Together they had written a political script that neither side had anticipated. Would uncivil society accept its defeat, something it had always said it would never do? Would Solidarity seek to take power, something it had said it would never do? Amid the uncertainty, on July 3, Michnik—as was his style—raised a scandal. He wrote an editorial in the opposition newspaper he edited, *Gazeta Wyborcza*, entitled "Your President, our Prime Minister." Michnik's closest colleagues jumped on him for "prematurely" advocating a Solidarity government. One of his most eloquent critics was Tadeusz Mazowiecki. But it turned out that opportunists were opportunistic, for when Wałęsa approached the forgotten United Peasant Party and the Democratic Party—the "historical allies" of the ruling Communists—both eagerly accepted Solidarity's offer of alliance *against* the Communists. Wałęsa then tapped his trusted adviser, General Kiszczak's former detainee, to lead the governing coalition; Mazowiecki was duly confirmed as Poland's prime minister. During his inaugural speech on September 12, 1989, the first postwar head of government in Poland not assigned to the office by the Communist regime fainted on the rostrum of the Sejm. Doctors took him for a short walk in the park, whence he returned to the parliament chamber. "Excuse me, but I have reached the same state as the Polish economy," Mazowiecki quipped. "But I have recovered, and I hope the economy will recover too."[62] In the 1990s, half of Poland's then $45 billion in foreign debt to Western governments and commercial banks was forgiven, in what at the time was the most generous treatment ever extended to a debtor country.

EPILOGUE

Is it true that when we reach full communism, there won't be any more political jokes? Yes, except for this one.

The political run on the bank that crashed the Berlin Wall blew everything open. East Germany was utterly central to the stability of the USSR, and any change in Germany's status could only be momentous, as everyone understood—at least after it happened. "I would be less than sincere," Mikhail Gorbachev later wrote of 1989–90, "if I said that I had foreseen the course of events and the problems that the German question would eventually create." As late as 1987 the Soviet leader, whose home province of Stavropol had fallen under Nazi occupation, underscored the durability of two German states, noting "what there will be in a hundred years' time is for history to decide."[1] Then, poof. The endgame of World War II—a Soviet victory in history's greatest-ever conflict—was rewritten. Germany began an ineluctable process of reunification, on Western terms. Hundreds of thousands of Soviet troops would begin retreating eastward, along the same roads used by Napoleon during his humiliating retreat westward from Moscow in 1813. The "loss" of East Germany stunned and demoralized Soviet uncivil society, especially the huge military and security wings. Romania's simultaneous political bank run delivered a further warning: everywhere, even in the USSR, the Communist system could be doomed. With Ceaușescu's execution after a hasty "trial," followed by people killing or being killed in the streets for no evident reason, Romania's chaotic example worried even those in the USSR who advocated shedding blood to hold on.

That said, the knock-on effects of Poland's liberation were even more immediate. On August 23, 1989—five days after the Solidarity prime minister assumed office in Poland—nearly 2 million people across the three Soviet Baltic republics (out of just 8 million total population) joined hands to form a 350-mile human chain dubbed "the Baltic Way." The date marked the fiftieth anniversary of the Hitler-Stalin Pact. Back in 1918, Estonia, Latvia, and Lithuania had managed to break free of the tsarist empire, but in 1940, following adoption of the pact, the three independent states had been occupied by the Soviet Union. (They had then fallen under Nazi occupation in 1941 but been retaken by the Soviets in 1944.) Initially, Gorbachev's reforms had sparked calls for "sovereignty" in the Baltics—Estonia led the way, in 1987, by developing a program for full "economic autonomy." But by March 1990, the democratically elected deputies of the Lithuanian Supreme Soviet, or parliament, proclaimed "restitution" of the country's *independence*. The Kremlin demanded revocation of this "illegal" act and, after toying with imposition of martial law, imposed an economic blockade. But in May 1990, the Latvian Supreme Soviet, which was also democratically elected, passed its own declaration restoring independence, to be preceded by a fig-leaf transition period of "autonomy." All three Baltic states insisted that on their territory, republic laws superseded Union ones (Lithuania formally adopted a "temporary" Constitution). Just as Poland's opposition had acted *as if* it were an autonomous civil society, so the Baltic states began acting *as if* they were sovereign states.

"The events in Eastern Europe," Jacques Lévesque has written, constituted "the breaking point between the success and failure of Gorbachev's great, historic endeavor."[2] This is an exaggeration. Gorbachev's "socialism with a human face" was a bundle of contradictions that were impossible to reconcile. But the bloc's implosion vastly accelerated the *exposure* of those contradictions and emboldened many people, from the Baltic states to Ukraine to Russia, to seek the formerly unthinkable: namely, full emancipation. Gorbachev had introduced—absent any societal pressure to do so—competitive multicandidate elections for the all-Union and then the republic Supreme Soviets, empowering new popular leaders such as Russia's Boris Yeltsin (1931–2007). Until that point, uncivil society had lacked any corrective mechanisms of its own. But it had long been subject to some not of its own creation, such as the capitalist world economy. Another important factor was the steadfast Western containment stance—whatever the mistakes and excesses, a united West properly opposed communism in the Cold War—and the powerful example of post–World War II capitalist democracy and prosperity. Uncivil society's own media transmitted information about the capitalist world, and so did the Western media that penetrated uncivil society's airwaves. The latter included not only West German broadcasts into East Germany, which were unimpeded, but also Voice of America, the BBC, and others, which managed to circumvent jamming and restrictions, especially during the spiraling year of 1989. Then, just as Eastern Europe was about to break away, the elections in the USSR added an additional impulse to the popular mobilization and sovereignty drives of the Soviet borderlands. Still, what most facilitated the stunning Soviet crackup was the circumstance that the Soviet Union was organized as a conglomerate of national states.

THE FAULT LINES

The United States had never recognized the Soviet annexation of the Baltic states, making them unique among the USSR's fifteen Union republics. Gorbachev, looking to the Baltic states as leading edges in his fight against hard-liners, had instructed the party machines and KGB to facilitate the formation of "popular fronts in support of perestroika" in each Baltic republic. This Kremlin initiative in 1988, meant to isolate "extremists," was at first met coolly by locals.[3] Soon enough, though, more and more Baltic activists grasped how to use the new umbrella organizations to advance long-standing agendas, first and foremost ecology. In 1983 in Estonia, a sociological survey had found that some 90 percent agreed with the statement that "environmental problems are so critical and significant that immediate remedies must be taken." In Lithuania that same year, membership in the official Nature Protection Society reached 320,000, compared with 20,000 in 1971. In April 1986, the Chernobyl nuclear accident—history's worst—seemed to confirm everyone's worst fears as thousands of Baltic youths were conscripted for dangerous cleanup work in Ukraine, while thousands of contaminated Belarusan and Ukrainian villagers were relocated temporarily to the Baltic states. For the regime, environmental issues had seemed a safe way to depoliticize social activism. But now, a groundswell for "republic sovereignty" took aim at Moscow's unilateral plans for a new phosphate plant in Estonia, a river-damming hydroelectric station in Latvia, and a fourth reactor at Lithuania's Chernobyl-style Ignalina power plant. Baltic high school students began to organize protests. As a prominent Latvian activist remarked in October 1988, "everything began with the movement to save nature."[4]

Everything might have stayed there, too, had it not been for the new competitive elections, Gorbachev's gift, which further galvanized the inhabitants of the Soviet republics beginning in spring 1989, before Eastern Europe fell. Then, as the bloc imploded, in November 1989, a member of Gorbachev's staff warned that "the Soviet Union will not allow its Baltic republics to copy the dramatic political reforms in Eastern Europe."[5] Gorbachev then brought hardliners back into the Soviet government. In January 1990, Soviet defense minister Dmitri Yazov executed a demonstrative crackdown on the "popular front" in the Soviet republic of Azerbaijan. But by far the bigger "demonstration" was Eastern Europe's conspicuous escape. What is more, Eastern Europe became a springboard against the USSR. Poland—which Gorbachev had shielded from a repeat of the December 1981 imposition of martial law—began signing state-to-state agreements with its close neighbor Lithuania (which had once been part of a Polish-Lithuanian Commonwealth). Adam Michnik of Solidarity, a newly minted parliamentarian, led a Polish delegation to Kiev in September 1989 for the inaugural congress of the small but resolute Ukrainian Independence movement called Rukh. When Michnik shouted out in Ukrainian, "*Khai zhyve Ukraina!*" (Long live Ukraine!), the 1,200 delegates erupted; some were further emboldened to speak of the Soviet "occupation" of Ukraine. Gorbachev's reward for having allowed the people of Poland to decide their own fate was Poles intervening to help decide the fate of the Baltics and Ukraine.[6]

The Communist establishments in the Baltic states defied Moscow, sided with the demonstrators, and helped lead the drives for self-rule, but crucially it was only after the Polish opposition's breakthrough to government in 1989 that Lithuania became the first Soviet republic to declare not sovereignty but independence. And it would be in Lithuania that Moscow's response to the Baltic challenge would play out most dramatically. In January 1991, forces in the Kremlin set into motion a crackdown in Lithuania's capital of Vilnius (Polish Wilno, Yiddish Vilna), which the Soviets had taken from Poland in World War II and given to Lithuania. The many Soviet troops and tanks permanently stationed in the Lithuanian Soviet Socialist Republic had been augmented, and probes were launched to take over various buildings, as young Lithuanians walked around ready to defend their capital, carrying sticks. Then Soviet riot police (known as OMON) stormed the parliament building and the broadcast tower of Lithuanian television, where they met considerable resistance, resulting in thirteen Lithuanian deaths. "The OMON," wrote two scholars sympathetic to the cause of Baltic independence, "could easily have sniffed out whatever resistance the Balts were able to put up."[7] But the crackdown was botched. Moscow failed to rally the Baltic states' combined 2 million ethnic Russians—the fewest (350,000) were in Lithuania—into pro-Soviet "National Salvation Committees." At the same time, the Baltic "fronts," following the influence that Eastern Europe had exerted on them, "exported their revolutions." That is, they aimed to fortify themselves by aiding potential allies, targeting the Soviet Union's Slavic republics, where they found a small but receptive audience whose impact was vastly magnified by the Soviet Union's national-state internal structure.

This was not a nationalist brush fire. On January 21, 1990, some 250,000 Ukrainians organized their own Baltic-style human chain, from western Ukraine's Lviv to Kiev, and by July 1990, the Ukrainian Supreme Soviet (or Verkhovna Rada) declared "sovereignty." Although significant, the number of participants was drastically smaller on a per capita basis than in the Baltics (one twentieth as opposed to one quarter). Moreover, every Soviet republic declared its "sovereignty," and the term itself was ambiguous: sovereignty originated in Ukraine too with ecology but also involved mass miners' strikes in the Russified eastern Ukraine from 1989.[8] Ukraine had the largest nationalist dissident movement in the USSR, but it had never exceeded around 950 people (out of the republic's 50 million). Ukrainian nationalists had long been in despair, claiming that Ukrainian culture had been destroyed; they themselves were decimated by waves of arrests (1965–66, 1972–73, 1976–80), and forced to serve some of the post–Stalin era's longest sentences—Levko Lukyanenko (1928–) spent twenty-five years in the Gulag for interpreting Lenin as supporting Ukrainian independence.[9] Ukraine had an entire establishment of committed antinationalist Soviet Ukrainian officials, and the republic was still under the grip of the Brezhnev-era Ukrainian party boss late into 1989. That was when Rukh was founded as Ukraine's "Popular Front in Support of Perestroika." Despite Rukh's eventual emulation of the Baltic "fronts" in seeking independence, however, Ukraine's proindependence political elite came from the uncivil society, and it came very late: when central authority disintegrated utterly in Moscow, Ukraine's establishment retrofitted itself as "national Communists" favoring independence.[10]

Still, empires topple not in the periphery but in the center. Ukraine's sovereignty declaration had come the month after the declaration of sovereignty from Moscow by, of all places, Russia. Russia's move is what shattered the Soviet Union. Back in 1983, the American scholar John Dunlop had advised U.S. policy makers to add Russia to the list of "captive nations" within the Soviet Union.[11] The U.S. government failed to take heed, but the Russian Republic's government under Boris Yeltsin would follow exactly that strategy, tapping into the Russian sentiment that they lived worse in their own empire than did the other peoples. Yeltsin condemned the Soviet crackdown in Azerbaijan in January 1990 ("It is a mistake to dispatch troops and suppress ethnic problems by armed force," he said), and in June 1990, as the elected chairman of the Russian Republic's new parliament, Yeltsin led Russia in breaking the Soviet blockade against Lithuania. In early July, he sent state-to-state diplomatic notes to the three Baltic Union republics.[12] In June 1991, running against the "dictatorship of the center," meaning Moscow, Yeltsin was elected to the new post of president of the Russian Republic. In August, Kryuchkov—the Soviet KGB head who had been sent to congratulate Prime Minister Mazowiecki in Poland in 1989—organized a coup. But the KGB-led putsch to save the Soviet state was bungled; the Soviet Union's president (Gorbachev) was arrested but not the republics' presidents (Yeltsin or his Ukraine counterpart). The coup achieved the opposite result of its intention: every Union republic that had yet to declare its independence from the USSR did so, including Russia. Soviet uncivil society in Moscow, too, abandoned the crippled Union for the republic state structures. The bank runs that began in the bloc found their completion in Moscow.

Even under the peculiarities of totalitarian monopoly, unsanctioned mass societal mobilization was not ipso facto state disintegration. The Baltic mobilizations around ecology, and then around the anniversary of the Hitler-Stalin Pact, influenced events in other Soviet republics, but the sine qua non of their impact was the Soviet Union's ethnoterritorial state structure.[13] Mark Beissinger has argued that "nationalism" allowed for very quick mobilizations, without societal organization.[14] But large numbers of ethnic Russians in Latvia, Lithuania, Estonia, and Ukraine went into the streets to support sovereignty and eventually independence for these republics vis-à-vis the Soviet Union, too. In Siberia, miners went on mass strikes in 1989 and called for "sovereignty"—but for Siberia, which lacked an ethnoterritorial structure; the miners' demands soon became absorbed in the calls for the sovereignty of the Russian Republic. In other words, the nationalisms were not always strong (as in Ukraine or Russia), but, decisively, the Soviet state was organized as a group of national states. Even all the "popular fronts for the support of perestroika" were national; there was no "all-Union" popular front.[15] The USSR's "titular-nation" internal structure was so extreme that it often made no allowance for ethnic minorities. Ethnic groups that had their own Union republic—as Russia did—were denied their own "autonomous" enclaves in other Union republics even where they formed sizable minorities. Thus, despite the fact that there were more than 10 million ethnic Russians in Ukraine (20 percent of the population), there was no "Autonomous Republic" for Russians inside Ukraine. Meanwhile, Ukraine, which was far from 100 percent Ukrainian in composition, was 100 percent Ukrainian in terms of its state structure. Nor were there autonomous Russian entities in Lithuania (almost 10 percent Russian), Estonia (33 percent Russian), or Latvia (nearly 40 percent Russian). In sum, with exceptions—the tangled Caucasus and in the Russian Republic itself—the Union republics were structurally single nation-states, whatever their ethnic composition. These nation-state structures became the key fault lines after the eruptions in Eastern Europe. That is how the repudiation of communism also turned into dissolution of the Soviet Union.

THE LIES

Before Gorbachev came to power in 1985, the bloc was not in upheaval—not even in Poland, where in 1980–81 the system had been clinically dead for sixteen months until reanimated by martial law. The new Soviet general secretary caused the destabilization. Underlying it were momentous structural shifts. Germany and Japan's huge shift from Great Depression and goose-stepping militarism to middle-class prosperity and democracy, followed by the reentry of some 400 million Chinese (in southern and coastal China) into the capitalist world economy beginning in 1978, was earth-shattering. Soviet-style socialism—the supposed antidote to capitalism—did not decline; it was crushed in a competition that was its raison d'être. The uncivil societies began to lose the courage of their convictions. True, right into 1989, the leaders of the uncivil societies were not giving up: not Erich Honecker and the East German regime, not Nicolae Ceauşescu and the Romanian regime, and, at least initially, not Wojciech Jaruzelski and the establishment in Poland. Jaruzelski, who had instituted martial law in 1981, found himself eight years later stuck in the same place but, this time, demurred on the use of force. Honecker tried to crack down in 1989 but failed, owing to a lack of grit, some telling procedural snafus, and local resistance as well as foot-dragging. In Romania, bloody repressions in 1989 brought out more demonstrators, and then the defense minister committed suicide, which, on top of the massing crowds, snapped the buckling army brass. In all three cases, the breaking factor was the double whammy of Gorbachev and the altered international context: the transformed capitalist world. Every uncivil society had plenty of police and loyalists, yet none could find—in the face of the postwar capitalist challenge—a stable equilibrium between sclerosis and dissolution. Reform was destabilizing; lack of reform, self-entrapping. Both were predicated on ideological adherence to socialism in the economy, meaning rejection of the market. In the end, the collapse of communism was a collapse of the establishments, and the establishments' collapse was rooted in the world conjuncture—the success of capitalism and the failure of socialism.

Could it have turned out differently? Adam Michnik likes to compare communism to a pair of old underpants: you put them in the washing machine, they come out clean but in pieces. The impulse to reform, however, was far from arbitrary. Rather, reform impulses were constantly generated by the system itself, flowing from the comparisons with the West and the social perfecting inherent in Marxism-Leninism. The conservatives' warnings about reform being autoliquidation were correct, but the conservatives had no answer to the competition with post–World War II capitalism either. They pushed greater discipline and refinement of planning, throwing money at panaceas such as technology, but mostly the conservatives held on, waiting for the West to nose-dive again, as in the 1930s. Trends in the outside world, however, especially in East Asia, moved against the conservatives. The East Asians helped clobber the East bloc manufacturers, undercutting the quixotic borrowing-and-export gamble that Gierek in Poland and Ulbricht in East Germany had launched in the early 1970s, and that others, such as Ceauşescu in Romania, had emulated. The resultant "Polish disease"—massive convertible-currency debt—was compounded by deficits in political legitimacy. At the same time, however, it was East Asia that seemed to have the cure. The persistence of Communist regimes well past 1989 in China and Vietnam (not to mention North Korea) showed how "market Leninism" could save the party. And yet, even had the East bloc uncivil societies realized that police-state market economies might work, they were ideologically opposed. Moreover, such a strategy was utterly out of the question for East Germany, given West Germany's existence (North Korea, facing South Korea, has hesitated to follow the China-Vietnam marketizing course). Keep in mind also that China's market Leninism was predicated on integrating into the capitalist global order, which required acceptance of the dominance of U.S. power. Unlike China, the Soviet Union was an alternative global order, a status it could not simply walk away from. And the USSR's fate was intimately tied to the disposition of its clone-regime satellites formed in the wake of World War II. The bind was nearly total.

The endgame could have been catastrophic. Driven by an idealistic belief in the viability of socialism, notwithstanding everything, Gorbachev sought to democratize the Soviet system, helping take it down peaceably. Of course, Leninist regimes were dictatorships, and the survival of dictatorships depends on the perception that they remain ready and able to "show their teeth." As soon as they waver in using force when challenged, their subject peoples can begin withdrawing their fear, and a political "run" on the system can escalate geometrically. In the Leninist cases the monopoly vanishes, bringing an end to the system seemingly overnight. So it was in Hungary in 1956. So it was in East Germany and Romania in 1989. As for Poland, most observers had long understood that the country was different; it had a peasantry with its own land, churches controlling public spaces, a pious populace for whom authority signified the local priest and the Polish pope, a working class with its own organizational forms, and a varied opposition that became the East bloc's only counterelite. But in Poland in 1989, the exact same cause as elsewhere in the bloc—a debt spiral that was unfixable because of the political bankruptcy—pushed the uncivil society to invite the opposition to a roundtable. Arguably, the resultant elections in Poland constituted something of a bank run, too, with Poland's voting booths substituting for street demonstrations. In the event, Poland's uncivil society passed the burden of governing to the imagined "civil society" in a peaceful bargain that allowed the Communist establishment a kind of immunity. The relatively uncatastrophic dénouement was providential, even if the outcome in Poland, as in Romania, would provoke accusations of a "stolen revolution." The people fumed as they watched Communist regimes fold the same way they had originally unfolded: namely, in a spasm of asset and property redistribution.

Post-1989, there were three basic paths for uncivil society: its members could be largely fired and retired in a bloodless mass purge (East Germany); they could mostly survive in positions of power (Romania); or they could be compelled to compete with an opposition counterelite (Poland). Therefore, East Germany aside, uncivil-society networks and insider knowledge proved of great value in the new circumstances.[16] No surprise there. All revolutions are in some sense revolutions of the deputies, who suddenly seize an opening. In the case of the Communist bloc's opportunists, some analysts have suggested differentiating between the more "modern" technocrats and the political hacks (apparatchiks), arguing that it was the former who flourished after 1989 because of their technical skills (particularly in the Hungarian case).[17] This retrospective view was an echo of 1950s–1960s modernization theory: one such theorist had imagined that "although vital decisions remain the monopoly of party leaders, the growing importance of technical problems in the governing of the state has forced an informal sharing of power with scientists, engineers . . . and other crucial technically skilled personnel" because such were the demands of "complex" modern societies.[18] In the same vein, two Hungarian intellectuals, György Konrád and Iván Szelényi, had argued in *Intellectuals on the Road to Class Power* (1979) that partocrats could share power with a supposedly professional elite—technocratic and humanistic intellectuals—and thereby produce a rational socialism. It was bunk. There was no Communist "technocracy" at the expense of the party's domination. Konrád himself, five years on, bitingly wrote, "Communism has sanctioned a system in which the more stupid lead the more intelligent, because it has made political reliability a more important job requirement than ability."[19] Still, in 1989 there was a structural change—the end of total state ownership and management of the economy. The breakthrough to legal private property benefited large swaths of the uncivil societies, often the worst of the worse, but, like the corresponding breakthrough to open political pluralism, privatization altered the possibilities for the rest of society, too.

Communist systems combined an all-encompassing idea (a new world that transcended capitalism) with a novel organization (monopoly over the economy and public life)—a heady mix that held awesome power but then disintegrated with uncanny velocity. Their most vulnerable aspect was the endemic lying, which magnified the power of Leipzig's Lutheran Church, Timişoara's Reformed (Calvinist) Church, and Poland's Catholic Church. The paragons of uncivil society certainly can be scorned for their prevarications and casuistry, as well as, in many cases, their devotion to the cause even after their own imprisonment for nonexistent crimes (Gomułka, Nagy, Kádár, Husák). Teresa Torańska (1944–), a Polish journalist, used Solidarity's breakthrough in 1980 to interview and disparage five of the highest surviving officials from Stalinist-era Poland (1945–56). Exemplary in her lineup was Jakub Berman, whose Jewish father had died in Treblinka and who became part of Poland's ruling troika with economic boss Hilary Minc and party chief Bolesław Bierut. Berman lorded over Polish culture as Politburo overseer of state security, with an office that had a direct phone line to Stalin. But in 1956, following Bierut's fatal heart attack (some two weeks after Khrushchev's secret speech), Berman was ousted from the leadership and, the next year, from the party for "distortions and errors." He got a lowly publishing-house job, petitioned the party for reinstatement, was twice refused, and gave up petitioning—but evidently not believing. Berman conceded to Torańska that "these things aren't simple," but he insisted that after the Soviets ejected the Germans from Poland "we wanted to get this country moving, to breathe life into it; all our hopes were tied up with the new model of Poland, which was without historical precedent and was the only chance it had throughout its thousand years of history." And, Berman concluded, "we succeeded. In any case, we were bound to succeed, because we were right.... History was on our side."[20] Only it wasn't, and they failed.

NOTES

PREFACE

1. Vladimir Tismăneanu (ed.), *The Revolutions of 1989* (New York: Routledge, 1999).
2. Mark Kramer, "The Collapse of East European Communism and the Repercussions within the Soviet Union," *Journal of Cold War Studies,* 5/4 (2003): 178–256, 6/4 (2004): 3–64, 7/1 (2005): 3–96.
3. Susanne Lohmann, "Dynamics of Informational Cascades: The Monday Demonstrations in Leipzig, East Germany, 1989–91," *World Politics,* 47/1 (1994): 42–101. Generalizing about social movements from the Communist experience can be hazardous because of the nature of the Communist state.
4. The underling, General Vitaly Pavlov, added that "the positions of Andropov Iu. V. in relation to Poland were to a great extent decisive, especially in the crisis years." V. G. Pavlov, *Rukovoditeli Pol'shi glazami razvedchika: krizisnye 1973–1984 gody* (Moscow: Terra, 1998), 330. In the transcript of a Soviet politburo session on December 10, 1981—three days before Poland's General Jaruzelski would introduce martial law—there is a tantalizing moment when Andropov argues against any possible Soviet military intervention in Poland, whatever happens. This position finds an echo in the memoirs of the KGB's chief analyst. Mark Kramer, "Soviet Deliberations during the Polish Crisis, 1980–1981," Cold War International History Project, Special Working Paper No. 1 (Washington, D.C., 1999), 164–5, available at www.wilsoncenter.org/topics/pubs/ACF56F.PDF); Nikolai Leonov, *Likholet'e* (Moscow: Mezhdunarodnye Otnosheniia, 1995), 212.
5. One of the authors of the present volume has written such a book: Stephen Kotkin, *Armageddon Averted: The Soviet Collapse, 1970–2000,* updated edition (New York: Oxford University, 2008).

I. BANK RUN

1. "Curiously enough the moment when people in the West finally thought there was a revolution was when they saw television pictures of Romania: crowds, tanks, shooting, blood in the streets. They said, 'That—we know that is a revolution,' and of course the joke is that it was the only one that wasn't [*sic*]."

Timothy Garton Ash, "Conclusions," in Sorin Antohi and Vladimir Tismăneanu (eds.), *Between Past and Present* (Budapest: Central European University, 2000), 395. On the stolen-revolution thesis, see Tom Gallagher, *Modern Romania: The End of Communism, the Failure of Democratic Reform, and the Theft of a Nation* (New York: New York University, 2005). See also Vladimir Tismăneanu, "The Quasi-Revolution and its Discontents: Emerging Political Pluralism in Post-Ceauşescu Romania," *East European Politics and Societies,* 7/2 (1993): 309–48.

2. Adam Przeworski, "The Man of Iron and Men of Power in Poland," *Political Science* 15 (1982): 18–31. Przeworski criticized—in advance—the myriad scholars who "will write thousands of books and articles correlating background conditions with outcomes in each 'East European' country, but... they will be wasting their time, for the entire event was one single snowball." Adam Przeworski, *Democracy and the Market: Political and Economic Reforms in Eastern Europe and Latin America* (New York: Cambridge University, 1991), 3.

3. "Civil Society" in D. Miller, *The Blackwell Encyclopedia of Political Thought* (Oxford, England: Basil Blackwell, 1987), 77; John Keane (ed.), *Civil Society and the State: New European Perspectives* (London: Verso, 1988); Zbigniew Rau (ed.), *The Reemergence of Civil Society in Eastern Europe and the Soviet Union* (Boulder, Colo.: Westview, 1991); Grzegorz Ekiert and Jan Kubik, *Rebellious Civil Society: Popular Protest and Democratic Consolidation in Poland, 1989–1993* (Ann Arbor: University of Michigan, 1999); Detlef Pollack and Jan Wielgohs (eds.), *Dissent and Opposition in Communist Eastern Europe: Origins of Civil Society and Democratic Transition* (Burlington, Vt.: Ashgate, 2004). The civil-society paradigm remains enormously influential, but some analysts have questioned "the common generalisation that an active civil society is necessarily good for democracy," noting the conspicuous exclusion of antiliberal and antidemocratic examples from the studies of social organizations. See Petr Kopecký and Cas Mudde (eds.), *Uncivil Society? Contentious Politics in Post-Communist Europe* (New York: Routledge, 2003), xvi.

4. Thomas Carothers, "Think Again: Civil Society," *Foreign Policy,* 1999–2000: 18–29, and "The End of the Transition Paradigm," *Journal of Democracy,* 13/1 (2002): 5–21. In the international aid community, the notion of "civil society" has been extraordinarily pervasive, but it has usually been reduced to a synonym for nongovernmental organizations (NGOs).

5. The priceless "bank run" metaphor was elaborated for the Soviet case by Steven L. Solnick, *Stealing the State: Control and Collapse in Communist Institutions* (Cambridge, Mass.: Harvard University, 1999).

6. Jacques Rupnik picked up on the Polish break with the strategy of reforming communism, but the key disseminator of the concept of civil society for Eastern Europe was Andrew Arato. For Arato and others on the left, "civil society" supposedly offered a mode of sociopolitical organization that would counteract what they saw as the bureaucratic dominance and consumerism of market

societies. Rupnik, "Dissent in Poland, 1968–1978: The End of Revisionism and the Rebirth of Civil Society," in Rudolf Tőkés (ed.), *Opposition in Eastern Europe* (Baltimore: Johns Hopkins University, 1979), 60–112; Arato, "Civil Society against the State: Poland, 1980–81," *Telos* 47 (1981): 23–47; and Jean L. Cohen and Andrew Arato, *Civil Society and Political Theory* (Cambridge, Mass.: MIT, 1992).

7. One example: Michael D. Kennedy, "The Intelligentsia in the Constitution of Civil Societies and Post-Communist Regimes in Hungary and Poland," *Theory and Society,* 21/1 (1992): 29–76.

8. Krishan Kumar, "Civil Society: An Inquiry into the Usefulness of an Historical Term," *British Journal of Sociology,* 44/3 (1993): 375–95. See also Petr Kopecký and E. Barnfield, "Charting the Decline of Civil Society: Explaining the Changing Roles and Conceptions of Civil Society in East Central Europe," in Jean Grugel (ed.), *Democracy without Borders: State and Non-state Actors in Eastern Europe, Africa and Latin America* (London: Routledge, 1999), 76–91.

9. Geremek, interviewed by Piotr Kosicki, July 2, 2007. After 1989, Geremek wrote, "We must ask whether the idea of a civil society—however effective it was in helping to bring down communism—will turn out to be useless in the building of a democracy." Geremek, "Civil Society in Historical Context," in Geremek et al., *The Idea of a Civil Society* (Research Triangle Park, N.C.: National Humanities Center, 1992), 11–18 (at 18).

10. Konrád, *Antipolitics: An Essay* (San Diego: Harcourt Brace Jovanovich, 1984), 82.

11. "New Forum did not want to be a party," Charles Maier has written. "In this goal it succeeded." Charles S. Maier, *Dissolution: The Crisis of Communism and the End of East Germany* (Princeton, N.J.: Princeton University, 1997), 169.

12. Mark R. Thompson, "Why and How East Germans Rebelled," *Theory and Society,* 25/2 (1996): 263–99 (at 276), citing Jan Urban, "The Powerlessness of the Powerful," unpublished manuscript (Prague, November 1992). The estimated size of the organized opposition in Czechoslovakia would be higher if one included all 1,883 signatories of the Charter 77 human rights appeal some twelve years before. John F. N. Bradley, *Czechoslovakia's Velvet Revolution: A Political Analysis* (Boulder, Colo.: East European Monographs, 1992), 21.

13. Communist China in 1989 offers another graphic example that exposes the limitations of the civil-society paradigm. See, e.g., the phantasmagorical essays by David Strand, "Protest in Beijing: Civil Society and the Public Sphere in China," *Problems of Communism* 39 (1990): 1–19; and Larry Sullivan, "The Emergence of Civil Society in China, Spring 1989," in Tony Saich (ed.), *The Chinese People's Movement: Perspectives on Spring 1989* (Armonk, N.Y.: M. E. Sharpe, 1990): 126–44.

14. What seems decisive was that, as Sájo added, by 1988 "Hungary's economic difficulties had increased to the extent that even the Communists had to acknowledge them." András Sájo, "The Roundtable Talks in Hungary," in Jon Elster (ed.), *The Roundtable Talks and the Breakdown of Communism* (Chicago:

University of Chicago, 1996), 69–98 (at 69–70). See also Rudolf L. Tőkés, *Hungary's Negotiated Revolution: Economic Reform, Social Change, and Political Succession, 1957–1990* (New York: Cambridge University, 1996); and András Bozóki (ed.), *The Roundtable Talks of 1989: The Genesis of Hungarian Democracy* (Budapest: Central European University, 2002). For analogies between Poland and Hungary, see Janina Frentzel-Zagorska, "Civil Society in Poland and Hungary," *Soviet Studies,* 42/4 (1990): 759–77.

15. Iván Szelényi, *Socialist Entrepreneurs* (New York: Cambridge University, 1988); Elemér Hankiss, "What the Hungarians Saw First," in Gwyn Prins (ed.), *Spring in Winter: The 1989 Revolutions* (Manchester: Manchester University, 1990), 13–36 (at 31); David Stark, "Privatization in Hungary: From Plan to Market or from Plan to Clan?," *East European Politics and Societies,* 4/3 (1990): 351–92. But cf. C. M. Hann, "Second Economy and Civil Society," *Journal of Communist Studies,* 6/2 (1990): 21–44; and Hann (ed.), *Market Economy and Civil Society in Hungary* (London: Frank Cass, 1990).

16. Zbigniew Brzezinski, *The Grand Failure: The Birth and Death of Communism in the Twentieth Century* (New York: Scribner, 1989), 2–3.

17. Helga A. Welsh, "The Elite Conundrum in the GDR: Lessons from the District Level," *German Studies Review,* 24/1 (2001): 19–33; John Connelly, "Internal Bolshevisation? Elite Social Science Training in Stalinist Poland," *Minerva,* 34/4 (1996): 323–46 (esp. 344); Ioana Angelescu, "A Few Features of the Nomenklatura in Romania," Radio Free Europe/Radio Liberty, Background Report (1983), available at http://files.osa.ceu.hu/holdings/300/8/3/text/53-5-26.shtml; Gheorghe Boldur-Lățescu, *The Communist Genocide in Romania* (New York: Nova, 2005), 55–60.

18. Katherine Anne Lebow, "Nowa Huta, 1949–1957: Stalinism and the Transformation of Everyday Life in Poland's 'First Socialist City,' " Ph.D. dissertation, Columbia University, New York (2002); Timothy Dowling, "Stalinstadt/Eisenhüttenstadt: A Model for (Socialist) Life in the German Democratic Republic, 1950–1968," Ph.D. dissertation, Tulane University, New Orleans (1999). In Eisenhüttenstadt, more than 50,000 artifacts of the GDR's material culture have been preserved at a Center for the Documentation of East German Daily Life.

19. Elemér Hankiss, who originated the idea, ended up concluding that by and large there was no coherent "second society," just a "no-man's-land" rather than a full alternative to the official or "first society." Hankiss, "The 'Second Society': Is There an Alternative Social Model Emerging in Hungary?," *Social Research,* 55/1–2 (1988): 13–42, reprinted in Ference Fehér and Andrew Arato (eds.), *Crisis and Reform in Eastern Europe* (New Brunswick, N.J.: Transaction, 1991), 303–34; and Hankiss, *East European Alternatives* (Oxford, England: Clarendon, 1990).

20. In a nod to Rudolf Bahro, *The Alternative in Eastern Europe: An Analysis of Actually-Existing Socialism* (London: Verso, 1978; German original, 1977).

21. See also Iván Szelényi, "The Position of the Intelligentsia in the Class Structure of State Socialist Societies," *Critique,* 10–11 (1978): 51–76; and György Konrád and Iván Szelényi, *The Intellectuals on the Road to Class Power* (Brighton, Sussex: Harvester, 1979).

22. Sam Dolgoff (ed.), *Bakunin Anarchy* (New York: Knopf, 1973), 319; Leon Trotsky, *The Revolution Betrayed: What Is the Soviet Union and Where Is It Going?* (New York: Pioneer, 1945), 289.

23. Jacek Kuroń and Karol Modzelewski, *List otwarty do partii* (Paris: Instytut Literacki, 1966), 76–89. Other analysts would note that the new class—sometimes called the *nomenklatura* (i.e., the regime "lists" of key personnel)—carefully looked after their children, closing access to the better educational institutions to others and thereby forming a caste. See Michael Voslensky, *Nomenklatura: The Soviet Ruling Class, an Insider's Report* (New York: Doubleday, 1984). The "new class" idea made a leap to America and then to the entire world. See David Bazelon, *Power in America: The Politics of the New Class* (New York: New American Library, 1967); and Alvin Gouldner, *The Future of Intellectuals and the Rise of the New Class* (New York: Seabury, 1979). But cf. B. Bruce-Briggs (ed.), *The New Class?* (New York: McGraw-Hill, 1981).

24. Milovan Djilas, *The Unperfect Society: Beyond the New Class* (New York: Harcourt, Brace & World, 1969).

25. Jan T. Gross, "Thirty Years of Crisis Management in Poland," in Teresa Rakowska-Harmstone (ed.), *Perspectives for Change in Communist Societies* (Boulder, Colo.: Westview, 1979), 145–67.

26. "Up to the actual outbreak of the revolution," one scholar wrote of Hungary in 1956, "the stirring of the opposition and agitation for reform had very much the character of an internal family affair within the party itself." Paul Kecskeméti, *Unexpected Revolution: Social Forces in the Hungarian Uprising* (Stanford, Calif.: Stanford University, 1961), 1–2. Even the famed Petőfi Circle of intellectuals was set up (in March 1956) by the regime as a hoped-for safety valve for grievances.

27. Peter Kenez, *Hungary from the Nazis to the Soviets: The Establishment of the Communist Regime in Hungary, 1944–1948* (New York: Cambridge University, 2006), 157.

28. Roi Medvedev, *Neizvestnyi Andropov: politicheskaia biografiia Iuria Andropova* (Moscow: Prava Cheloveka, 1999), 33.

29. Paul E. Zinner, *National Communism and Popular Revolt in Eastern Europe* (New York: Columbia University, 1956), 429, 454; Csaba Békés et al. (eds.), *The 1956 Hungarian Revolution: A History in Documents* (Budapest: Central European University, 2002), 290–1.

30. Medvedev, *Neizvestnyi Andropov,* 46–7.

31. Djilas, "Hungary and Yugoslavia," in Béla Király et al. (eds.), *The First War between Socialist States: The Hungarian Revolution of 1956 and Its Impact* (New York: Brooklyn College, 1984), 92–3. Many socialists managed to swallow the crack-

down in Hungary at the time because of the uprising's nationalist rhetoric and the fact that Hungary had been allied with Nazi Germany only twelve years before. Such leftist excuse making would not be evident during the suppression of the Prague Spring. Mikhail Gorbachev and Zdeněk Mlynář, *Conversations with Gorbachev: On Perestroika, the Prague Spring, and the Crossroads of Socialism* (New York: Columbia University, 2002).

32. Katalin Sinko, "Political Rituals: The Raising and Demolition of Monuments," in Peter Gyorgy and Hedvig Tura (eds.), *Art and Society in the Age of Stalin* (Budapest: Corvina, 1992), 81. See also Gregorz Ekiert, *The State against Society: Political Crises and Their Aftermath in East Central Europe* (Princeton, N.J.: Princeton University, 1996), esp. 95–8.

33. One scholar who grasped both the centrality of ideology and its crucial link to geopolitics was Zbigniew Brzezinski, *The Soviet Bloc: Unity and Conflict* (Cambridge, Mass.: Harvard University, 1960, 1967).

34. Mark Kramer, "The Soviet Union and the 1956 Crises in Hungary and Poland: A Reassessment and New Findings," *Journal of Contemporary History*, 33/2 (1998): 163–214 (quotes at 173, 191). See also Amir Weiner, "The Empires Pay a Visit: Gulag Returnees, East European Rebellions, and Soviet Frontier Politics," *Journal of Modern History*, 78/2 (2006): 333–76.

35. Charles Gati, *Failed Illusions: Moscow, Washington, Budapest, and the 1956 Hungarian Revolution* (Stanford, Calif.: Stanford University, 2006), 12; Békés, *The 1956 Hungarian Revolution*, 375. Gati notes that contrary to myth, not every Hungarian supported the uprising in 1956; many were disturbed by it.

36. Paul Lendvai, *Hungary: The Art of Survival* (London: I. B. Tauris, 1988), 127–55 ("The Many Faces of Károly Grósz").

37. Václav Havel, "The Power of the Powerless" (1978), in Gale Stokes (ed.), *From Stalinism to Pluralism* (New York: Oxford University, 1996), 168–74. Many dissidents were not just pessimistic but despairing—for example, the Hungarian Miklós Haraszti (1945–), who had to admit that freedom was not an essential condition of cultural production and that even the advent of some pluralism seemed to strengthen the state's grip. Miklós Haraszti, *The Velvet Prison: Artists under State Socialism* (New York: Basic, 1987). The text was originally self-published in the Hungarian underground in 1986.

38. Adam Michnik, "A New Evolutionism" (1976), in *Letters from Prison and Other Essays* (Berkeley: University of California, 1985), 135–148.

39. Sidney Tarrow, " 'Aiming at a Moving Target': Social Science and the Recent Rebellions in Eastern Europe," *PS: Political Science and Politics* 24 (1991): 12. In Czechoslovakia, as late as mid-November 1989, during enormous street protests, Jan Urban, a high-profile activist, suggested that Civic Forum seek to contest elections—for June 1991. Even this humble suggestion was dismissed by some of Urban's colleagues as unrealistic. Timur Kuran, " 'Now Out of Nowhere': The Element of Surprise in the East European Revolutions in 1989," *World Politics*, 44/1 (1991): 7–48 (at 13).

40. Timothy Garton Ash, *The Magic Lantern: The Revolution of '89 Witnessed in Warsaw, Budapest, Berlin, and Prague* (New York: Random House, 1990), 25.

41. Bilak, *Paměti Vasila Bilak* (Prague: Agentura Cesty, 1991). Originally serialized in the Slovak Communist-party newspaper, Bilak's memoirs were discontinued as too revealing after a pair of installments. He was preoccupied with his role in 1968 ("1968 etched such a strong scar in my thought, heart, and memory that I must continuously turn to it" [I: 5]).

42. Zdeněk Mlynář, *Nightfrost in Prague: The End of Humane Socialism* (New York: Karz, 1980), 1–2.

43. Igor Lukes argues that in 1948, Czechoslovakia's betrayal by the Western European powers at Munich in 1938 was still seared into people's minds. There was also the illusion that the Soviets would allow the Czechoslovaks to develop their own version of socialism. Igor Lukes, "The Czech Road to Communism," in Norman Naimark and Leonid Gibianskii (eds.), *The Establishment of Communist Regimes in Eastern Europe, 1944–1949* (Boulder, Colo.: Westview, 1997), 243–65; Robert Bruce Lockhart, *My Europe* (London: Putnam, 1952), 125.

44. Kieran Williams, *The Prague Spring and Its Aftermath* (Cambridge, England: Cambridge University, 1997), 5.

45. Heda Margolius Kovály, *Under a Cruel Star: A Life in Prague, 1941–1968* (Cambridge, Mass.: Plunkett Lake, 1986), 62, 25. Czechoslovakia's Stalinist-era political trials resulted in more deaths than in the rest of the bloc *combined*. Several hundred people were executed between 1948 and 1955 (a few hundred more were shot while trying to cross the border); another 3,000 died in camps and prisons. Czechoslovak political prisoners peaked in 1953 at nearly 16,000. By comparison, in the five years after 1968, 1,142 people were imprisoned. Kieran Williams and Dennis Deletant, *Security Intelligence Services in New Democracies: The Czech Republic, Slovakia and Romania* (Houndmills, England: Palgrave, 2001), 25–6.

46. Quoted in William Shawcross, *Dubcek* (London: Weidenfeld and Nicholson, 1973), 63. Dubček's father, a worker, had joined the Communist party and in the 1920s immigrated to the Soviet Union. As a result, the young Dubček spent the years aged four to seventeen in Soviet schools, returning to Slovakia in 1938 and becoming a factory worker and a Communist himself. He was twice wounded in the 1944 Slovak uprising (his brother was killed). In 1955–58, i.e., the years of the secret speech and thaw, Dubček was sent for training at the Moscow Higher Party School. Therefore, as of 1968, he had spent sixteen of his forty-seven years in the Soviet Union. Still, Gordon Skilling concluded that "There was nothing in Dubček's background that distinguished him as a person of unusual standpoint, even on the Slovak question." H. Gordon Skilling, *Czechoslovakia's Interrupted Revolution* (Princeton, N.J.: Princeton University, 1976), 185.

47. Half a million Czechoslovak Communists were expelled from the party in the years 1945–50. After the Prague Spring, in the early 1970s, another 327,000 Communists were expelled from the party, while 150,000 resigned voluntar-

ily, cutting party membership by one third. Such a shrinkage was unprecedented in the Communist world in the post–World War II period, outside Mao's catastrophic Cultural Revolution. Counting all expellees, a quarter of the Czechoslovak adult population was in the Communist ranks at one time or another. Jacques Rupnik, "The Roots of Czech Stalinism," in Raphael Samuel and Gareth Stedman-Jones (eds.), *Culture, Ideology, and Politics: Essays for Eric Hobsbawm* (London: Routledge & Kegan Paul, 1982), 302–20 (at 320).

48. Rupnik, "The Roots of Czech Stalinism," 312; Williams, *The Prague Spring*, 5–6.

49. Williams and Deletant, *Security Intelligence Services*, 32. By then, Czechoslovakia's Státní Bezpečnost ("State Security"; StB) employed around 9,000 people for a population of around 15 million, meaning the political police were staffed at a norm of one officer per 1,200 to 1,700 inhabitants (rising in later years to one for every 867). Two thirds had entered the security ranks before 1956, that is, before Khrushchev's denunciation of Stalin. Note that some 30 million pieces of mail crossed the border daily, and the StB could not cope with its assigned task of perlustration. Half the listening devices they planted in foreign embassies did not even function (and not all embassies were penetrated to begin with). The largest group of people under investigation for antistate crimes were grumbling manual workers. Williams, *The Prague Spring*, 214–5. The StB had a dozen or so Soviet KGB liaisons, who were privy to all internal information and analyses.

50. Alexander Dubček, *Hope Dies Last: The Autobiography of Alexander Dubček* (New York: Kodansha, 1993), 112.

51. Jaromír Navratíl et al. (eds.), *The Prague Spring 1968* (Budapest: Central European University, 1998), 92–5.

52. Robin Alison Remington (ed.), *Winter in Prague: Documents on Czechoslovak Communism in Crisis* (Cambridge, Mass.: MIT, 1969), 252–3.

53. Z. A. B. Zeman, *Prague Spring: A Report on Czechoslovakia 1968* (London: Penguin, 1969), 112–3.

54. Mlynář, *Nightfrost in Prague*, 199.

55. "Vasil Bilak, the Grey Eminence" and "Pytor Shelest, Diary and Interview," in Miklós Kun, *Prague Spring—Prague Fall: Blank Spots of 1968* (Budapest: Akademiai Kiado, 1999), 69–98, 99–133 (esp. 89, 127). See also Mark Kramer (ed.), "Ukraine and the Soviet-Czechoslovak Crisis of 1968, Part 1: New Evidence from the Diary of Petro Shelest," *Cold War International History Project Bulletin* 10 (1998) 234–247; and P. Iu. Shelest, *Da ne sudimy budete: dnevnikovye zapisi, vospominaiia chlena Politbiuro TsK KPSS* (Moscow: Edition q., 1995).

56. Mlynář claims he warned the Soviet leadership that unless the kidnapped Czechoslovak group was allowed to return to power, "Czechoslovakia will quickly become bourgeois." As cited in Williams, *The Prague Spring*, 134. See also Navratíl, *The Prague Spring 1968*, 465–86. After August 1968, the borders were kept open for some thirteen months, and tens of thousands of Czechoslovaks emigrated, especially young people and professionals.

57. S. Kovalev, "Suverenitet i internatsional'nye obiazannosti sotsialisticheskikh stran," *Pravda,* September 26, 1968. In November 1968, Brezhnev told the Fifth Congress of the Polish United Workers' Party (i.e., the Communists), that "when internal and external forces hostile to socialism are threatening to turn a socialist country back to capitalism, this becomes the common problem and concern of all socialist countries." See www.cnn.com/SPECIALS/cold.war/ episodes/14/documents/doctrine. See also Navratíl, *The Prague Spring 1968,* 547–54; Skilling, *Czechoslovakia's Interrupted Revolution,* 663–4 (citing Bilak); Mlynář, *Nightfrost in Prague,* 238–40; Matthew J. Ouimet, *The Rise and Fall of the Brezhnev Doctrine in Soviet Foreign Policy* (Chapel Hill and London: University of North Carolina, 2003); and "My spasli sotsializm v etoi strane: iz zapisi peregovorov delegatsii TsK KPSS s delegatsici ital'ianskoi kompartii," *Istochnik,* 1994, no. 5: 77–86.

58. Kun, *Prague Spring,* 28–31, 74–5. As of 1986, twelve of the Czechoslovak Communist Presidium's fourteen members had been in power since 1971, as had nine of the eleven members of the Slovak Presidium. The next year, when the aging and infirm Husák was shunted aside as general secretary (but not head of state), Bilak became the party's number two. He remained a Central Committee secretary and member of the Czechoslovak Presidium until December 1988 and a member of the National Assembly into 1989. In December 1989, Bilak was suspended from the party pending an investigation into his role in the events of 1968.

59. http://files.osa.ceu.hu/holdings/300/8/3/text/117-2-145.shtml. By "foreign interference" Bilak understood not the Soviet Union, of course, but "the imperialist forces."

60. Quoted in Mlynář, *Nightfrost in Prague,* 143.

61. Much of the scholarly literature blames the Eastern European relative backwardness on Soviet backwardness. By contrast, Iván Berend has argued that in the twentieth century Eastern Europe mounted two revolts against the West out of humiliation: an antiliberal right-wing rebellion in the interwar years and an antiliberal left-wing rebellion in the postwar years, both motivated by "economic backwardness and the increasing gap which separated them from the advanced Western core." Iván T. Berend, *Central and Eastern Europe, 1944–1993: Detour from the Periphery to the Periphery* (New York: Cambridge University, 1996), x.

62. Charles Gati, *The Bloc That Failed: Soviet-East European Relations in Transition* (Bloomington: Indiana University, 1990), 119; Paul Marer, "Has Eastern Europe Become a Liability to the Soviet Union? III. The Economic Aspect," in Charles Gati (ed.), *The International Politics of Eastern Europe* (New York: Praeger, 1976): 59–81 (at 70). Romania imported oil from the USSR but not at subsidized prices.

63. Hajna Istvanffy Lorinc, "Foreign Debt, Debt Management Policy, and Implications for Hungary's Development," *Soviet Studies,* 44/6 (1992): 997–1013;

J. Vanous, "East European Economic Slowdown," *Problems of Communism*, 31/4 (1982): 1–19; Gati, *The Bloc That Failed*, 108–9; Katherine Verdery, "What Was Socialism, and Why Did It Fail?," in Tismăneanu, *The Revolutions of 1989*, 63–85 (at 81).

64. Derek H. Aldcroft and Steven Morewood, *Economic Change in Eastern Europe since 1918* (Aldershot, England: Edward Elgar, 1995), 170; Valerie Bunce, "The Empire Strikes Back: The Evolution of the Eastern Bloc from a Soviet Asset to a Soviet Liability," *International Organization*, 39/1 (1985): 1–46 (at 39).

65. Aldcroft and Morewood, *Economic Change in Eastern Europe*, 137. For a high-end estimate ($87 billion) of Soviet trade subsidies to Eastern Europe between 1960 and 1980, see Michael Marrese and J. Vanous, *Soviet Subsidization of Trade with Eastern Europe* (Berkeley: University of California, 1983).

66. Valerie Bunce suggested that the choice had narrowed to two unpalatable options: liberalize and thereby destroy the system, or put off reforms and purchase short-term stability but long-term doom. Jeffrey Kopstein wrote that "leaders throughout the bloc faced two alternatives, either retreat to a conservative immobilism or proceed down the road of gradual capitalist restoration." Bunce, *Subversive Institutions: The Design and Destruction of Socialism and the State* (New York: Cambridge University, 1999), 37; Jeffrey Kopstein, *The Politics of Economic Decline in East Germany, 1945–1989* (Chapel Hill: University of North Carolina, 1997), 46.

67. In 1966, a pro-Chinese "Polish Communist Party" in exile was announced in Albania, advocating for a return to orthodoxy (Stalinism) at home and a more revolutionary policy abroad, against Gomułka's "revisionism" and alleged "renunciation of socialist conquests." See http://files.osa.ceu.hu/holdings/300/8/3/text/44-5-8.shtml.

68. Bruce J. Dickson, *Democratization in China and Taiwan: The Adaptability of Leninist Parties* (Oxford, England: Clarendon, 1998).

69. http://files.osa.ceu.hu/holdings/300/8/3/text/120-4-215.shtml.

70. Jason McDonald, "Transition to Utopia: A Reinterpretation of Economics, Ideas, and Politics in Hungary, 1984 to 1990," *East European Politics and Societies*, 7/2 (1993): 203–39 (Kádár quote at 214).

71. Hankiss, *East European Alternatives*, 203; McDonald, "Transition to Utopia," 217–28; Tőkés, *Hungary's Negotiated Revolution*, 297–8.

72. Mark Kramer, "The Collapse of East European Communism," 192–200.

73. Konrád, *Antipolitics*, 84–5.

II. No Exit

1. *1980 World Bank Atlas: Population, Per Capita Product, and Growth Rates* (Washington, D.C.: World Bank, 1980), 16.

2. Jeffrey Kopstein, *The Politics of Economic Decline in East Germany, 1945–1989* (Chapel Hill and London: University of North Carolina, 1997).

3. Even before its formation as a state, the territory of the future GDR was wired

to be able to receive Western programming. East Germany never switched to the North Korean approach of prohibiting the manufacture of radios and TVs that were capable of receiving Western signals. East Germans could also talk with millions of visitors from the West, part of East–West détente. One scholar has argued that the GDR's "dearth of independent publishing reflected the availability to the GDR's dissidents of the ersatz public sphere of the Federal Republic." John Torpey, *Intellectuals, Socialism and Dissent: The East German Opposition and Its Legacy* (Minneapolis: University of Minnesota, 1995), 97. On East German television, see Anna Funder, *Stasiland: Stories from behind the Berlin Wall* (London: Granta, 2003), 121–38.

4. Christian Joppke, *East German Dissidents and the Revolution of 1989* (New York: New York University, 1995), esp. chap. 6 ("Why Was There No 'Dissidence' in East Germany?").

5. Jens Reich, "Reflections on Becoming an East German Dissident, on Losing the Wall and a Country," in Gwyn Prins (ed.), *Spring in Winter: The 1989 Revolutions* (Manchester and New York: Manchester University, 1990): 65–98 (at 68).

6. Michael Bric, as cited in Steven Pfaff, *Exit-Voice Dynamics and the Collapse of East Germany: The Crisis of Leninism and the Revolution of 1989* (Durham, N.C.: Duke University, 2006), 235.

7. By contrast, Poland's Adam Michnik wrote, "In my opinion, an unceasing struggle for... an expansion of civil liberties and human rights is the only course East European dissidents can take." *Letters from Prison and Other Essays* (Berkeley: University of California, 1985), 142.

8. "One month before the opening of the Berlin wall, most East Germans were busy getting on with their lives," Kopstein has suggested. "In the industrial provinces, what little protest did occur was largely nonpolitical, directed against the inconveniences of purchasing the staples of everyday life under socialism"—for example, on October 6, 1989, workers in Altenburg demanded fruit, jam, and bread. Kopstein, *Politics of Economic Decline*, 1.

9. Whereas Albert Hirschmann had argued that the exit option (emigration) had diminished voice (protest), Pfaff argues that the former enhanced the latter: in the summer and fall of 1989, emigration (exit) helped protest (voice), but this also undermined reformed socialism as a possibility. Pfaff, *Exit-Voice Dynamics*, 32, 252; Hirschmann, "Exit, Voice and the Fate of the German Democratic Republic," *World Politics*, 45/2 (1993): 173–202 (at 176). Cf. Gareth Dale, *Popular Protest in East Germany, 1945–1989* (London and New York: Routledge, 2005), 156–61, 180. Charles Maier also suggested that exit promoted voice: "The growing flight compelled those unprepared"—or unwilling—"to uproot themselves to demand reforms that might justify their remaining." Charles S. Maier, *Dissolution: The Crisis of Communism and the End of East Germany* (Princeton, N. J.: Princeton University, 1997), 131, 136.

10. Charles Maier, for all his book's homage to "agency" and his desire to credit the populace in some way, nonetheless argues that the system cratered be-

cause socialism's "guardians discarded it." He asks the key question "How does the determination to rule falter among the ruling elite of an imperial system?" Maier, *Dissolution*, 58, 34, 38.

11. Kopstein, *Politics of Economic Decline*, 13. Mary Fulbrook, while straining to assert the existence of "an emerging, if very limited, 'civil society,' " nonetheless makes the important point that "the East German regime was perhaps sustained to a greater degree by widespread participation in its structures and functioning." This circumstance helps account for both the GDR's relative stability and its precipitous collapse. Fulbrook, *Anatomy of a Dictatorship: Inside the GDR, 1949–1989* (New York: Oxford University, 1995), 202, 276.

12. According to Günter Schabowski, as quoted in Dale, *Popular Protest in East Germany*, 121.

13. Norman Naimark, *The Russians in Germany: A History of the Soviet Occupation Zone, 1945–1949* (Cambridge, Mass.: Harvard University, 1995), 181.

14. John L. Chase, "The Development of the Morgenthau Plan through the Quebec Conference," *Journal of Politics*, 16/2 (1954): 324–59.

15. Melvin Leffler rightly argues that the United States moved first on formally dividing Germany, but he does not recognize that this move entailed proper recognition of political realities. As Mark Kramer has noted, "clandestine progress toward the formation of an East German army was under way long before the GDR was formally created." Leffler, "The Struggle for Germany and the Origins of the Cold War," German Historical Institute, Washington, D.C., Occasional Paper No. 16 (1996); Kramer, "The Soviet Union and the Founding of the German Democratic Republic: Fifty Years Later—A Review Article," *Europe-Asia Studies*, 51/6 (1999): 1092–1106 (at 1102).

16. Naimark, *Russians in Germany*, 467.

17. Gareth Pritchard, *The Making of the GDR, 1945–53: From Antifascism to Stalinism* (Manchester: Manchester University, 2000), 129.

18. Arthur Koestler, *The Invisible Writing: An Autobiography* (Boston: Beacon, 1954), 154–5.

19. Eric Weitz, *Creating German Communism, 1890–1990: From Popular Protest to Socialist State* (Princeton, N.J.: Princeton University, 1996).

20. Christian F. Ostermann, ed., *Uprising in East Germany, 1953: The Cold War, the German Question, and the First Major Upheaval behind the Iron Curtain* (Budapest: Central European University, 2003); Gary Bruce, *Resistance with the People: Repression and Resistance in Eastern Germany, 1945–1955* (Lanham, Md.: Rowman & Littlefield, 2003). Kramer shows that the charge that Lavrenty Beria had wanted to abandon East Germany was an invention of the Kremlin power struggle. Mark Kramer, "The Early Post-Stalin Succession Struggle and Upheavals in East-Central Europe: Internal-External Linkages in Soviet Policy Making," *Journal of Cold War Studies*, 1/1 (1999): 3–55, 1/2 (1999): 3–38, 1/3 (1999): 3–66; comments on Kramer by James Richter and Gerhard Wettig (www.fas.harvard.edu/~hpcws/comment11.htm, www.fas.harvard.edu/~hpcws/comment10.htm).

21. Alan L. Nothnagle, *Building the East German Myth: Historical Mythology and Youth Propaganda in the German Democratic Republic, 1945–1989* (Ann Arbor: University of Michigan, 1999); John Rodden, *Repainting the Little Red Schoolhouse: A History of Eastern German Education, 1945–1995* (New York: Oxford University, 2002); Silke Satjukow and Rainer Gries (eds.), *Sozialistische Helden: eine Kulturgeschichte von Propagandafiguren in Osteuropa und der DDR* (Berlin: Links, 2002). East German Communists—no less than the country's Soviet military administration (or Communists elsewhere)—took an inordinate interest in cultural affairs. See David Pike, *The Politics of Culture in Soviet-Occupied Germany, 1945–1949* (Stanford, Calif.: Stanford University, 1992).

22. *What Is Life Like in the GDR? The Way of Life and Standard of Living under Socialism* (East Berlin: Panorama DDR, 1977), 17.

23. On the supposedly normal life in the GDR, see Mark Allinson, *Politics and Popular Opinion in East Germany, 1945–68* (Manchester: Manchester University, 2000), and Mary Fulbrook, *The People's State: East German Society from Hitler to Honecker* (New Haven, Conn.: Yale University, 2005). But cf. Konrad H. Jarausch (ed.), *Dictatorship as Experience: Towards a Socio-Cultural History of the GDR* (New York: Berghan, 1999); and A. James McAdams, *East Germany and Détente: Building Authority after the Wall* (New York: Cambridge University, 1985).

24. Katherine Pence and Paul Betts (eds.), *Socialist Modern: East German Everyday Culture and Politics* (Ann Arbor: University of Michigan, 2008), and Jonathan Grix and Paul Cooke (eds.), *East German Distinctiveness in a Unified Germany* (Birmingham, England: University of Birmingham, 2002).

25. Even cybernetics, the science of complex systems, was deemed threatening, because it left insufficient room for a political avant-garde. Peter C. Caldwell, *Dictatorship, State Planning, and Social Theory in the German Democratic Republic* (New York: Cambridge University, 2003).

26. Kopstein, *Politics of Economic Decline*, 64, 66. Ackermann, whose political highwater mark was well behind him, may have written the letter as a craven effort to return himself to Ulbricht's good graces and to a position of authority. Eric Weitz, personal communication, September 2008.

27. As cited in Kopstein, *Politics of Economic Decline*, 43–4. Between 1949 and 1990, approximately 2.7 million people permanently crossed from East Germany to West Germany, almost all of them before 1961; about 200,000 people crossed in the other direction.

28. Hope M. Harrison, *Driving the Soviets up the Wall: Soviet–East German Relations, 1953–1961* (Princeton, N.J.: Princeton University, 2003). In 1963, on a visit to Moscow, Ulbricht remarked that "even after the closing of the state borders, the high living standard [in West Germany] strongly affects the population of the GDR and its political attitudes." Kopstein, *Politics of Economic Decline*, 48.

29. Kopstein, *Politics of Economic Decline*, 68–9.

30. André Steiner, *Von Plan zu Plan: eine Wirtschaftsgeschichte der DDR* (Munich: Deutsche Verlags-Anstalt, 2004), 190.

31. Kopstein argues that the regime *was* responsive to society: it sought labor peace, and bought off the working class, paying a price. But he overplays the causality of the regime's fear of a reprise of the June 1953 uprising in condemning the GDR to low productivity. Soviet-style regimes *everywhere* were stuck with low labor productivity. Kopstein, *Politics of Economic Decline*, 37. See also H. Klodt, "Industrial Policy and the East German Productivity Puzzle," *German Economic Review*, 1/3 (2000): 315–33.

32. Kopstein, *Politics of Economic Decline*, 93–4.

33. Schürer blamed the Eighth Party Congress of 1971, when Honecker had taken over, for deciding that the GDR must underwrite a consumer society and welfare state. Maier, *Dissolution*, 60.

34. Lutz Niethammer et al., *Die volkseigene Erfahrung: eine Archäologie des Lebens in der Industrieprovinz der DDR. 30 biografische Eröffnungen* (Berlin: Rowohlt, 1991); Dorothee Wierling, *Geboren im Jahr eins: der Jahrgang 1949 in der DDR. Versuch einer Kollektivbiographie* (Berlin: Links, 2002).

35. Steiner, *Von Plan zu Plan*, 165–96; Philip J. Bryson, "East German Traditional Centralism: An Alternative Route to Economic Reconstruction," *Annals of the American Academy of Political and Social Science*, 507 (1990): 133–41.

36. "The contradictions of central planning," Kopstein has written, "justified and gave meaning to their existence." Kopstein, *Politics of Economic Decline*, 153. On East German electronics and computing, see Raymond G. Stokes, *Constructing Socialism: Technology and Change in East Germany, 1945–1990* (Baltimore: Johns Hopkins University, 2000), 177–94.

37. The main proponent of this view, Peter Ludz, did note the sclerosis at the top. Peter C. Ludz, *The Changing Party Elite in East Germany* (Cambridge, Mass.: MIT, 1972; German original 1968). See also Thomas Arthur Baylis, *The Technical Intelligentsia and the East German Elite* (Berkeley: University of California, 1974). In 1979, Norman Naimark questioned the view of the GDR as a success. Naimark, "Is It True What They're Saying about East Germany?" *Orbis*, no. 3 (1979): 549–77.

38. Thomas Steger and Rainhart Lang, "Career Paths of the Former GDR Combinates during the Postsocialist Transformation Process," *Journal of World Business*, 38/3 (2003): 168–81; Heinrich Best, "Cadres into Managers: Structural Changes of East German Economic Elites before and after Reunification," *Historical Social Research*, 30/2 (2005): 6–24.

39. Kopstein argues that "in many ways the structure of authority in East Germany became more ideological and less technocratic over time." Kopstein, *Politics of Economic Decline*, 111. See also Corey Ross, *Constructing Socialism at the Grass-Roots: The Transformation of East Germany, 1945–65* (New York: St. Martin's, 2000), 3.

40. As Kopstein has noted, "Leninist structures regularly reproduce the same bureaucratic cultures and developmental outcomes in significantly different cultural contexts." Kopstein, *Politics of Economic Decline*, 9.

41. A. James McAdams, "GDR Oral History Project," *AAASS Newsletter,* March 1994: 5. On the paralysis at the top, see also Dale, *Popular Protest in East Germany,* 142.

42. By 1944, in Germany proper and in the sprawling Nazi-occupied territories, the Gestapo had mushroomed to 31,000. Catherine Epstein, "The Stasi: New Research on the East German Ministry of State Security," *Kritika,* 5/2 (2004): 321–48.

43. David Childs and Richard Popplewell, *The Stasi: The East German Intelligence and Security Service* (New York: New York University, 1996), 82.

44. Maier, *Dissolution,* 173.

45. "Beyond a certain level," remarked one Stasi officer in 1991, "the leaders lived cut off from reality"; he added that "much that we informed them about was put to one side." Quoted in Childs and Popplewell, *The Stasi,* 174.

46. In March 1978, after two pastors had immolated themselves, the East German regime had signed an agreement with the Union of Evangelical (Lutheran) Churches. The Churches foreswore opposition in exchange for the right to assembly and to publish their own materials, as well as state funding. This produced, in the words of the agreement, "the Church within socialism." But many pastors, especially younger ones, mobilized their parishioners on behalf of peace, the environment, and women's rights. Repression of these actions for going too far—e.g., for deploring not just NATO missiles but Soviet ones—often radicalized the protesters. Still, pastors varied. A number were pressured or recruited to be Stasi informers. On the Church, see David Rock (ed.), *Voices in Times of Change: The Role of Writers, Opposition Movements, and Churches in the Transformation of East Germany* (New York and Oxford: Berghahn, 2000), esp. chap. 2. Even though a 1965 religious census recorded almost 80 percent of the GDR populace as claiming to belong to the Evangelical (Lutheran) Church, by the 1980s East Germany was deeply secularized.

47. Wayne Bartee, *A Time to Speak Out: The Leipzig Citizen Protests and the Fall of East Germany* (Westport, Conn.: Praeger, 2000), 11–4, 121–3; Reiner Tetzner, *Leipziger Ring: Aufzeichnungen eines Montagsdemonstranten, Oktober 1989 bis 1. Mai 1990* (Frankfurt: Luchterhand Literaturverlag, 1990).

48. Pfaff, *Exit-Voice Dynamics,* 79.

49. Maier, *Dissolution,* 126.

50. The Hungarian government had passed a new passport law in 1988 and publicly called the 150-mile fence "outdated," promising to remove all of it by the end of 1990 (the Austrian government welcomed the announcement, even as it feared a flood of Eastern Europeans). In any case, to upgrade the obsolete electronic system, Hungary would have had to begin importing Western parts, paid for with hard currency, since the Soviets had stopped producing them; see www.berliner-mauer.de/laszlo-nagy/lazslonagy-en.htm. There was also the cost of the Hungarian border guards (who had to check the documents of some 50 million people visiting or transiting Hungary through sixty-six highway, rail, river, and air border-crossing points).

51. Timothy Garton Ash, *In Europe's Name: Germany and the Divided Continent* (New York: Random House, 1993), 371, 600n; Maier, *Dissolution,* 129.

52. One of seven children—his father, a Communist, had been arrested by the Nazis and killed on the way to a concentration camp—Horn had been able to graduate from an institution of higher education in the Soviet Union during the last years of Stalin's rule. In 2006, Horn would tell *Die Welt,* a German newspaper, that "I would like to make it clear that 1956 was not a fight against communism. Even the rebels did not want to wipe it out." One American journalist absurdly dramatized the decision to "open" the border as a solitary one by Horn made in the privacy of his Budapest home ("After a sleepless night, pacing up and down his sitting room, the 57 year old foreign minister made up his mind. He decided to abrogate the treaty with East Berlin and let the refugees go"). Michael Dobbs, *Down with Big Brother,* 277–8. By contrast, Horn admitted that he had acted along with Hungary's prime minister, Miklós Németh, and Interior Minister István Horváth. "First Person, Gyula Horn," *Time,* available at www.time.com/time/europe50/hor.html; and Zsolt Estefán, "Who Let the East Germans Out of the Country?" (2008), available at www.hetivalasz.hu/index.php?eng&page=pages/cikk&englishcikk_id=31.

53. Hartmut Zwahr, *Das Ende einer Selbstzerstörung: Leipzig und die Revolution in der DDR* (Göttingen, Germany: Vandenhoeck & Ruprecht, 1993), 23–102; Carol Mueller, "Claim 'Radicalization'? The 1989 Protest Cycle in the GDR," *Social Problems,* 46/4 (1999): 528–47. Between September 1989 and March 1990, close to 400,000 people—nearly 3 percent of the population—emigrated, while the state recorded more than 1,500 public protests. "Had there not been those people ready to exit," recalled one GDR official in 1990, "then we would still be sitting here and getting ready for the forty-first anniversary" of the GDR. Maier, *Dissolution,* 125.

54. Bartee, *A Time to Speak Out,* 21. The superintendent politely declined invitations to participate in the GDR's fortieth-anniversary celebrations.

55. Childs and Popplewell, *The Stasi,* 188. On the eve of his fortieth-anniversary celebration, Honecker needed some face saving vis-à-vis the 2,500 East Germans in the West German embassy in Prague: they were allowed to exit to West Germany, but only via the GDR—in locked trains to keep others from clambering in.

56. Elizabeth Pond, *Beyond the Wall: Germany's Road to Unification* (Washington, D.C.: Brookings Institution, 1993), 111–29; Pfaff, *Exit-Voice Dynamics,* 123–7; Derek Philipsen, *We Were the People: Voices from East Germany's Revolutionary Autumn of 1989* (Durham, N.C.: Duke University, 1993), 354; Zwahr, *Das Ende einer Selbstzerstörung,* 76–96. An announcement in Leipzig's main newspaper on October 6 had read, "Law and order would be restored once and for all."

57. Maier, *Dissolution,* 145. On Honecker's instructions to district party chiefs on September 22, see Pfaff, *Exit-Voice Dynamics,* 170.

58. Fulbrook, *Anatomy of a Dictatorship,* 252–7. On October 8, the Soviet ambassa-

dor had warned Egon Krenz that "the most important thing is to avoid bloodshed." Pfaff, *Exit-Voice Dynamics,* 171; Philip D. Zelikow and Condoleezza Rice, *Germany Unified and Europe Transformed: A Study in Statecraft* (Cambridge, Mass.: Harvard University, 1995), 84–5.

59. The militia commander added, "We were not there to start shooting; we were there to dissolve counterrevolutionary groups. Only if they provoked us, only in this instance [would we shoot]." Pfaff, *Exit-Voice Dynamics,* 174–5. At least one commander apparently informed his superiors that he and his men were unwilling to fight, if so ordered. Some party militia may have failed to muster.

60. The Leipzig district party secretary, Kurt Meyer, two weeks later, explained, "We had already experienced the 7th and 8th of October and knew there was real danger that things could escalate. We Communists did not want that, but the security forces were independent of us, and they were prepared for a provocation." Pfaff, *Exit-Voice Dynamics,* 183–4.

61. Pfaff, *Exit-Voice Dynamics,* 128.

62. Even though the police had just been purged of supposed softies in anticipation of being ordered into action, some of those being exhorted to crack down are said to have cried. Pond, *Beyond the Wall,* 112. Pfaff wrote, "Leipzigers were brave on October 9, but they were hardly foolhardy." Pfaff, *Exit-Voice Dynamics,* 136.

63. Childs and Popplewell, *The Stasi,* 189.

64. Pfaff, *Exit-Voice Dynamics,* 172.

65. Some 67 percent joined via niches, according to a professional poll of 1,300 respondents in Leipzig done in late 1990. Karl-Dieter Opp et al., *Origins of a Spontaneous Revolution: East Germany, 1989* (Ann Arbor: University of Michigan, 1995). Pfaff contends that failure to take to the streets would have been seen as a betrayal of one's "niche."

66. Jan Werner Müller, *Another Country: German Intellectuals, Unification, and National Identity* (New Haven, Conn., and London: Yale University, 2000), 69. This strategy was the very "antipolitics" championed by György Konrád, the Hungarian intellectual, who stressed "networks of friends" and concluded "let the Government stay on top" and "we will live our own lives underneath it." George [György] Konrád, *Antipolitics: An Essay* (San Diego: Harcourt Brace Jovanovich, 1984).

67. "We had a little dacha, and this is where we talked and complained and got angry," one East German woman recalled, adding that "this is exactly how every other GDR citizen did it as well. Everybody had a niche in which he sat quietly and complained." Derek Philipsen, *We Were the People: Voices from East Germany's Revolutionary Autumn of 1989* (Durham, N.C.: Duke University, 1993), 117. Only about 15 percent of the East German population owned dachas, but most knew someone who had one.

68. As for the organized "opposition," it had too few contacts across society to organize demonstrations. In Leipzig, the Stasi tapped around 1,000 telephones

and opened some 2,000 letters per day (invariably, those with cash inside were not delivered, becoming self-awarded bonuses for Stasi staff). Childs and Popplewell, *The Stasi*, 91. "Throughout the revolution, the opposition remained marginal, weak, and divided." Pfaff, *Exit-Voice Dynamics*, 4.

69. Niels C. Nielsen, *Revolutions in Eastern Europe: The Religious Roots* (Maryknoll, N.Y.: Orbis, 1991), 27.

70. Dale, *Popular Protest in East Germany*, 179. When told that the mood in the factories was "a very complicated question at the moment," Mielke retorted, "It is a very simple question. It is a question of power." Pfaff, *Exit-Voice Dynamics*, 151. By 1988, 80 percent of GDR university students were children of white-collar workers; only 10 percent were children of the working class.

71. Mike Dennis, *The Rise and Fall of the German Democratic Republic, 1945–1990* (Harlow, England, and New York: Longman, 2000), 278.

72. As cited in Trish Davie, "Leipzig, 9 October 1989: When the Church Led a Peaceful Revolution," sermon at All Hallows Church, Leeds, England, October 13, 2002, available at www.allhallowsleeds.org.uk/worship/sermons/TrishDavie021013.shtml.

73. Childs and Popplewell, *The Stasi*, 81, 190–191. "Our main problem," one Stasi official said, "was that we tried to solve political problems by police methods, problems which we as an organization were not able to solve." Childs and Popplewell, *The Stasi*, 192.

74. Angela E. Stent, *Germany and Russia Reborn: Unification, the Soviet Collapse, and the New Europe* (Princeton, N.J.: Princeton University, 1999), 94–6; Ann Tusa, "A Fatal Error," *Media Studies Journal*, 13/3 (1999): 26–9; Pond, *Beyond the Wall*, 1–3, 130–4; translated (partial) transcript available at www.wilsoncenter.org/cwihp/documentreaders/eotcw/891109c.pdf.

75. Cited in Mark Kramer, "The Soviet Union and the Founding of the German Democratic Republic: 50 Years Later—A Review Article," *Europe-Asia Studies*, 51/6 (1999): 1093–1106 (at 1100).

76. Garton Ash, based on his own observations in Leipzig on Monday, November 21, has written that calls for unification already began to dominate the post-services processionals. Timothy Garton Ash, *The Magic Lantern: The Revolution of '89 Witnessed in Warsaw, Budapest, Berlin, and Prague* (New York: Vintage, 1990, 1993), 71–2.

77. Pfaff, *Exit-Voice Dynamics*, 197.

78. Mielke added, "I always think about what we lived through. I couldn't eat and buy bananas." Childs and Popplewell, *The Stasi*, 187. As Chief Planner Gerhard Schürer told the East German Politburo in 1989, "There are poorer countries than the GDR with a much richer offering of goods in the stores," adding that "when the people have a lot of money and can't buy the goods they want, they curse socialism." Kopstein, *Politics of Economic Decline*, 192.

79. Kopstein has pointed out that "the East German leadership was hamstrung by its rejection of market ideology." True enough. But, as Kopstein himself adds,

the problem was even deeper: "Who, after all, needed a second capitalist Germany, given that one was already so successful?" Kopstein, *Politics of Economic Decline,* 95, 103.

80. Pfaff, *Exit-Voice Dynamics,* 222; Childs and Popplewell, *The Stasi,* 174.

81. Maier argues that the East German leadership could have sought gradual reform, mixing market and planning. But was there a stable equilibrium in such mixed reform? Where is the example where it worked? Maier also suggests pointedly that the GDR leadership "did not know how to extricate themselves or devise decisive reforms." Maier, *Dissolution,* 79, 57.

82. Iván T. Berend, *The Hungarian Economic Reforms, 1953–1988* (New York: Cambridge University, 1990); Berend, *Central and Eastern Europe, 1944–1993,* 151–2; David Stark, "Privatization in Hungary: From Plan to Market or from Plant to Clan?," *East European Politics and Societies,* 4/3 (1990): 351–92.

III. BREAKTHROUGH

1. Marvin R. Jackson, "Romania's Debt Crisis, Its Causes and Consequences," in *East European Economies: Slow Growth in the 1980's* (Washington, D.C.: U.S. Government Printing Office, 1986), III: 489–542; Trond Gilberg, "Romania's Growing Difficulties," *Current History* 83, no. 496 (1984): 375–9, 389–91; anon., "Birth and Death in Romania," *The New York Review of Books,* October 23, 1986. See also Keith Hitchins, "Historiography of the Countries of Eastern Europe: Romania," *American Historical Review,* 97/4 (1992): 1064–83; Şerban Papacostea, "Captive Clio: Romanian Historiography under Communist Rule," *European History Quarterly,* 26/2 (1996): 181–208.

2. Gail Kligman, "The Politics of Reproduction in Ceauşescu's Romania: A Case Study in Political Culture," *Eastern European Politics and Societies,* 6/3 (1992): 364–418.

3. Dan Ionescu, "The Fourteenth RCP Congress," *RFE Research,* SR/9 (December 14, 1989). The day after the party congress concluded, Dennis Deletant, one of the foremost Romanian-regime experts, wrote that Ceauşescu "will continue to dominate his country because the conditions for change in the rest of Eastern Europe...do not apply in Romania's case." *The Times* [London], November 25, 1989.

4. Peter Siani-Davies, *The Romanian Revolution of December 1989* (Ithaca, N.Y.: Cornell University, 2005), 56. Siani-Davies, like Steven Pfaff for the GDR, is dealing with the same problem, namely, how to explain societal mobilization without an organized society (opposition). But whereas records in the GDR are extensive and accessible, in Romania, there are few comparable sources.

5. Irina Livezeanu, *Cultural Politics in Greater Romania: Regionalism, Nation Building, and Ethnic Struggle* (Ithaca, N.Y.: Cornell University, 1995). Note also the Lucian Pintilie film *An Unforgettable Summer* (1994), set in Greater Romania in the year 1925.

6. Robert R. King, *History of the Romanian Communist Party* (Stanford, Calif.: Hoover Institution, 1980), 64; Tismăneanu, *Stalinism*, 87.

7. Henry L. Roberts, *Rumania: Political Problems of an Agrarian State* (New Haven, Conn.: Yale University, 1951), 259–66. Hugh Seton-Watson laid down an influential schematic model of Communist takeovers in Eastern Europe that proceeded through three stages: genuine coalition (including Communists), bogus coalition, Communist monopoly. Others noted the further factor of how the war had broken the previous order. Seton-Watson, *The East European Revolution*, 3rd ed. (New York: Praeger, 1956), 161–71; Thomas T. Hammond (ed.), *The Anatomy of Communist Takeovers* (New Haven, Conn.: Yale University, 1975); Jan T. Gross, "War as Revolution," in Norman Naimark and Leonid Gibianskii (eds.), *The Establishment of Communist Regimes in Eastern Europe, 1944–1949* (Boulder, Colo.: Westview, 1997), 17–41.

8. Official internal figures for 1933 enumerated Romanian Communist-party membership as 26.68 percent ethnic Hungarian, 22.65 ethnic Romanian, and 18.12 Jewish. Doubtless the number of Jews was higher, perhaps as high as 50 percent, given that many of those listed as Hungarians had Jewish origins. Vasile Luca, at a party meeting in fall 1945, said, "What a disaster we had in Moldavia. The party was made up only of Jews, the various organizations, the police and the administrative apparatus were all Jewish. And then the people began asking: 'What's going on here? Is this a Jewish state or a Romanian state?' And this is continuing to go on in a lot of places." Robert Levy, *Ana Pauker: The Rise and Fall of a Jewish Communist* (Berkeley: University of California, 2001), 5, 236–7. Richard Voyles Burks, noting the preponderance of Jews, Hungarians, and other non-Romanians in the interwar Communist party of Romania, underscored "the tendency of all Communism in power to become national Communism." He also pointed out that in the 1920s, the Communist vote "was significant only in the Slavic countries." R. V. Burks, *The Dynamics of Communism in Eastern Europe* (Princeton, N.J.: Princeton University, 1961), xxv, 78.

9. Luca died in prison; Pauker was saved from a show trial by Stalin's death but was politically marginalized, along with the ethnic Romanian Teohari Georgescu. Emil Bodnariuc, known as Bodnăraş (1904–76)—who had been born in Habsburg Bukovina to a Ukrainian father and German mother and as the head of secret intelligence had helped orchestrate the Communist takeover—was one high-profile non-Romanian who would survive Dej.

10. Robert R. King, "Rumania and the Sino-Soviet Conflict," *Studies in Comparative Communism* no. 4 (1972): 373–93.

11. Dennis Deletant, *Communist Terror in Romania: Gheorghiu-Dej and the Police State 1948–1965* (New York: St. Martin's, 1999), ix.

12. Ghiţă Ionescu, even before Dej's death, had foreseen the likely succession of Ceauşescu. Ionescu, *Communism in Romania, 1944–1962* (New York: Oxford University, 1964), 351.

13. See, for example, the recollections by Ion Iliescu, who succeeded Ceauşescu

following the 1989 revolution and who had accompanied the dictator on the 1971 Asia trip. George Galloway and Bob Wylie, *Downfall: The Ceausescus and the Romanian Revolution* (London: Futura, 1991), 88–9.

14. Romania's patriarch had the birthdays of the Ceauşescus inserted into the Church calendar and even agreed to the demolition of some two dozen Orthodox churches in Bucharest alone. On Ceauşescu's manipulation of personnel, see Mary Ellen Fischer, *Nicolae Ceauşescu: A Study in Political Leadership* (Boulder, Colo.: Lynne Riener, 1989). The dynastic setup and attendant corruption were derided as "socialism in one family." Tismăneanu, *Stalinism*, 206–7.

15. Michael Shafir, *Romania: Politics, Economics, and Society* (London: Pinter, 1985), 168. As one scholar has written, "None of the few intellectuals who did protest against the regime during the late 1980s played a major role in the final demise of the regime." Cristina Petrescu, "Romania," in Detlef Pollack and Jan Wieloghs (eds.), *Dissent and Opposition in Communist Eastern Europe: Origins of Civil Society and Democratic Transition* (Burlington, Vt.: Ashgate, 2004), 141–60 (at 152).

16. Mihai Botez, *Romania: A Case of Dynastic Communism* (New York: Freedom House, 1989), 43. Ceauşescu further burnished his image by allowing Jews to emigrate—for which he received ransoms and a country that was more Romanian Orthodox, not to mention many houses and jobs to redistribute. He also allowed the Jews who remained in Romania a degree of autonomy. Shafir, *Romania*, 157; Ion Mihai Pacepa, *Red Horizons: Chronicles of a Communist Spy Chief* (Washington, D.C.: Regnery Gateway, 1987), 73; Dennis Deletant, *Ceauşescu and the Securitate: Coercion and Dissent in Romania, 1965–1989* (Armonk, N.Y.: M. E. Sharpe, 1996), 206–10.

17. Tismăneanu, *Stalinism*, 233.

18. "A whole new elite had arisen," wrote the sociologist Daniel Chirot, "with its own interests, its own internal divisions, and a greater sense of security than it had possessed a few years before." Chirot, "Social Change in Communist Romania," *Social Forces*, 57/2 (1978): 457–99.

19. Vlad Georgescu, *The Romanians: A History* (Columbus: Ohio State University, 1991), 272.

20. Pacepa, *Red Horizons*, 155–60.

21. Silviu Brucan, *The Wasted Generation: Memoirs of a Romanian Journey from Capitalism to Socialism and Back* (Boulder, Colo.: Westview, 1993), 84, 82. The memoir contains revelations (some perhaps true) about various unrealized plots to unseat Ceauşescu (1976, 1984). Brucan also conveys strong affection for his mentor, the Stalinist Dej, and an acquired adherence to a reformed Communist outlook. He claims no credit for the events of 1989.

22. Norman Manea, *On Clowns: The Dictator and the Artist* (New York: Grove, 1992), 140, 147–8. Czesław Miłosz, in *The Captive Mind* (New York: Knopf, 1953), analyzed four intellectuals who remained in Poland under the Communist system: Alpha, the Moralist; Beta, the Disappointed Lover; Gamma, the Slave of

History; and Delta, the Troubadour. Miłosz did not further name them, but they are recognizable as Jerzy Andrzejewski (Alpha), Tadeusz Borowski (Beta), Jerzy Putrament (Gamma), and Konstanty Ildefons Gałczyński (Delta).

23. Whether nationalism ultimately discredited Marxism-Leninism and the party's legitimacy can be debated. Katherine Verdery's argument that the nationalist "discourse," promoted by the party, became "a major element in destroying the Party's legitimacy" needs to be placed alongside the economic catastrophe, the radically shifting international context, and the party's record in power. Verdery, *National Ideology under Socialism: Identity and Cultural Politics in Ceausescu's Romania* (Berkeley: University of California, 1991), 4. The book went to press in November 1989.

24. King, *History of the Romanian Communist Party,* 64. By social origin, the largest categories were "workers" and "others," meaning neither worker nor peasant but white collar and intelligentsia. The party had many peasants, but peasants were underrepresented compared with their proportion of the overall population.

25. Manea dismissed Romania's Communist legions, scoffing "it would have been difficult to find a thousand true believers." Norman Manea, "Blasphemy and Carnival," *World Policy Journal,* 13/1 (1996): 71–82 (at 76).

26. Robert R. King, *History of the Romanian Communist Party,* 117–8.

27. David Granick, *Enterprise Guidance in Eastern Europe: A Comparison of Four Socialist Economies* (Princeton, N.J.: Princeton University, 1975). One scholar judged the Romanian economy to be among the most centralized and least flexible in the bloc. Evan E. Anderson, "Central Planning and Production Instabilities in Eastern Europe," *Slavic Review,* 42/2 (1983): 221–9 (at 226). On the formation of Communist Romania's economy, see John Michael Montias, *Economic Development in Communist Romania* (Cambridge, Mass.: MIT, 1967).

28. Tismăneanu further argues that Romania's intellectuals, who were close to their counterparts in France, nonetheless remained largely immune to the passion for leftist ideas. He writes of "a political culture based on fear, suspicion, problematic legitimacy, spurious internationalism, populist manipulation of national symbols, unabashed personalization of power, and persecution mania." Vladimir Tismăneanu, *Stalinism for All Seasons: A Political History of Romanian Communism* (Berkeley: University of California, 2003), 5.

29. The letter, which was read over the BBC, also stated that "Romania is and remains a European country.... You have begun to change the geography of the rural areas but you cannot move Romania into Africa." For the text, see Brucan, *The Wasted Generation,* 153–5. See also Vladimir Tismăneanu, "The Rebellion of the Old Guard," *East European Reporter,* 3/4 (1989): 23–4; and Siani-Davies, *The Romanian Revolution,* 27–8.

30. "Breaking through," Kenneth Jowitt wrote, "means the decisive alteration or destruction of values, structures, and behaviors which are perceived by a revolutionary elite as comprising or contributing to the actual or potential exis-

tence of alternative centers of political power." Jowitt, *Revolutionary Break-throughs and National Development: The Case of Romania, 1944–1965* (Berkeley: University of California, 1971), 7.

31. Roberts, *Romania: Political Problems,* 329.

32. Michael Kaser, *Comecon: Integration Problems of the Planned Economies,* 2nd ed. (London: Royal Institute of International Affairs, 1967), 201–23.

33. William E. Crowther, "Romanian Politics and the International Economy," *Orbis,* 28 (1984): 553–74; Crowther, *The Political Economy of Romanian Socialism* (New York: Praeger, 1988); David Turnock, *The Romanian Economy in the Twentieth Century* (London: Croom Helm, 1986); Andreas C. Tsantis and Roy Pepper, *Romania, the Industrialization of an Agrarian Economy under Socialist Planning: Report of a Mission Sent to Romania by the World Bank* (Washington, D.C.: World Bank, 1979).

34. Deletant, *Ceaușescu and the Securitate,* 339.

35. Ibid., 233–4.

36. L. Tőkés, as told to David Porter, *With God, for the People: The Autobiography of Laszlo Tőkés* (London: Hodder and Stoughton, 1990); Michael Shafir, "The Revolution: An Initial Assessment," *Report on Eastern Europe,* 1/4 (January 26, 1990): 34–42; Vladimir Socor, "Pastor Tőkés and the Outbreak of the Revolution in Timișoara," *Report on Eastern Europe,* 1/5 (February 2, 1990): 19–26. On popular anger at the regime's policies of destruction, see Dinu C. Giurescu, *The Razing of Romania's Past* (Washington, D.C.: United States Committee, International Council on Monuments and Sites, 1989).

37. The Timișoara region, by 1977, had become 71 percent Romanian versus 13 percent Hungarian and 12 percent German, and "among those arrested," wrote Siani-Davies, "each ethnic group was represented more or less in proportion to its numbers in the city as a whole." Siani-Davies, *The Romanian Revolution,* 55.

38. On how shared misery lent itself to a certain amount of social solidarity in Romania, see Steven L. Sampson, "Regime and Society in Romania," *International Journal of Rumanian Studies,* 4/1 (1984–6): 41–51 (at 44).

39. Siani-Davies, *The Romanian Revolution,* 44.

40. Galloway and Wylie, *Downfall,* 109.

41. *The Times* (London), December 20, 1989.

42. Richard Andrew Hall, "Theories of Collective Action and Revolution: Evidence from the 1989 Romanian Transition," *Europe-Asia Studies,* 52/6 (2000): 1069–93.

43. Interview with General Ștefan Gușă taken by Colonel Valeriu Pricina on March 20, 1990, available at www.fundatiagusa.ro/en/interviu.

44. Vladimir Socor, "The Workers' Protest in Brașov: Assessment and Aftermath," RAD Background Report/231, December 4, 1987, available at http://files.osa .ceu.hu/holdings/300/8/3/text/53-9-5.shtml; Dennis Deletant and Mihail Ionescu, "Romania and the Warsaw Pact: 1955–1989," Cold War International History Project, Washington, D.C., Working Paper No. 43 (2004).

45. Silviu Brucan dared issue a statement to the foreign press (broadcast to Romania on foreign radio) about Braşov, warning that "the situation of the workers has deteriorated and the explosion in Braşov is a sign that the cup of anger is now full and the working class is no longer prepared to be treated like an obedient servant." Brucan was briefly put under house arrest. Brucan, *The Wasted Generation.*

46. One analyst pointed out that the protests broke out not where the misery was greatest but where the shame was greatest. Siani-Davies, *The Romanian Revolution,* 56.

47. "Television was the decisive factor of the revolution," wrote Brucan. "Every important act, from the popular uprising in the Palace Square to the trial and execution of Ceauşescu, was seen live." Brucan, *The Wasted Generation,* 171.

48. Most of the Romanian territories of Wallachia and Moldavia, however, remained calm. Only in Timişoara (in the Banat) and Cluj (in Transylvania) did the bulk of the deaths in 1989 occur before December 22.

49. Harvey Morris, "When the Workers of Romania Said No," *The Independent,* January 13, 1990, citing Viktor Carausu of the Braşov Salvation Front, whose boss, Ion Flora, the local commander, was the man who allegedly received the telex.

50. *Le Monde,* April 26, 1990, p. 5. Colonel Dumitru Pavelescu of the Securitate, although not the top Securitate chief, may have ordered his troops withdrawn on his own volition. Siani-Davies, *The Romanian Revolution,* 91–2. At some point, the army high command also removed the party's operational archive from the Central Committee building.

51. Deletant, *Ceauşescu and the Securitate,* 353–9.

52. According to the Soviet Union's TASS correspondent, in *The Current Digest of the Soviet Press,* 41/51 (1989): 14.

53. Siani-Davies, *The Romanian Revolution,* 92. See also Hall, "Romania in December 1989," 1085 ("The army's arbitrary [*sic*] and anarchic defection was the key to the collapse of the regime"). More broadly, see Charles Tilly, *From Mobilization to Revolution* (New York: Random House, 1978), 214–6.

54. Siani-Davies, *The Romanian Revolution,* 37; Kieran Williams and Dennis Deletant, *Security Intelligence Services in New Democracies: The Czech Republic, Slovakia and Romania* (Houndmills, England: Palgrave, 2001), 198, 216.

55. Deletant, *Ceauşescu and the Securitate,* 393.

56. Tismăneanu, "The Tragicomedy of Romanian Communism," *Eastern European Politics and Societies,* 3/2 (1989): 329–76 (at 330).

57. Brucan bluntly noted, "If the so-called plot organized by the front and the army had been true, we, its leaders, would have had every reason to boast about it.... Why be so modest and not claim such a great historical achievement?... The truth is that there never was such a plan. The making of such a plan under Ceauşescu's police state would have been impossible. Surveillance was so effective that no political group could possibly take shape inside the

party or outside it, and even less involve the military." Brucan, on Radio Bucharest, as cited in Michael Shafir, "Ceauşescu's Overthrow: Popular Uprising or Moscow-Guided Conspiracy?," *Report on Eastern Europe,* 1/3 (January 19, 1990): 15–9 (at 17).

58. According to Brucan, following the 1987 Braşov events, Ceauşescu had formed units for urban warfare that were given keys to caches of arms and food, uniforms, and maps of the tunnels and bunkers under government buildings, and it was these mysterious men who were responsible for the 1989 sniper fire and killings, most of which took place after Ceauşescu fled the capital. Brucan, *The Wasted Generation,* 183–4.

59. Nonetheless, Siani-Davies underscores the demonstrations' "lack of formal organizations." Siani-Davies, *The Romanian Revolution,* 44–5.

60. Brucan, a prominent member of the Front, told an American reporter in 1999 that "our only merit was that we were in the railway station when the train of the revolution arrived." Donald G. McNeil, Jr., "Romania's Revolution of 1989: An Enduring Enigma," *The New York Times,* December 31, 1999.

61. *The Guardian,* June 5, 1998.

62. Robert Cullen, "Report from Romania," *The New Yorker,* April 2, 1990, 100, 104.

63. Cullen, "Report from Romania," 112.

IV. As If

1. Andrzej Paczkowski, *Zdobycie władzy, 1945–1947* (Warsaw: Wydawnictwa Szkolne i Pedagogiczne, 1993), 5; Andrzej Garlicki, *Bolesław Bierut* (Warsaw: Wydawnictwa Szkolne i Pedagogiczne, 1994), 43.

2. In the 1960s, one Polish sociologist began to argue that because of the country's unusual circumstances, Poland's Communist party actually ruled via hegemony, not monopoly. Jerzy J. Wiatr, "The Hegemonic Party System in Poland," in Jerzy J. Wiatr (ed.), *Studies in Polish Political System* (Wroclaw: Ossolineum, 1967), 108–23. On "pluralism" in Communist Poland, see Stanisław Ehrlich, *Oblicza pluralizmów,* 2nd ed. (Warsaw: PWN, 1985).

3. Andrzej Korbonski, *The Politics of Socialist Agriculture, 1945–1960* (New York: Columbia University, 1965). See also Adolf Dobieszewski, *Kolektywizacja wsi polskiej, 1948–1956* (Warsaw: Fundacja im. Kazimierza Kelles-Krauza, 1993), and Franciszka Gryciuka (ed.), *Opór chłopów przeciw kolektywizacji wsi polskiej: 1948–1956* (Siedlce, Poland: IH WSRP, 1997).

4. Andrzej Friszke, *Polska: Losy panstwa i narodu, 1939–1989* (Warsaw: Iskry, 2003), 352. On the distinguishing features of Communist-era university milieus in Poland, see John Connelly, *Captive University: The Sovietization of East German, Czech, and Polish Higher Education, 1945–1956* (Chapel Hill: University of North Carolina, 2000). On the Catholic Church's organizational structure in Poland, see Peter Raina, *Kościół w Polsce 1981–1984* (London: Veritas, 1985), chap. 6. Communist-era Poland had just 400,000 Orthodox and 150,000 Protestants

(predominantly Augsburg-Evangelical denomination) and only several thousand surviving or returning Jews. In Hungary, 65 percent of the population was Catholic; far fewer than in Poland attended church regularly.

5. Friszke, *Polska,* 219. Estimates concerning the numbers of fatalities in Poznań vary; some are lower.

6. The literature on the workers is exceptionally rich, offering a shop-floor view: Roman Laba, *The Roots of Solidarity: A Political Sociology of Poland's Working Class Democratization* (Princeton, N.J.: Princeton University, 1991); David Ost, *Solidarity and the Politics of Anti-Politics: Opposition and Reform in Poland since 1968* (Philadelphia: Temple University, 1990); Beata Chmiel and Elżbieta Kaczyńska (eds.), *Postulaty: Materialy do dziejów wystapien pracowniczych w iatach 1970/71 i 1980* (Warsaw: Warsaw University, 1988). Occupation strikes and interfactory strike committees had been important elements of worker militancy in interwar Poland.

7. Jan Józef Lipski, *KOR: A History of the Workers' Defense Committee in Poland, 1976–1981* (Berkeley: University of California, 1985). Lipski was one of the founders of KOR.

8. Timothy Garton Ash, *The Polish Revolution: Solidarity,* 3rd ed. (New Haven, Conn.: Yale University, 2002; original edition 1984), 26.

9. Lipski, *KOR,* 339–40.

10. The uprisings inspired great literature, troves of family stories, and a Great Emigration—patriotic Poles who had escaped abroad cultivated a tradition of freedom struggles and conveyed these messages back to the Motherland. "Dabrowski's Mazurka," composed in 1797 and adopted as the national anthem in 1926, recapitulates this story every time it is played before a Polish audience. Two national poets, Adam Mickiewicz (1798–1855) and Juliusz Słowacki (1809–1849), were part of the Great Emigration. Thus, an easy-to-memorize canon of patriotic virtues—including an injunction to stand up "for yours and our freedom"—is imbibed by sons and daughters of the Polish intelligentsia as soon as they learn how to read.

11. Jonathan Schell, "Reflections," *The New Yorker,* February 3, 1986, reprinted as "Introduction" in Adam Michnik, *Letters from Prison and Other Essays* (Berkeley: University of California, 1985), xvii–xlii (at xxx–xxxi).

12. James P. McGregor, "Economic Reform and Polish Public Opinion," *Soviet Studies,* 41/2 (1989): 215–27.

13. Jan Karski, *Story of a Secret State* (Boston: Houghton Mifflin, 1944). The book, whose author was a courier of the Polish underground, was launched at the Waldorf-Astoria in October 1944 and became a best seller in the United States. Jan Karski (1914–2000), who was born Jan Kozielewski, took direct evidence to Churchill and Roosevelt that the Nazis were exterminating European Jews. During his book tour, he was told by the State Department not to mention the involvement of the Soviet Union (a key U.S. wartime ally) in the Katyń massacre. See also Jan T. Gross, *Polish Society under German Occupation:*

The Generalgouvernement, 1939–1944 (Princeton, N.J.: Princeton University, 1979), and Gross, *Revolution from Abroad: The Soviet Conquest of Poland's Western Ukraine and Western Belorussia* (Princeton, N.J.: Princeton University, 2003).

14. Stalin's signature, together with those of Vyacheslav Molotov, Kliment Voroshilov, and Anastas Mikoyan, appears on the document. Anna Cienciala et al. (eds.), *Katyn: A Crime Without Punishment* (New Haven, Conn.: Yale University, 2007), 26, 28, 29, 30, 31; *Katyn—Dokumenty ludobojstwa. Dokumenty i materialy archiwalne przekazane Polsce 14 pazdziernika 1992 r.* (Warsaw: Instytut Nauk Politycznych PAN, 1992), 34–46. In 1990, Soviet President Gorbachev finally made a tacit admission of Soviet responsibility. In 1992, Russian President Yeltsin passed copies of the 1940 Politburo execution order to Polish President Lech Wałęsa.

15. "Khrushchev's Second Secret Speech" (introduced and edited by L. W. Gluchowski), in *Cold War International History Project Bulletin*, 10 (1998): 44–9.

16. In the period 1946–70, 359 permits were issued for construction or renovation of church buildings. Out of this number 270 permits were made available immediately after October 1956. Friszke, *Polska*, 352. On church construction, see also Adam Łopatka, "Zsady polityki wyznaniowej w Polsce," *Nowe drogi*, 4/407 (April 1982): 14–25.

17. Stefan Wyszyński, *A Freedom Within: The Prison Notes of Stefan Cardinal Wyszyński* (San Diego: Harcourt Brace Jovanovich, 1983), 246–7.

18. In 1962, the sociologist Anna Rudzinska was sentenced to prison for translating a book for the émigré Institut Littéraire (Polish: Instytut Literacki) in Paris, which was the publisher of the monthly *Kultura*. Rudzinska and her three defense attorneys—Aniela Steinsbergowa, Ludwik Cohn (both of them would be founding members of KOR in 1976), and Jan Olszewski—were active members of the Crooked Circle. Jerzy Giedroyc (1906–2000) founded the Institut Littéraire and edited *Kultura*, which not only kept alive Poland's non-Communist literary traditions in publications smuggled into Poland but provided a forum for contacts with independent Ukrainian, Russian, and Lithuanian writers and thinkers. Another émigré institution of outstanding and perhaps unique quality was the Polish section of Radio Free Europe, under its director, Jan Nowak-Jeziorański (1914–2005), a former underground courier during the war.

19. Tony Kemp-Welch, "Dethroning Stalin: Poland 1956 and Its Legacy," *Europe-Asia Studies*, 58/8 (2006): 1261–84 (at 1263).

20. Martin Malia, "Poland's Eternal Return," *The New York Review of Books*, September 29, 1983, 18–27; Maryjane Osa, *Solidarity and Contention: Networks of Polish Opposition* (Minneapolis: University of Minnesota, 2003), 67–75; Andrzej Micewski, *Cardinal Wyszyński: A Biography* (San Diego: Harcourt Brace Jovanovich, 1984), 157–70.

21. The holy painting was credited with miraculously protecting the shrine when it was besieged by Protestant Swedes during a seventeenth-century war,

thereby saving Poland from the "Swedish Deluge." The Black Madonna was then "crowned" in gratitude by the Polish king Jan II Kazimierz as the Queen and Protector of Poland. The story was popularized by Henryk Sienkiewicz in the best-selling novel *The Deluge* (1891).

22. Michael H. Bernhard, *The Origins of Democratization in Poland: Workers, Intellectuals, and Oppositional Politics, 1976–1980* (New York: Columbia University, 1993), 77.

23. Adam Michnik, *Kościół, lewica, dialog* (Paris: Instytut Literacki, 1977); translated as *The Church and the Left* (Chicago: University of Chicago, 1993).

24. Kołakowski was joined as a speaker at the event by a younger colleague, Krzysztof Pomian. Both lost their jobs two years later in 1970 after being dismissed with a group of university professors whom the regime wanted to get rid of in the wake of the student protests of March 1968. Pomian took up an academic career in France, Kołakowski in the United States and England. In 1976–78, Kołakowski published his monumental critical study of Marxism in Polish with the Institut Littéraire in Paris. The English translation is *Main Currents of Marxism: Its Rise, Growth, and Dissolution*, 3 vols. (Oxford: Clarendon, 1978).

25. Polish Communists always strained credulity as supposed true patriots and bearers of national interest, one reason that Gomułka launched the anti-Semitic campaign of 1967–68. But General Mieczysław Moczar (1913–86), the feared interior minister who also ran the Veterans' Association, seized it to promote himself and his "partisans" (many of them career security police personnel) as "true patriots." In the event, Gomułka was able to fight off the challenge to his position by Moczar, but thousands of people lost their positions. The last wave of "Jewish" emigration from Poland, upwards of 15,000, then took place, mostly people who had been completely assimilated, including numerous highly educated professionals and students attending universities. See Paul Lendvai, *Anti-Semitism without Jews: Communist Eastern Europe* (Garden City, N.Y.: Doubleday, 1971). One of the authors of the present book, Jan Gross, was expelled from Warsaw University as a result of the events of March 1968 and jailed for five months before immigrating to the United States with his parents in 1969.

26. Friszke, *Polska*, 300–2.

27. These insights of the Polish opposition would eventually reverberate in the Anglophone historiography: Jan Gross, "A Note on the Nature of Soviet Totalitarianism," *Soviet Studies*, 34/3 (1982): 367–76.

28. Kazimierz Z. Poznański, *Poland's Protracted Transition: Institutional Change and Economic Growth, 1970–1994* (New York: Cambridge University, 1996), 3–4. See also Włodzimierz Brus, "Economics and Politics: The Fatal Link," in Abraham Brumberg (ed.), *Poland: Genesis of a Revolution* (New York: Vintage, 1983), 26–41, and Alex Pravda, "Poland 1980: From 'Premature Consumerism' to Labour Solidarity," *Soviet Studies*, 34/3 (1982): 167–99.

29. Adam Michnik, "A New Evolutionism" (1976), in *Letters from Prison and Other Essays* (Berkeley: University of California, 1985), 135–44 (at 144). Leszek Kołakowski, "Hope and Hopelessness," *Survey,* 17/3 (1971): 42–8. Michnik was also influenced by Jacek Kuroń's essay "Political Opposition in Poland," published in *Kultura* in 1974, in which Kuroń renounced his earlier approach of writing "an open letter to the party" in favor of addressing society. See Ost, *Solidarity,* 58–73. Compare the general advocacy for "incrementalism" in public policy making by Charles E. Lindblom, "The Science of Muddling Through," *Public Administration Review,* 19 (1959): 79–88.

30. Schell, "Reflections," xxx.

31. Micewski, *Cardinal Wyszyński,* 265–6.

32. Andrzej Stasiuk, *Fado* (Wołowiec, Poland: Wydawnictwo Czarne, 2006), 141–5.

33. Michnik, "A Lesson in Dignity," in *Letters from Prison,* 163, 166.

34. Osa, *Solidarity and Contention,* 143–5; Ost, *Solidarity,* 79–80.

35. Marek Sterlingow, "Wałęsa, ty zes przegral," third segment of a seven-part publication series, "Siedem wyborow Walesy," in *Gazeta Wyborcza,* July 2, 2008. KOR's role has been laid out by Lipski. "Sometimes one meets with the opinion that KOR organized the strikes," he wrote. "This is not true. If it were so, I would surely emphasize this fact." Lipski added, though, that KOR provided an indispensable information service for use by the strikers. Lipski, *KOR,* 423–4.

36. In Gdańsk, a permanent monument was soon erected: three huge steel crosses linked at the top with an anchor, at the shipyard gates, and a verse by the Nobel Laureate poet Czesław Miłosz chiseled into the pedestal (Milosz, *Collected Poems* [Hopewell, N.J.: Ecco, 1988], 106). Jankowski, the long-serving provost of St. Bridget's in Gdańsk and Wałęsa's confessor, became the chaplain of Solidarity. In 1997, he was suspended from preaching for a year for making anti-Semitic remarks.

37. Andrzej Paczkowski and Malcom Byrne (eds.), *From Solidarity to Martial Law: The Polish Crisis of 1980–1981. A Documentary History* (Budapest and New York: Central European University, 2007), 66–80; Ost, *Solidarity,* 80–90.

38. On workers in Hungary—their powerful sense of class consciousness, their self-organization strategies on the shop floor, and their absolute political demobilization—see Michael Burawoy and János Lukács, *The Radiant Past: Ideology and Reality in Hungary's Road to Capitalism* (Chicago: University of Chicago, 1992).

39. Roman Laba, *The Roots of Solidarity.* See also Lawrence Goodwyn, *Breaking the Barrier: The Rise of Solidarity in Poland* (New York: Oxford University, 1991). Workers had demanded a free trade union beginning in 1970 and insisted on the union in 1980, whereas some intellectuals, such as Kuroń and Michnik, deemed such a demand too radical; the latter were both arrested in Warsaw and did not make it to Gdańsk. Garton Ash, *The Polish Revolution: Solidarity,* 364–66. Michael Bernhard suggested that there were neither workers nor in-

tellectuals but "oppositionists." Still he concluded, echoing Laba, that "the Polish opposition of the 1970s and 1980s was unique because, unlike its counterparts in the rest of East Central Europe, it included a large number of industrial workers." Bernhard, *The Origins of Democratization in Poland,* 151.

40. Martin Malia, "Poland's Eternal Return," *The New York Review of Books,* September 29, 1983. For Solidarity's program, see Peter Raina, *Poland, 1981: Towards Social Renewal* (London: Allen & Unwin, 1985), 326–47.

41. Osa, *Solidarity and Contention,* 175–9. See also Christopher Civic, "The Church," in Abraham Brumberg (ed.), *Poland: Genesis of a Revolution* (New York: Vintage, 1983), 92–108.

42. As always, the Soviet leadership did not want to intervene if it could avoid it. On Poland's tortured path to martial law, see Paczkowski and Byrne, *From Solidarity to Martial Law;* Mark Kramer, "Soviet Deliberations during the Polish Crisis, 1980–1981," Special Working Paper No. 1, Cold War International History Project (Washington, D.C., 1999), available at www.wilsoncenter.org/topics/pubs/ACF56F.PDF; Stanisław Kania with Andrzej Urbańczyk, *Zatrzymać konfrontacje* (Warsaw: BGW, 1992).

43. Hannah Arendt, *On Revolution* (New York: Penguin, 1965), 119.

44. For an English transcript of the Solidarity congress proceedings, see George Sanford (ed.), *The Solidarity Congress, 1981: The Great Debate* (Houndmills, England: Macmillan, 1990).

45. Jadwiga Staniszkis, *Poland's Self-Limiting Revolution,* ed. Jan T. Gross (Princeton, N.J.: Princeton University, 1984). But the Solidarity congress of September 1981 did formally call upon other East bloc countries to recognize independent (non-Communist) trade unions, which set off a furor in the Soviet Politburo on September 10, 1981 ("they're mocking us").

46. Jerzy J. Wiatr, "Mobilization of Non-Participants during the Political Crisis in Poland, 1980–1981," *International Political Science Review,* 5/3 (1984): 233–44.

47. George Sanford, *Polish Communism in Crisis* (New York: St. Martin's, 1983).

48. For a published version of his speech, see *Jaruzelski, Prime Minister of Poland: Selected Speeches* (Oxford, England, and New York: Pergamon, 1985), 28–35. For his subsequent efforts to justify martial law, see Wojciech Jaruzelski, Marek Jaworski, and Włodzimierz Łoziński, *Stan wojenny dlaczego* (Warsaw: BGW, 1992); and especially Jaruzelski, *Les chaînes et le refuge: mémoires* (Paris: Jean-Claude Lattes, 1992), which includes an illuminating dialogue with Michnik. See also Mark Kramer, "Jaruzelski, the Soviet Union, and the Imposition of Martial Law in Poland: New Light on the Mystery of December 1981," and W. Jaruzelski, "Commentary," *Cold War International History Project Bulletin,* 11 (1998): 5–31, 32–9; and Andrzej Paczkowski, *Wojna polsko-jaruzelska: stan wojenny w Polsce 13 XII 1981–22 VII 1983* (Warsaw: Prószyński i S-ka, 2006). Others in the regime, such as Mieczysław Rakowski, the main regime negotiator with Wałęsa and Solidarity in 1980, firmly believed that the Soviet Union would never allow Poland to go and thus would intervene militarily if necessary.

49. George Sanford, *Military Rule in Poland: The Rebuilding of Communist Power, 1981–1983* (New York: St. Martin's, 1986), 67–8. On the military displacing the party, see A. Ross Johnson, *Poland in Crisis* (Santa Monica, Calif.: Rand, 1982), available at www.rand.org/pubs/notes/2007/N1891.pdf.

50. Laba, *The Roots of Solidarity,* 148. More broadly, see Jan Kubik, *The Power of Symbols against the Symbols of Power: The Rise of Solidarity and the Fall of State Socialism in Poland* (University Park: Pennsylvania State University, 1994). See also Leopold Labedz (ed.), *Poland under Jaruzelski: A Comprehensive Sourcebook on Poland during and after Martial Law* (New York: Scribner, 1984).

51. *Wejdą nie wejdą. Polska 1980–1982: wewnętrzny kryzys, międzynarodowe uwarunkowania. Konferencja w Jachrance, listopad 1997* (London: Aneks, 1999), 191.

52. Thanks to Piotr Kosicki, personal communication, citing Archiwum Akt Nowych KC PZPR V/409.

53. Mieczysław F. Rakowski, *Dzienniki polityczne,* 10 vols. (Warsaw: Iskry, 2005), X: 186. Both of Rakowski's parents had been executed by the Nazis. His diary entries encompass more than four decades.

54. Rakowski, *Dzienniki,* X: 222.

55. Ibid., 303, 306.

56. Wiktor Osiatynski, "The Roundtable Talks in Poland," in Jan Elster (ed.), *The Roundtable Talks and the Breakdown of Communism* (Chicago: University of Chicago, 1996), 21–68 (at 26).

57. *Geremek opowiada, Zakowski pyta. Rok 1989* (Warsaw: Plejada, 1990), 23, 75, 14.

58. Rakowski, *Dzienniki,* X: 395.

59. Ibid., 452.

60. "After all," Kiszczak wrote, "only experienced diplomats and trusted activists of the PUWP [Polish United Workers' Party, i.e., the Communist party] and proregime allied parties were employed there." "Prawda wedlug Kiszczaka. Dokument, 1988 rok. Relacja generala Czeslawa Kiszczaka," *Gazeta Wyborcza,* August 22, 2008.

61. Rakowski, *Dzienniki,* X: 452.

62. John Tagliabue, "Poles Approve Solidarity-Led Cabinet," *The New York Times,* September 13, 1989.

Epilogue

1. Mikhail Gorbachev, *Memoirs* (New York: Doubleday, 1996), 516; Gorbachev, *Perestroika: New Thinking for Our Country and the World* (New York: Harper and Row, 1988), 200. See also Jacques Lévesque, *The Enigma of 1989: The USSR and the Liberation of Eastern Europe* (Berkeley: University of California, 1997), 37–99, 144–6; and Angela Stent, *Russia and Germany Reborn: Unification, the Soviet Collapse, and the New Europe* (Princeton, N.J.: Princeton University, 2000). Note that back in April 1989, Vyacheslav Dashichev, a Soviet expert on Germany close to Gorbachev's Kremlin, had written an internal memorandum proclaiming the unequivocal victory of West Germany over East Germany in

"standard of living, social security, development of democratic institutions, the rights and freedoms [of its citizens], but also in the possibility for further dynamic development." Jeffrey Gedmin, *The Hidden Hand: Gorbachev and the Collapse of East Germany* (Washington, D.C.: American Enterprise Institute, 1992), 50–1. Dashichev had spent two years as a visiting professor in West Germany.

2. Lévesque, *The Enigma of 1989,* 1.

3. Kristian Gerner and Stefan Hedlund, *The Baltic States and the End of the Soviet Empire* (London: Routledge, 1993), 80.

4. Nils Raymond Muiznieks, "The Baltic Popular Movements and the Disintegration of the Soviet Union," Ph.D. dissertation, University of California, Berkeley (1993), 150–1, 162–70. At the Ignalina nuclear power plant, units three and four were never completed, while unit one was finally closed in 2004, as a condition for Lithuania's entry into the EU, and unit two was scheduled for closure in 2009 or 2010. That would finally terminate the plant's existence.

5. Mark Kramer, "The Collapse of East European Communism and the Repercussions within the Soviet Union," *Journal of Cold War Studies,* 5/4 (2003): 178–256 (at 209). For Lévesque, the " 'permissiveness' of the USSR must therefore be considered the great enigma of 1989." He adds that "rarely in history have we witnessed the policy of a great power continue, throughout so many difficulties and reversals, to be guided by such an idealistic view of the world." Lévesque, *The Enigma,* 5, 252.

6. Kramer, "The Collapse," 255–6. Dmitri Volkogonov, the Soviet general and historian of the military, told Kramer, "The scope and intensity of the ideological disillusionment increased drastically as a result of the events in Eastern Europe." Kramer, "The Collapse of East European Communism and the Repercussions within the Soviet Union," *Journal of Cold War Studies,* 6/4 (2004): 3–64 (at 8). In spring 1990, Lech Wałęsa sent a letter protesting the Soviet economic blockade of Lithuania.

7. Gerner and Hedlund, *The Baltic States,* 151. For an unsentimental eyewitness portrait of Baltic (especially Lithuanian) nationalists, see Anatol Lieven, *The Baltic Revolution: Estonia, Latvia, Lithuania and the Path to Independence* (New Haven, Conn., and London: Yale University, 1993).

8. David R. Marples, *Ukraine under Perestroika: Ecology, Economics and the Workers' Revolt* (New York: St. Martin's, 1991).

9. In 1959, Lukyanenko and two others organized an underground Ukrainian Workers' and Peasants' Union to uphold the right of Ukraine to secede from the Union (as specified in the 1936 Soviet Constitution); he was arrested in 1961 and given the death penalty, which was commuted to fifteen years' imprisonment. No sooner was Lukyanenko out then he was rearrested, in 1977, and given another ten years in the camps. Andrew Wilson, *Ukrainian Nationalism in the 1990s: A Minority Faith* (New York: Cambridge University, 1996). On

the wartime origins of Ukraine's post–World War II nationalist resistance, see Danylo Shumuk, *Life Sentence: Memoirs of a Ukrainian Political Prisoner* (Edmonton: Canadian Institute of Ukrainian Studies, University of Alberta, 1984).

10. "Ukrainian independence," wrote Andrew Wilson, "arrived as much by accident as by design, and largely as a result of events occurring elsewhere." Wilson, *The Ukrainians: Unexpected Nation,* 2nd ed. (New Haven, Conn.: Yale University, 2002), 152–72 (at 172). See also Roman Szporluk, "National Building in Ukraine: Problems and Prospects," in Szporluk, *Russia, Ukraine, and the Breakup of the Soviet Union* (Stanford, Calif.: Hoover Institution, 2000), 315–26. On Ukraine's Brezhnev-era party boss, the highly capable Volodymyr Shcherbytsky, and on the nationalist-come-lately Leonid Kravchuk, see Boydan Nahaylo, *Ukrainian Resurgence* (Toronto: University of Toronto, 1999).

11. John B. Dunlop, *The Faces of Contemporary Russian Nationalism* (Princeton, N.J.: Princeton University, 1983), 286–7. See also Yitzhak M. Brudny, *Reinventing Russia: Russian Nationalism and the Soviet State, 1953–1991* (Cambridge, Mass.: Harvard University, 1998).

12. John B. Dunlop, *The Rise of Russia and the Fall of the Soviet Union* (Princeton, N.J.: Princeton University, 1993).

13. As Nils Raymond Muiznieks wrote, "The Soviet regime institutionalized ethnicity, then used it as an important criterion in the distribution of economic, political, and social records and opportunities." He added that "even ostensibly non-ethnic issues, such as the all-important ecology and the urge for 'sovereignty' became *framed* in ethnic terms." Muiznieks, "The Baltic Popular Movements," 2, 99. More broadly, Joseph Rothschild argued "a general tendency for other lines of conflict to be displaced into ethnic ones." Rothschild, *Ethnopolitics: A Conceptual Framework* (New York: Columbia University, 1981), 4.

14. Mark Beissinger, *Nationalist Mobilization and the Collapse of the Soviet State* (New York: Cambridge University, 2002). Beissinger codes just about every action as "nationalism," but to explain the collapse he also has to introduce the question of establishment psychology, which, he rightly notes, was shattered by "failed reform" (p. 40).

15. A cofounder and leader of the Estonian Popular Front, Marju Lauristin, discussing the ties among the various republic popular fronts, remarked at a conference in New York in May 1990 that "it is our principled position not to create an all-union popular front. It would be a disaster, as was the all-union Communist party." *Nationalities Papers,* 18/1 (1990): 77.

16. Martin Diewald et al. (eds.), *After the Fall of the Wall: Life Courses in the Transformation of East Germany* (Stanford, Calif.: Stanford University, 2006); Jacek Wasilewski, *Communist Nomenklatura in Post-Communist Eastern Europe: Winners or Losers of Transformation?* (Warsaw: Polish Academy of Sciences, 1995); Tom Gallagher, *Modern Romania: The End of Communism, the Failure of Democratic Reform, and the Theft of a Nation* (New York: New York University, 2005). Gallagher argues that the post-1989 dominance and looting by Romania's former

Communist elites were "consolidated" in Romania's accession to the European Union. In passing, he suggests that Romania, though an EU member, be compared not to Poland or Slovakia but to Angola or countries in Central Asia (p. 16). See also Marius Oprea, "The Fifth Power: Transition of the Romanian Securitate from Communism to Nato," *New Europe College Yearbook*, 11 (2003–4): 151–72, available at www.ceeol.com.

17. Erzsebet Szalai, "The Power Structure in Hungary after the Political Transition," in Christopher G. A. Bryant and Edmund Mokrzycki (eds.), *The New Great Transformation? Change and Continuity in East-Central Europe* (London and New York: Routledge, 1994); Andrew G. Walder, "Career Mobility and the Communist Political Order," *American Sociological Review* 60 (1995): 309–28; Eric Hanley et al., "The Making of Post-Communist Elites in Eastern Europe," working papers of the research project Social Trends, April 1998, available at www.soc.cas.cz/articles/en/5/1134/Hanley-Eric-a-Petr-Mateju-Klara-Vlachova-Jindrich-Krejci-1998-.--The-Making-of-Post-Communist-Elites-in-Eastern-Europe-Sociologicky-ustav-AV-CR-Praha-.-Working-Papers-of-the-Project-Social-Trends-1998-5.html; Eric Hanley and Donald J. Treiman, "Recruitment into the East European Elite: Dual Career Paths," *Research in Social Stratification and Mobility*, 23 (2005): 35–66. See also Jadwiga Staniszkis, *The Dynamics of Breakthrough in Eastern Europe* (Berkeley: University of California, 1991).

18. Alex Inkeles, "Social Stratification and the Modernization of Russia," in Cyril Black (ed.), *The Transformation of Russian Society* (Cambridge, Mass.: Harvard University, 1960), 338–50 (at 346).

19. Konrád, *Antipolitics,* 134. Konrád's coauthor also cogently repudiated their earlier arguments. See Iván Szelényi, "The Prospects and Limits of the East European New Class Project: An Autocritical Reflection on 'The Intellectuals on the Road to Class Power,'" *Politics and Society,* 15/2 (1986–7): 103–44; and Szelényi, "An Outline of the Social History of Socialism or an Auto-critique of an Auto-critique," in *Research in Social Stratification and Mobility* 19 (2002): 39–65. This same point had been made by Zbigniew Brzezinski in *Ideology and Power in Soviet Politics* (New York: Praeger, 1962), 71–82.

20. Teresa Torańska, *"Them": Stalin's Polish Puppets* (New York: Harper and Row, 1987), 139, 257; the interviews were first published in the Polish underground. Only one of the five interviewees renounced Marxism-Leninism. By the way, in the 2000s, the Slovak Communist party was led by Jozef Ševc, the son-in-law of Vasil Bilak.

GUIDE TO FURTHER READING

On East Germany and 1989, the outstanding books include Jeffrey Kopstein, *The Politics of Economic Decline in East Germany, 1945–1989* (Chapel Hill: University of North Carolina, 1997); Charles S. Maier, *Dissolution: The Crisis of Communism and the End of East Germany* (Princeton, N.J.: Princeton University, 1997); Eric Weitz, *Creating German Communism, 1890–1990: From Popular Protest to Socialist State* (Princeton, N.J.: Princeton University, 1996); and Steven Pfaff, *Exit-Voice Dynamics and the Collapse of East Germany: The Crisis of Leninism and the Revolution of 1989* (Durham, N.C.: Duke University, 2006). For Romania, major works include Kenneth Jowitt, *Revolutionary Breakthroughs and National Development: The Case of Romania, 1944–1965* (Berkeley: University of California, 1971); Dennis Deletant, *Ceauşescu and the Securitate: Coercion and Dissent in Romania, 1965–1989* (Armonk, N.Y.: M. E. Sharpe, 1996); Vladimir Tismăneanu, *Stalinism for All Seasons: A Political History of Romanian Communism* (Berkeley: University of California, 2003); and Peter Siani-Davies, *The Romanian Revolution of December 1989* (Ithaca, N.Y.: Cornell University, 2005). For Poland, key texts include Martin Malia, "Poland's Eternal Return," *The New York Review of Books,* September 29, 1983, 18–27; Jan Józef Lipski, *KOR: A History of the Workers' Defense Committee in Poland, 1976–1981* (Berkeley: University of California, 1985); Roman Laba, *The Roots of Solidarity: A Political Sociology of Poland's Working-Class Democratization* (Princeton, N.J.: Princeton University, 1991); and

George Sanford, *Military Rule in Poland: The Rebuilding of Communist Power, 1981–1983* (New York: St. Martin's, 1986). For the republics of the Soviet Union, important studies include Nils Raymond Muiznieks, "The Baltic Popular Movements and the Disintegration of the Soviet Union," Ph.D. dissertation, University of California, Berkeley (1993); Andrew Wilson, *The Ukrainians: Unexpected Nation,* 2nd ed. (New Haven, Conn.: Yale University, 2002); and John B. Dunlop, *The Rise of Russia and the Fall of the Soviet Union* (Princeton, N.J.: Princeton University, 1993).

Standout general studies on communism's downfall include Steven L. Solnick, *Stealing the State: Control and Collapse in Communist Institutions* (Cambridge, Mass.: Harvard University, 1999), and Mark Kramer, "The Collapse of East European Communism and the Repercussions within the Soviet Union," *Journal of Cold War Studies,* 5/4 (2003): 178–256, 6/4 (2004): 3–64, 7/1 (2005): 3–96. Also valuable is Niels C. Nielsen, *Revolutions in Eastern Europe: The Religious Roots* (Maryknoll, N.Y.: Orbis, 1991). Many classic analyses retain their salience, notably Zbigniew Brzezinski, *The Soviet Bloc: Unity and Conflict* (Cambridge, Mass.: Harvard University, 1960, 1967), and Paul Marer, "Has Eastern Europe Become a Liability to the Soviet Union? III. The Economic Aspect," in Charles Gati (ed.), *The International Politics of Eastern Europe* (New York: Praeger, 1976): 59–81. Mention might also be made of the authors' own contributions, such as Jan T. Gross, "Thirty Years of Crisis Management in Poland," in Teresa Rakowska-Harmstone (ed.), *Perspectives for Change in Communist Societies* (Boulder, Colo.: Westview, 1979), 145–67; and Stephen Kotkin, *Armageddon Averted: The Soviet Collapse, 1970–2000,* updated edition (New York: Oxford University, 2008). For insights into the Yugoslav case and beyond, see Valerie Bunce, *Subversive Institutions: The Design and Destruction of Socialism and the State* (New York: Cambridge University, 1999); and C. P. Gagnon, Jr., *The Myth of Ethnic War: Serbia and Croatia in the 1990s* (Ithaca, N.Y.: Cornell University, 2004).

Within the vast dissident or opposition literature, among the most important texts are Czesław Miłosz, *The Captive Mind* (New York: Knopf, 1953); Milovan Djilas, *The New Class: An Analysis of the Communist System* (New York: Praeger, 1957); Leszek Kołakowski, "Hope and

Hopelessness," *Survey,* 17/3 (1971); Adam Michnik, "A New Evolutionism" (1976), in *Letters from Prison and Other Essays* (Berkeley: University of California, 1985), 135–48; Václav Havel, "The Power of the Powerless" (1978), in Gale Stokes (ed.), *From Stalinism to Pluralism* (New York: Oxford University, 1996), 168–74; and George Konrád, *Antipolitics: An Essay* (San Diego: Harcourt Brace Jovanovich, 1984). Notable memoirs include Zdeněk Mlynář, *Nightfrost in Prague: The End of Humane Socialism* (New York: Karz, 1980); Mikhail Gorbachev and Zdeněk Mlynář, *Conversations with Gorbachev: On Perestroika, the Prague Spring, and the Crossroads of Socialism* (New York: Columbia University, 2002); Laszlo Tőkés, as told to David Porter, *With God, for the People: The Autobiography of Laszlo Tőkés* (London: Hodder and Stoughton, 1990); Silviu Brucan, *The Wasted Generation: Memoirs of a Romanian Journey from Capitalism to Socialism and Back* (Boulder, Colo.: Westview, 1993); and Stefan Wyszyński, *A Freedom Within: The Prison Notes of Stefan Cardinal Wyszyński* (San Diego: Harcourt Brace Jovanovich, 1983). Some valuable collections of interviews are Miklós Kun, *Prague Spring—Prague Fall: Blank Spots of 1968* (Budapest: Akademiai Kiado, 1999); Derek Philipsen, *We Were the People: Voices from East Germany's Revolutionary Autumn of 1989* (Durham, N.C.: Duke University, 1993); and Teresa Torańska, *"Them": Stalin's Polish Puppets* (New York: Harper and Row, 1987).

INDEX

About the Authors

STEPHEN KOTKIN is Rosengarten Professor of Modern and Contemporary History at Princeton University, with a joint appointment as Professor of International Affairs in the Woodrow Wilson School. He is the author of the influential books *Magnetic Mountain: Stalinism as a Civilization* (1995) and *Armageddon Averted: The Soviet Collapse 1970–2000* (rev. ed. 2008) and contributes regularly to *The New York Times, The New Republic,* and the BBC.

JAN T. GROSS, a native of Poland, also teaches at Princeton, where he is the Norman B. Tomlinson '16 and '48 Professor of War and Society. He was a 2001 National Book Award nominee for his widely acclaimed *Neighbors: The Destruction of the Jewish Community in Jedwabne, Poland.* His previous book, *Fear: Anti-Semitism in Poland After Auschwitz,* was named one of the best books of the year by *The Washington Post.*

A Note on the Type

The principal text of this Modern Library edition was set in a digitized version of Janson, a typeface that dates from about 1690 and was cut by Nicholas Kis, a Hungarian working in Amsterdam. The original matrices have survived and are held by the Stempel foundry in Germany. Hermann Zapf redesigned some of the weights and sizes for Stempel, basing his revisions on the original design.